COLLECTIONS AND RECOLLECTIONS;

George William Erskine Russell

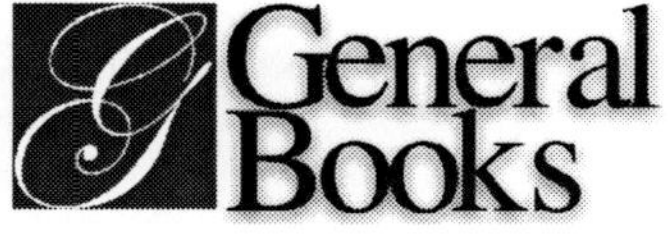

www.General-Books.net

Publication Data:

Title: Collections and Recollections
Author: George William Erskine Russell
General Books publication date: 2009
Original publication date: 1898
Original Publisher: Harper brothers
Subjects: Great Britain
Fiction / Short Stories
History / General
History / Europe / Great Britain
Literary Collections / General
Literary Collections / Essays
Literary Criticism / European / English, Irish, Scottish, Welsh
Reference / Quotations
Social Science / Customs Traditions

CONTENTS

COLLECTIONS AND RECOLLECTIONS;

1

SECTION 1

THE MOST GENIAL OF COMPANIONS

JAMES PAYN

AT WHOSE SUGGESTION THESE PAPERS WERE 'WRITTEN AND TO WHOM THEY WEEE INSCRIBED

psy"D2le$ flBarcb 25, 1808

Is he gone to a land of no laughter –
This man that mado mirth for us all?
Proves Death but a silence hereafter,
Where the echoes of Earth cannot fall?
Once closed, have the lips no more duty?
No more pleasure the exquisite ears?
Has the heart done o'crflowing with beauty,
As the eyes have with tears?
Nay, If aught bo sure, what can be surer
Than that earth's good decays not with earth?
And of all the heart's springs none are purer
Than the spring of the fountains of mirth?
He that sounds them has pierced the heart's hollow.

The places where tears are and sleep ;
For tho foam-flakes that dance in life's shallows
Are wrung from life's deep.
J. Rhoades

NOTE

These Papers appeared in the *Manehester Guardian* during the year 1897, and are hero reproduced by the kind permission of Mr. C. P. Scott, M. P. It Las not been thought necessary to alter some phrases which imply that they were published periodically.

The Papers are exactly what the title implies. They consist in part of traditions and anecdotes which the writer has collected from people and books; in part of incidents which " he personally recollects. With respect to the traditional part,

the usual crop of contradictions and disproofs may be anticipated, and may also be disregarded. Except in his own Recollections, the writer does not vouch for accuracy, but only "tells the tale

as 'twas told to him." Some of the Links with the Past on which he relied have been snapped by death while the pages were passing through the press.

Easter, 1833.

2

SECTION 2

COLLECTIONS AND RECOLLECTIONS

LIXKS WITH THE PAST

Of the celebrated Mrs. Disraeli her husband is reported to have said : " She is an excellent creature, but she never can remember which came first, the Greeks or the Romans." In my walk through life I hare constantly found myself among excellent creatures of this sort. The world is full of vague people, and in the average man, and still more in the average woman, the chronological sense seems to be entirely wanting. Thus, when I have occasionally stated in a mixed company that my first distinct recollection was the burning of Covent Garden Theatre, I have seen a general expression of surprised interest, and have been told, in a tone meant to be kind and complimentary, that my hearers would hardly have thought that my memory went back so far. The explanation has been that these excellent creatures had some vague notions of *Rejected Addresses* floating in their minds, and confounded the burning of Covent Garden Theatre in 1856 with that of Drury Lane Theatre in 1809. It was pleasant to feel that one bore one's years so well as to make the error possible.

But events, however striking, are only landmarks in memory. They are isolated and detached, and begin and end in themselves. The real interest of one's early life is in its Links with the Past, through the old people whom one has known. Though I place my first distinct recollection in 1856, I have memories more or less hazy of an earlier date.

There was an old Lady Robert Seymour, who lived in Portland Place, and died there in 1855, in her ninety- first year. Probably she is my most direct link with the past, for she carried down to the time of the Crimean War the habits and phraseology of Queen Charlotte's early Court. "Goold"of course she said for gold, and "yal- ler"for yellow, and "laylock" for lilac. She laid the stress on the second syllable of balcony. She called her maid her "'ooman"; instead of sleeping at a place, she "lay" there, and when she consulted the doctor she spoke of having " used the 'potticary."

There still lives, in full possession of all her faculties, a venerable lady who can say that her husband was born at Boston when America was a British dependency. This is the widow of Lord Chancellor Lyndhurst, who was born in 1772, and helped to defeat Mr. Gladstone's Paper Bill in the House of Lords on his eighty-eighth birthday. He died in 1862.

A conspicuous figure in my early recollections is Sir Henry Holland, M. D., father of the present Lord Knuts- ford. He was born in 1788, and died in 1873. The stories of his superhuman vigor and activity would fill a volume. In 1863 Bishop Wilberforce wrote to a friend abroad: " Sir Henry Holland, who got back safe from all his American rambles, has been taken by Palmerston through the river at Broadlands, and lies very ill." However, he completely threw off the effects of this mischance, and survived his aquatic host for some eight years. I well remember his telling me in 1868 that his first famouspatient was the mysterious "Pamela," who became the wife of the Irish patriot, Lord Edward Fitzgerald.

Every one who went about in London in the sixties and seventies will remember the dyed locks and crimson velvet waistcoat of William, fifth Earl Bathurst, who was born in 1791 and died in 1878. lie told me that he was at a private school at Sunbury-on-Thames with William and John Russell, the latter of whom became the author of the Reform Bill and Prime Minister. At this delightful seminar)', the peers' sons, including my informant, who was then the Hon. William Bathurst, had a bench to themselves. William and John Russell were not peers' sons, as their father had not then succeeded to the Dukedom of Bedford. In 1802 he succeeded, on the sudden death of his elder brother, and became sixth Duke of Bedford; and his sons, becoming *Lord* William and *Lord* John, were duly promoted to the privileged bench. Nothing in *Pelham* or *Vivian Grey* quite equals this.

When I went to Harrow, in 1867, there was an old woman, by name Polly Arnold, still keeping a stationer's shop in the town, who had sold cribs to Byron when he was a Harrow boy; and Byron's fag, a funny old gentleman in a brown wig – called Baron Heath – was a standing dish on our school speech-day.

Once at a London dinner I happened to mention in the hearing of Mrs. Procter (widow of " Barry Cornwall," and mother of the poetess) that I was going next day to the Harrow speeches. "Ah,"said Mrs. Procter, "that used to be a pleasant outing. The last time I went I drove down with Lord Byron and Dr. Parr, who had been breakfasting with my father." Mrs. Procter died in 1888.

Among the remarkable women of our time, if merely in respect of longevity, must be enumerated Lady Louisa Stuart, sister and heir of the last Earl of Traquair. Shewas a friend and correspondent of Sir Walter Scott, who, in describing " Tally Veolan," drew Traquair House with literal exactness, even down to the rampant bears which still guard the locked entrance-gates against all comers until the Royal Stuarts shall return to claim their own. Lady Louisa Stuart lived to be a hundred, and died in 1876.

Perhaps the most remarkable old lady whom I knew intimately was Caroline Lowther, Duchess of Cleveland, who was born in 1792 and died in 1883. She had been presented to Queen Charlotte when there were only forty people at the drawing-room, had danced with the Prince of Orange, and had attended the "breakfasts" given by Albinia Countess of Buckinghamshire (who died in 1816), at her villa just outside London. The site of that villa is now Hobart Place, having taken its name from that of the Buckinghamshire family; and under the trees of its orchard, still discoverable in the back gardens of the Hobart Place houses, Sir Hamilton Seymour, who lived to become Ambassador at Vienna, was stopped by a highwayman when travelling in his father's carriage. He died in 1880 – certainly a good link with the past.

Another story of highway-robbery which excited me when I was a boy was that of the fifth Earl of Berkeley, who died in 1810. He had always declared that any one might without disgrace be overcome by superior numbers, but that he would never surrender to a single highwayman. As he was crossing Hounslow Heath one night, on his way from Berkeley Castle to London, his travelling-carriage was stopped by a man on horseback, who put his head in at the window and said : "I believe you are Lord Berkeley ?" " I am." "*I* believe you have always boasted that you would never surrender to a single highwayman?" "I have." "Well," presenting a

pistol, " I am a single highwayman, and I say, 'Yourmoney or your life.'" "Yon cowardly dog," said Lord Berkeley, "do you think I can't see your confederate skulking behind you ?" The highwayman, who was really alone, looked hurriedly round, and Lord Berkeley shot him through the head. I asked Lady Caroline Maxse (1803-1886), who was born a Berkeley, if this story was true. I can never forget my thrill when she replied : " Yes; and I am proud to say that I am that man's daughter !"

Sir Moses Montefiore was born in 1784, and died in 1885. It is a disheartening fact for the teetotalei-s that he had drunk a bottle of port-wine every day since he grew up. He had dined with Lord Nelson on board his ship, and vividly remembered the transcendent beauty of Lady Hamilton. The last time Sir Moses appeared in public was, if I mistake not, at a garden-party at Marl- borough House. The party was given on a Saturday. Sir Moses was restrained by religious scruples from using his horses, and was, of course, too feeble to walk, so he was conveyed to the party in a magnificent sedan- chair. That was the only occasion on which I have seen such an article in use in London.

When I began to go out in London, a conspicuous figure in dinner-society and on Protestant platforms was Captain Francis Maude, R. N. He was born in 1778, and died in 1886. He used to say: " My grandfather was twelve years old when Charles II. died." And so, if pedigrees may be trusted, he was. Charles II. died in 1685. Sir Robert Maude was born in 1673. His son, the first Lord Hawarden, was born in 1729, and Captain Francis Maude was Lord Hawarden's youngest son. The year of his death (1886) saw also the disappearance of a truly venerable woman, Mrs. Hodgson, mother of Kirk- man and Stewart Hodgson, the well-known partners in Barings' house. Her age was not precisely known, butwhen a school-girl in Paris she had seen Robespierre executed, and distinctly recollected the appearance of his bandaged face. Her grand - daughters, Mr. Stewart Hodgson's children, are quite young women, and if they live to the age which, with such ancestry, they are entitled to anticipate, they will carry down into the middle of the twentieth century the account, derived from an eye-witness, of the central event of the French Bev- olution.

One year later, in 1887, there died, at her family house in St. James's Square, Mrs. Anne Penelope Hoare, mother of the late Sir Henry Hoare, M. P. She recollected being at a children's party when the lady of the house came in and stopped the dancing because news had come that the King of France had been put to death. Her range of conscious knowledge extended from the execution of Louis XVI. to the Jubilee of Queen Victoria. So short a thing is history.

Sir Walter Stirling, who was born in 1802 and died in 1888, was a funny little old gentleman of ubiquitous activity, running about London with a brown wig, short trousers, and a cotton umbrella. I well remember his saying to me, when Mr. Bradlaugh was committed to the Clock Tower: "I don't like this. I am afraid it will mean mischief. I am old enough to remember seeing Sir Francis Burdett taken to the Tower by the Sergeant- at-Arms with a military force. I saw the riot then, and I am afraid I shall see a riot again."

In the same year (1888) died Mrs. Thomson Hankey, wife of a former M. P. for Peterborough. Her father, a Mr. Alexander, was born in 1729, and she had inherited from him traditions of London as it appeared to a young Scotsman in the year of the decapitation of the rebels after the rising of 1745.

One of the most venerable and interesting figures inLondon, down to his death in 1891, was George Thomas, sixth Earl of Albemarle. He was born in 1799. He had played bat-trap-and-ball at St. Anne's Hill with Mr. Fox, and shared with his old comrade Sir Thomas Which- cote, who survived him by a few months, the honor of being the last survivor of Waterloo. A man whom I knew longer and more intimately than any of those whom I have described was the late Lord Charles James Fox Russell. He was born in 1807, and died in 1894. His father's groom had led the uproar of London servants which in the last century damned the play " High Life Below Stairs." He remembered a Highlander who had followed the army of Prince Charles Edward in 1745, and had learned from another Highlander the Jacobite soldiers' song:

"I would I were at Manchester,
A-sitting on the grass,
And by my side a bottle of wine,
And on my lap a lass."

He had officiated as a page at the coronation of George IV.; had conversed with Sir Walter Scott about *The Bride of Lammermoor* before the authorship was disclosed ; had served in the Blues under Ernest Duke of Cumberland; and had lost his way in trying to find the newly developed quarter of London called Belgrave Square.

Among living links, I hope it is not ungallant to enumerate Lady Georgiana Grey, only surviving child of

"That Earl, who forced his compeers to be just,
And wrought in brave old age what youth had planned ;"

Lady Louisa Tighe, who, as Lady Louisa Lennoxbuckled the Duke of Wellington's sword when he set out from her mother's ball at Brussels for the field of Waterloo; and Miss Eliza Smith, of Brighton, the vivacious and evergreen daughter of Horace Smith, who wrote *Rejected Addresses.* But these admirable and accomplished ladies hate garrulity, and the mere mention of their names is a signal to bring these disjointed reminiscences to a close. n

LORD RUSSELL

These chapters are founded on Links with the Past. Let me now describe in rather fuller detail three or four remarkable people with whom I had more than a cur- sory acquaintance, and who allowed me for many years the privilege of drawing without restriction on the rich stores of their political and social recollections.

First among these in point of date, if of nothing else, I must place John Earl Russell, the only person I have ever known who knew Napoleon the Great. Lord Russell – or, to give him the name by which he was most familiar to his countrymen, Lord John Russell – was born in 1792,'and when I first knew him he was already old; but it might have been said of him with perfect truth that

"Votivii piituit veluti descripta tahella

Vita senis."

After he resigned the leadership of the Liberal party, at Christmas, 1867, Lord Russell spent the greater part of his time at Pembroke Lodge, a house in Richmond Park, which takes its name from Elizabeth Countess of Pembroke, familiar to all students of last century's memoirs as the object of King George Ill's hopeless and pathetic love. As a token of his affection the King allowed Lady Pembroke to build herself a "lodge " in the "vast wilderness" of Richmond Park, amid surroundings which went far to realize Cowper's idea of a " boundless contiguity of shade."

On her death, in 1831, Pembroke Lodge was assigned by William IV. to his son-in-law, Lord Erroll, and in 1847 it was offered by the Queen to her Prime Minister, Lord John Russell, who then had no home except his house in Chesham Place. It was gratefully accepted, for indeed it had already been coveted as an ideal residence for a busy politician who wanted fresh air, and could not safely be far from the House of Commons. As years went on Lord John spent more and more of his time in this delicious retreat, and in his declining years it was practically his only home.

A quarter of a century ago it was a curious and interesting privilege for a young man to sit in the trellised dining-room of Pembroke Lodge, or to pace its terrace-walk looking down upon the Thames, in intimate converse with a statesman who had enjoyed the genial society of Mr. Fox, and had been the travelling companion of Lord Holland, had corresponded with Tom Moore, debated with Francis Jeffrey, and dined with Dr. Parr; had visited Melrose Abbey in the company of Sir Walter Scott, and criticized the acting of Mrs. Siddons; conversed with Napoleon in his seclusion at Elba, and ridden with the Duke of Wellington along the lines of Torres Vedras.

The genius of John Leech, constantly exercised on the subject for twenty years, has made all students of *Punch* familiar with Lord John Russell's outward aspect. We know from his boyish diary that on his eleventh birthday he was "4 feet 2 inches high and 3 stone 12 Ib. weight"; and though, as time went on, these extremely modest dimensions were slightly exceeded, he was an unusually short man. His massive head and broad shoulders gave him when he sat theappearance of greater size, and when he rose to his feet the diminutive stature caused a feeling of surprise.

Sydney Smith declared that when Lord John first contested Devonshire the burly electors were disappointed by the exiguity of their candidate, but were satisfied when it was explained to them that he had once been much larger, but was worn away by the anxieties and struggles of the Reform Bill of 1832. Never was so robust a spirit enshrined in so fragile a form. He inherited the miserable legacy of congenital weakness. Even in those untender days he was considered too delicate to remain at a public school. It was thought impossible for him to live through his first session of Parliament.

When he was fighting the Reform Bill through the House of Commons he had to be fed with arrowroot by a benevolent lady who was moved to compassion by his pitiful appearance. For years afterwards he was liable to fainting fits, had a wretched digestion, and was easily upset by hot rooms, late hours, and bad air. These circumstances, combined with his love of domestic life and his fondness for the country, led him to spend every evening that he could spare in his seclusion at Pembroke Lodge, and consequently cut him off, very much to his political disadvantage, from constant and intimate association with official colleagues and parliamentary supporters.

There were other characteristics which enhanced this unfortunate impression of aloofness. His voice had what used to be described in satirical writings of the first half of the century as "an aristocratic drawl," and his pronunciation was archaic. Like other high-bred people of his time, he talked of "cowcnmbers" and "laylocks"; called a woman an "'ooman," and was "much obleeged" where a degenerate age is content tobe obliged. The frigidity of his address and the seeming stiffness of his manner, due really to an innate and incurable shyness, produced, even among people who ought to have known him well, a totally erroneous notion of his character and temperament. To Bulwer Lytton he seemed –

" How formed to lead, if not too proud to please !
His fame would fire you, but his manners freeze.
Like or dislike, he does not care a jot;
He wants your vote, but your affections not;
Yet human hearts need sun as well as oats –
So cold a climate plays the deuce with votes."

It must be admitted that in some of the small social arts which are so valuable an equipment for a political leader Lord John was funnily deficient. He had no memory for faces, and was painfully apt to ignore his political followers when he met them beyond the walls of Parliament. Once, staying in a Scotch country-house, he found himself thrown with young Lord D , now Earl of S . He liked the young man's conversation, and was pleased to find that he was a Whig. When the party broke up, Lord John conquered his shyness sufficiently to say to his new friend : "Well, Lord D , I am very glad to have made your acquaintance, and now you must come into the House of Commons and support me there." "I have been doing that for the last ten years, Lord John," was the reply of the gratified follower.

This inability to remember faces was allied in Lord John with a curious artlessness of disposition which made it impossible for him to feign a cordiality he did not feel. Once, at a concert at Buckingham Palace, he was seen to get up suddenly, turn his back on the Duchess of Sutherland, by whom he had been sitting, walk to the remotest part of the room, and sit down by the Duchess of Inverness. When questioned afterwards as to the cause of his unceremonious move, which had the look of a quarrel, he said: "I could not have sat any longer by that great fire; I should have fainted."

"Oh, that was a very good reason for moving; but I hope you told the Duchess of Sutherland why you left her."

" Well – no. I don't think I did that. But I told the Duchess of Inverness why I came and sate by her !"

Thus were the opportunities of paying harmless compliments recklessly thrown away.

It was once remarked by a competent critic that "there have been ministers who knew the springs of that public opinion which is delivered ready digested to the nation every morning, and who have not scrupled to work them for their own diurnal glorification, even although the recoil might injure their colleagues. But Lord Russell has never bowed the knee to the potentates of the press; he has offered no sacrifice of invitations to social editors; and social editors have accordingly failed to discover the merits of a statesman who so little appreciated them until they have almost made the nation forget the services that Lord Russell has so faithfully and courageously rendered."

Be this as it may, there is no doubt that the old Whig statesman lacked those gifts or arts which make a man widely popular in a large society of superficial acquaintances. On his death-bed he said with touching pathos, "I have seemed cold to my friends, but it was not in my heart." The friends needed no such assurance. He was the idol of those who were most closely associated with him by the ties of blood or duty. Even to people outside the innermost circle of intimacy there was something peculiarly attractive in his singular mixture ofgentleness and dignity. He excelled as a host, doing the honors of his table with the old-fashioned grace which he had learned at Woburn Abbey and at Holland House when the century was young; and in the charm of his conversation he was not easily equalled – never, in my experience, surpassed. He had the happy knack of expressing a judgment which might be antagonistic to the sentiments of those with whom he was dealing in language which, while perfectly void of offence, was calmly decisive. His reply to Sir Francis Burdett has been pronounced by Mr. Gladstone to be the best repartee ever made in Parliament. Sir Francis, an ex- Radical, attacking his former associates with all the bitterness of a renegade, had said, " The most offensive thing in the world is the cant of patriotism." Lord John replied, "I quite agree that the cant of patriotism is a very offensive thing; but the *recant* of patriotism is more offensive still." His letter to the Dean of Hereford about the election of Bishop Hampden is a classical instance of courteous controversy. Ouce a most illustrious personage asked him if it was true that he thought that under certain circumstances it was lawful for a subject to disobey the Sovereign. "Well, speaking of a Sovereign of the House of Hanover, I can only answer in the affirmative."

His copiousness of anecdote was inexhaustible. His stories always fitted the point, and the droll gravity of his way of telling them added greatly to their zest. Of his conversation with Napoleon at Elba I recollect only one question and answer. The Emperor took the little Englishman by the ear and asked him what was thought in England of his chance of returning to the throne of France. "I said, 'Sire, they think yon have no chance at all.' 'Then you can tell them from me that they are wrong.'"

This interview took place when Lord John was making a tour with Lord and Lady Holland, and much of his earlier life had been spent at Holland House, in the heart of that brilliant society which Macaulay so picturesquely described, and in which Luttrell and Samuel Rogers were conspicuous figures. Their conversation supplied Lord John with an anecdote which he used to bring out, with a twinkling eye and a chuckling laugh, whenever he heard that any public reform was regarded , with misgiving by sensible men. Luttrell and Rogers were passing in a wherry under old London Bridge when its destruction was contemplated, and Rogers said, " Some very sensible men think that the removal of these narrow arches will cause such a rush of water as will be very dangerous." " My dear Rogers," answered Luttrell, " if some very sensible men had been attended to, we should still be eating acorns."

Of William and John Scott, afterwards Lord Stowell and Lord Eldon, Lord John Russell used to tell with infinite zest a story which he declared to be highly characteristic of the methods by which they made their fortunes and position. When they were young men at the Bar, having had a stroke of professional luck, they determined to celebrate the occasion by having a dinner at a tavern and going to the play. When it was time to call for the reckoning William Scott dropped a guinea. He and his brother searched for it in vain, and came to the conclusion that it had fallen between the boards of the nncarpeted floor.

" This is a bad job," said William ; " we must give up the play."

" Stop a bit," said John ; " I know a trick worth two of that," and called the waitress.

"Betty," said he, "we've dropped two guineas. See if you can find them." Betty went down on her handsand knees, and found the one guinea, which had rolled under the fender.

" That's a very good girl, Betty," said John Scott, pocketing the coin, " and when you find the other you can keep it for your trouble." And the prudent brothers went with a light heart to the play, and so eventually to the Bench and the Woolsack.

In spite of profound differences of political opinion, Lord Russell had a high regard for the memory of the Duke of Wellington, and had been much in his society in early life. Travelling in the Peninsula in 1812, he visited Lord Wellington at his headquarters near Burgos. On the morning after his arrival he rode out with his host and an aide-de-camp, and surveyed the position of the French army. Lord Wellington, peering through his glass, suddenly exclaimed, " By God ! they've changed their position !" and said no more.

When they returned from their ride, the aide-de-camp said to Lord John, "Yon had better get away as quick as you can. I am confident that Lord Wellington means to make a move." Lord John took the hint, made his excuses, and went on his way. That evening the British army was in full retreat, and Lord Russell used to tell the story as illustrating the old Duke's extreme reticence when there was a chance of a military secret leaking out.

Lord Russell's father, the sixth Duke of Bedford, belonged to that section of the Whigs who thought that, while a Whig Ministry was impossible, it was wiser to support the Duke of Wellington, whom they believed to be a thoroughly honest man, than Canning, whom they regarded as an unscrupulous adventurer. Accordingly, the Duke of Wellington was a frequent visitor at Woburn Abbey, and showed consistent friendliness to Lord Russell and his many brothers, all of whom were full of anecdotes illustrative of his grim humor and robust common- sense. Let a few of them be recorded.

The Government was contemplating the despatch of an expedition to Burma, with a view to taking Rangoon, and a question arose as to who would be the fittest general to be sent in command of the expedition. The Cabinet sent for the Duke of Wellington, and asked his advice. He instantly replied, " Send Lord Combermere."

" But we have always understood that your grace thought Lord Combermere a fool."

" So he is a fool, and a damned fool; but he can take Rangoon."

At the time of Queen Caroline's trial the mob of London sided with the Queen, and the Duke's strong adhesion to the King made him extremely unpopular. Riding up Grosvenor Place one day towards Apsley House, he was beset by a gang of workmen who were mending the road. They formed a cordon, shouldered their pickaxes, and swore they would not let the Duke pass till he said "God save the Queen." "Well, gentlemen, since you will have it so – 'God save the Queen,' and may all your wives be like her !"

Mrs. Arbutlmot (wife of the Duke's private secretary, familiarly called " Gosh") was fond of parading her intimacy with the Duke before miscellaneous company. One day, in a large party, she said to him :

" Duke, I know you won't mind my asking you, but is it true that you were so much surprised when you found you had won the Battle of Waterloo ?"

" By God ! not half as much surprised as I am now, mum."

When the Queen came to the throne her first public act

was to go in state to St. James's Palace to be proclaimed.

She naturally wished to be accompanied in her State

coach only by the Duchess of Kent and one of the ladiesof the household; but Lord Albemarle, who was Master of the Horse, insisted that he had a right to travel with her Majesty in the coach, as he had done with William IV. The point was submitted to the Duke of Wellington, as a kind of universal referee in matters of precedent and usage. His judgment was delightfully unflattering to the outraged magnate – " The Queen can make you go inside the coach or outside the coach, or run behind like a damned tinker's dog."

And surely the whole literary profession, of which the present writer is a feeble unit, must cherish a sentiment of grateful respect for the memory of a man who, in refusing the dedication of a song, informed Mrs. Norton that he had been obliged to make a rule of refusing dedications, "because, in his situation as Chancellor of the University of Oxford, he had been *much exposed to authors."* m

LORD SHAFTESBURY

If the Christian Socialists ever frame a Calendar of Worthies (after the manner of Auguste Comte), it is to be hoped that they will mark among the most sacred and memorable of their anniversaries the day – April 28,1801 – which gave birth to Anthony Ashley, seventh Earl of Shaftesbury. His life of eighty-four years was consecrated, from boyhood till death, to the social service of humanity; and, for my own part, I must always regard the privilege of his friendship as among the highest honors of my life. Let me try to recall some of the outward and inward characteristics of this truly illustrious man.

Lord Shaftesbury was tall and spare – almost gaunt – in figure, but powerfully framed, and capable of great exertion. His features were handsome and strongly marked – an aquiline nose and very prominent chin. His complexion was as pale as marble, and contrasted effectively with a thick crop of jet-black hair which extreme old age scarcely tinged with silver.

When he first entered Parliament a contemporary observer of the House of Commons wrote : "It would be difficult to imagine a more complete bean-ideal of aristocracy. His whole countenance has the coldness as well as the grace of a chiselled one, and expresses precision, prudence, and determination in no common degree." The stateliness of bearing, the unbroken figure, the high glance of stern though melancholy resolve, he retainedto the end. But the incessant labor and anxiety of sixty years made their mark, and Sir John Millais's nohle portrait, painted in 1877, shows a countenance 011 which a lifelong contact with human suffering had written its tale in legible characters.

All temperament is, *I* suppose, largely hereditary. Lord Shaftesbury's father, who was for nearly forty years chairman of committees in the House of Lords, was distinguished by a strong intellect, an imperious temper, and a character singularly deficient in amiability. His mother (whose childish beauty is familiar to all lovers of Sir Joshua's art as the little girl frightened by the mask in the great " Maryborough Group") was the daughter of the third Duke of Marlborough by that Duchess whom Queen Charlotte pronounced to be the proudest woman in England. It is reasonable to suppose that from such a parentage and such an ancestry Lord Shatesbury derived some of the most conspicuous features of his character. From his father he inherited his keenness of intellect, his habits of laborious industry, and his iron tenacity of purpose. From his mother he may have acquired that strong sense of personal dignity – that intuitive and perhaps unconscious feeling of what was due to his station as well as to his individuality – which made his presence and address so impressive and sometimes alarming.

Dignity was indeed the quality which immediately struck one on one's first encounter with Lord Shaftes- bury ; and with dignity were associated a marked imperiousness and an eager rapidity of thought, utterance, and action. As one got to know him better, one began to realize his intense tenderness towards all weakness and suffering ; his overflowing affection for those who stood nearest to him ; his almost morbid sensitiveness; his passionate indignation against cruelty or oppression. Now and then his conversation was brightened by brief and sudden gleams of genuine humor, but these gleams were rare. He had seen too much of human misery to be habitually jocose, and his whole nature was underlain by a groundwork of melancholy.

The marble of manhood retained the impression stamped upon the wax of childhood. His early years had been profoundly miserable. His parents were stern disciplinarians of the antique type. His private school was a hell on earth ; and yet he used to say that he feared the master and the bullies less than he feared his parents. One element of joy, and one only, he recognized in looking back to those dark days, and that was the devotion of an old maid-servant, who comforted him in his childish sorrows, and taught him the rudiments of Christian faith. In all the struggles and distresses of boyhood and manhood, he used the words of prayer which he had learned from this good woman before he was seven years old, and of a keepsake which she left him – the gold watch which he wore to the last day of his life – he used to say, " That was given to me by the best friend I ever had in the world."

At twelve years old Anthony Ashley went to Harrow, where he boarded with the Head Master, Dr. Butler, father of the present Master of Trinity. I have heard him say that the master in whose form he was, being a bad sleeper, held " first school" at four o'clock on a winter's morning; and that the boy for whom he fagged, being anxious to shine as a reciter, and finding it difficult to secure an audience, compelled him and his fellow-fag to listen night after night to his recitations, perched on a high stool where a nap was impossible.

But in spite of these austerities, Anthony Ashley was happy at Harrow, and the place should be sacred in the eyes of all philanthropists, because it was there that, whenhe was fourteen years old, he consciously and definitely gave his life to the service of his fellow-men. He chanced to see a scene of drunken indecency and neglect at the funeral of one of the villagers, and exclaimed in horror, " Good heavens ! Can this be permitted simply because the man was poor and friendless ?" What followed is told by a tablet on the wall of the old school, which bears the following inscription :

Love. Serve.

NEAR THIS SPOT

ANTHONY ASHLEY COOPER

Afterwards 7th Earl Of Shaptesbury, K. g.

While Tet A Boy In Harrow School

Saw With Shame And Indignation

The Pauper's Funekal

Which Helped To Awaken His Lifelong

Devotion To The Service Op The Poor

And The Oppressed.

Blessed is he that considercth the poor.

After leaving Harrow, Lord Ashley (as he now was) spent two years at a private tutor's, and in 1819 he went up to Christ Church. In 1822 he took a First Class in Classics. The next four years were spent in study and travel, and in 1826 he was returned to Parliament, by the influence of his uncle, the Duke of Marlborough, for the Borough of Woodstock. On November 16th he recorded in his diary : "Took the oaths of Parliament with great good-will; a slight prayer for assistance in my thoughts and deeds." Never was a politician's prayer more abundantly granted.

In 1830 Lord Ashley married a daughter of Lord Cow- per, and this marriage, independently of the radiant happiness which it brought, had an important bearing on hispolitical career, for Lady Ashley's uncle was Lord Melbourne, and her mother became, by a second marriage, the wife of Lord Palmerston. Of Lord Melbourne and his strong common-sense, Lord Shaftesbury, in 1882, told me the following characteristic story. When the Queen became engaged to Prince Albert, she wished him to be made King Consort by Act of Parliament, and urged her wish upon the Prime Minister, Lord Melbourne. At first that sagacious man simply evaded the point, but when her Majesty insisted on a categorical answer, " I thought it my duty to be very plain with her. I said, 'For God's sake, let's hear no more of it, ma'am; for if you once get the English people into the way of making kings, you will get them into the way of unmaking them.'"

By this time Lord Ashley was deeply immersed in those philanthropic enterprises which he had deliberately chosen as the occupation of his lifetime. Reform of the Lunacy Law and a humaner treatment of lunatics were the earliest objects to which he devoted himself. To attain them the more effectually, he got himself made a member, and subsequently chairman, of the Lunacy Commission, and threw himself into the work with characteristic thoroughness. He used to pay " surprise visits " both by day and night to public and private asylums, and discovered by those means a system of regulated and sanctioned cruelty which, as he narrated it in his old age, seemed almost too horrible for credence.

The abolition of slavery all over the world was a cause which very early enlisted his sympathy, and he used to tell with grim humor how when, after he had become Lord Shaftesbury, he had signed an Open Letter to America in favor of emancipation, a Southern newspaper sarcastically inquired: "Where was this Lord Shaftesbury when the noble-hearted Lord Ashley was doing hissingle-handed work on behalf of the English slaves in the factories of Lancashire and Yorkshire '("

Sanitary reform and the promotion of the public health were objects at which, in the middle part of his life, he worked hard, both as a landowner and as the nnpaid Chairman of the Board of Health. The crusade against vivisection warmed his heart and woke his indignant eloquence in his declining years. His Memorial Service in Westminster Abbey was attended by representatives of nearly two hundred religious and philanthropic institutions with which he had been connected, and which, in one way or another, he had served. But, of course, it is with the reform of the Factory Laws that his name is most inseparably associated.

In 1833 Lord Ashley took up the Ten Hours Bill, previously in the charge of Mr. Sadler, who had now lost his seat. He carried his Bill through the Second Reading, but it was opposed by Lord Althorp, who threw it out, and carried a modified proposal in 1833. In 1844 the introduction of a new Bill for the regulation of labor in factories brought Lord Ashley back to his old battlefield. A desperate struggle was made to amend the Bill into a Ten Hours Bill, but this failed, owing to Sir Robert Peel's threat of resignation.

In 1845 Lord Ashley refused the Chief Secretaryship for Ireland, in order to be able to devote himself wholly to the Ten Hours Bill; and, as soon as Parliament rose, he went on a tour through the manufacturing districts, speaking in public, mediating between masters and men, and organizing the Ten Hours Movement.

In 1847 the Bill passed into law. On June 1st in that year Lord Ashley wrote in his diary: " News that the Factory Bill has just passed the Third Reading. I am humbled that my heart is not bursting with thankfulness to Almighty God – that I can find breath and sense toexpress my joy. "What reward shall we give nnto the Lord for all the benefits He hath conferred upon us ? God in His mercy prosper the work, and grant that these operatives may receive the cup of salvation and call upon the name of the Lord !"

The perfervid vein of philanthropic zeal which is apparent in this extract animated and dominated every part of Lord Shaftesbury's nature and every action of his life. He had, if ever man had, " the Enthusiasm of Humanity." His religion, on its interior side, was rapt, emotional, and sometimes mystic; but at the same time it was, in its outward manifestations, definite, tangible, and, beyond most men's, practical. At the age of twenty-seven he wrote in his diary: " On my soul, I believe that I desire the welfare of mankind !" At eighty-four he exclaimed, in view of his approaching end, " I cannot bear to leave the world with all the misery in it *I"* And this was no mere effusive declamation, but the genuine utterance of a zeal which condescended to the most minute and laborious forms of practical expression.

"Poor dear children!" he exclaimed to the superintendent of a ragged school, after hearing from some of the children their tale of cold and hunger. " What can we do for thorn ?"

" My God shall supply all their need," replied the superintendent, with easy faith.

"Yes," said Lord Shaftesbury, "He will, but they must have some food directly." He drove home, and instantly sent two churns of soup, enough to feed four hundred. That winter ten thousand basins of soup, made in Grosvenor Square, were distributed among the " dear little hearts " of Whitechapel.

And as in small things, so in great. One principle consecrated his whole life. The love of God constrained him to the service of men, and no earthly object or consideration – however natural, innocent, or even laudable – was allowed for a moment to interpose itself between him and the supreme purpose for which he lived. He was by nature a man of keen ambition, and yet he twice refused office in the Household, once the Chief Secretaryship, and three times a seat in the Cabinet, because acceptance would have hindered him in his social legislation and philanthropic business. When one considers his singular qualifications for public life – his physical gifts, his power of speech, his habits of business, his intimate connections with the official caste – when we remember that he did not succeed to his paternal property till he was fifty years old, and then found it grossly neglected and burdened with debt; and that his purse had been constantly drained by his philanthropic enterprises ; I feel justified in saying that very few men have ever sacrificed so much for a cause which brought neither honor, nor riches, nor power, nor any visible reward, except the diminished suffering and increased happiness of multitudes who were the least able to help themselves.

Lord Shaftesbury's devotion to the cause of Labor led him to make the Factory Acts a touchstone of character. To the end of his days his view of public men was largely governed by the part which they had played in that great controversy. " Gladstone voted against me," was a stern sentence not seldom on his lips. " Bright was the most malignant opponent the Factory Bill ever had." "Cobden, though bitterly hostile, was better than Bright." Even men whom, on general grounds, he disliked and despised – such as Lord Beaconsfield and Bishop Wilberforce – found a saving clause in his judgment if he could truthfully say, "He helped me with the chimney - sweeps," or, "He felt for the wretched operatives."

But even apart from questions of humane sentimentand the supreme interests of social legislation, I always felt in my intercourse with Lord Shaftesbury that it would have been impossible for him to act for long together in subordination to, or even in concert with, any political leader. Resolute, self-reliant, inflexible; hating compromise; never turning aside by a hair's-breadth from the path of duty, incapable of flattering high or low; dreading leaps in the dark, but dreading more than anything else the sacrifice of principle to party; he was essentially the type of politician who is the despair of the official wire-puller.

Oddly enough, Lord Palmerston was the statesman with whom, despite all ethical dissimilarity, he had the most sympathy, and this arose partly from their near relationship, and partly from Lord Palmerston's easy-going habit of placing his ecclesiastical patronage largely in Lord Shaftesbury's hands. It was this unseen but not unfelt power as a confidential but irresponsible adviser that Lord Shaftesbury really enjoyed ; and, indeed, his political opinions were too individual to have allowed of binding association with either political party. He was, in the truest and best sense of the word, a Conservative. To call him a Tory would be quite misleading. He was not averse from Roman Catholic emancipation. He took no prominent part against the first Reform Bill. His resistance to the admission of the Jews to Parliament was directed rather against the method than the principle. Though not friendly to Women's Suffrage, he said: " I shall feel myself bound to conform to the national will, but I am not prepared to stimulate it."

But, while no blind and unreasoning opponent of all change, he had a deep and lively veneration for the past. Institutions, doctrines, ceremonies, dignities, even social customs, which had descended from old time, had for him a fascination and an awe. In his high sense of theprivileges and the duties of kingship, of aristocracy, of territorial possession, of established religions, he recalled the doctrine of Burke ; and he resembled that illustrious man in his passionate love of principle ; in his proud hatred of shifts and compromises ; in his contempt for the whole race of mechanical politicians and their ignoble strife for place and power.

When Lord Derby formed his Government in 1866, on the defeat of Lord Russell's second Reform Bill, he endeavored to obtain the sanction of Lord Shaftesbury's name and authority by offering him a seat in his Cabinet. This offer was promptly declined ; had it been accepted, it might have had an important bearing on the following event, which was narrated to me by Lord Shaftesbury in 1882. One winter evening in 1867 he was sitting in his library in Grosvenor Square, when the servant told him that there was a poor man waiting to see him. The man was shown in, and proved to be a laborer from Clerken- well, and one of the innumerable recipients of the old Earl's charity. He said, " My Lord, you have been very good to me, and I have come to tell you what I have heard." It appeared that at the public-house which he frequented he had overheard some Irishmen of desperate character plotting to blow up Clerkenwell Prison. He gave Lord Shaftesbury the information to be used as he thought best, but made it a condition that his name should not be divulged. If it were, his life would not be worth an hour's purchase.

Lord Shaftesbury pledged himself to secrecy, ordered his carriage, and drove instantly to Whitehall. The authorities there refused, on grounds of official practice, to entertain the information without the name and address of the informant. These, of course, could not be given. The warning was rejected, and the jail blown up. Had Lord Shaftesbury been a Cabinet Minister, this triumph of officialism would probably not have occurred.

What I have said of this favorite hero of mine in his pnblic aspects will have prepared the sympathetic reader for the presentment of the man as he appeared in private life. For what he was abroad that he was at home. He was not a man who showed two natures or lived two lives. He was profoundly religious, eagerly benevolent, utterly impatient of whatever stood between him and the laudable object of the moment, warmly attached to those who shared his sympathies and helped his enterprises – *Fort comme le diamant; plus tendre qu'une mire.* The imperiousness which I described at the outset remained a leading characteristic to the last. His opinions were strong, his judgment was emphatic, his language unmeasured. He had been, all through his public life, surrounded by a cohort of admiring and obedient coadjutors, and he was unused to, and intolerant of, disagreement or opposition. It was a disconcerting experience to speak on a platform where he was chairman, and, just as one was warming to an impressive passage, to feel a vigorous pull at one's coat-tail, and to hear a quick, imperative voice say, in no muffled tone, " My dear fellow, are you never going to stop ? We shall be here all night."

But when due allowance was made for this natural habit of command, Lord Shaftesbury was delightful company. Given to hospitality, he did the honors with stately grace ; and, on the rare occasions when he could be induced to dine out, his presence was sure to make the party a success. In early life he had been pestered by a delicate digestion, and had accustomed himself to a regimen of rigid simplicity ; but, though the most abstemious of men, he knew and liked a good glass of wine, and in a small party would bring out of the treasures of his memory things new and old with a copiousness and avivacity which fairly fascinated his hearers. His conversation had a certain flavor of literature. His classical scholarship was easy and graceful. He had the Latin poets at his fingers' ends, spoke French fluently, knew Milton by heart, and was a great admirer of Crabbe. His own style, both in speech and writing, was copious, vigorous, and often really eloquent. It had the same ornamental precision as his exquisite handwriting. When he was among friends whom he thoroughly enjoyed, the sombre dignity of his conversation was constantly enlivened by flashes of a genuine humor, which relieved, by the force of vivid contrast, the habitual austerity of his demeanor.

A kind of proud humility was constantly present in his speech and bearing. Ostentation, display, lavish expenditure would have been abhorrent alike to his taste and his principles. The stately figure which bore itself so majestically in Courts and Parliaments naturally unbent among the costermongers of Whitechapel and the laborers of

Dorsetshire. His personal appointments were simple to a degree; his own expenditure was restricted within the narrowest limits. But he loved, and was honestly proud of, his beautiful home – St. Giles's House, near Cranbourne – and when he received his guests, gentle or simple, at " The Saint," as he affectionately called it, the mixture of stateliness and geniality in his bearing and address was an object-lesson in high breeding. Once Lord Beaconsfield, who was staying with Lord Alington at Crichel, was driven over to call on Lord Shaftesbury at St. Giles's. When he rose to take his leave, he said, with characteristic magniloquence, but not without an element of truth : "Good-bye, my dear Lord. You have given me the privilege of seeing one of the most impressive of all spectacles – a great English nobleman living in patriarchal state in his own hereditary halls." IV

CARDIKAL MANNING

I Have described a great philanthropist and a great statesman. My present subject is a man who combined in singular harmony the qualities of philanthropy and of statesmanship – Henry Edward, Cardinal Manning, and titular Archbishop of Westminster.

My acquaintance with Cardinal Manning began in 1883. Early in the Parliamentary session of that year he intimated, through a common friend, a desire to make my acquaintance. He wished to get an independent member of Parliament, and especially, if possible, a Liberal and a Churchman, to take up in the House of Commons the cause of Denominational Education. His scheme was much the same as that now adopted by the Government – the concurrent endowment of all denominational schools; which, as he remarked, would practically come to mean those of the Romans, the Anglicans, and the Wesleyans. In compliance with his request I presented myself at that strange, barrack-like building off the Vauxhall Bridge Road, which was formerly the Guards' Institute, and is now the Archbishop's House. Of course, I had long been familiar with the Cardinal's shrunken form and finely cut features, and that extraordinary dignity of bearing which gave him, though in reality below the middle height, the air and aspect of a tall man. But I only knew him as a conspicuous and impressive figure in society, on public platforms, and(where he specially loved to be) in the precincts of the House of Commons. I had never exchanged a word with him, and it was with a feeling of very special interest that I entered his presence.

We had little in common. I was still a yonng man, and the Cardinal was already old. I was a stanch Anglican ; he the most devoted of Papalists. I was strongly opposed both to his Ultramontane policy and to those dexterous methods by which he was commonly supposed to promote it; and, as far as the circumstances of my life had given me any insight into the interior of Romanism, I agreed with the great Oratorian of Birmingham rather than with his brother - Cardinal of Westminster. But though I hope that iriy principles stood firm, all my prejudices melted away in that fascinating presence. Though there was something like half a century's difference in our ages, I felt at once and completely at home with him.

What made our perfect ease of intercourse more remarkable was that, as far as the Cardinal's immediate object was concerned, my visit was a total failure. I had no sympathy with his scheme for the endowment of denominational teaching, and, with all the will in the world to please him, I could not even meet him half-way. But this untoward circumstance did not import the least difficulty or restraint into our conversation. He gently glided from business into general topics; knew all about my career, congratulated me on some recent success, remembered some of my belongings, inquired about my school and college, was interested to find that, like himself, I had been at Harrow and Oxford, and, after an hour's pleasant chat, said : " Now you must stay and have some luncheon." From that day to the end of his life I was a frequent visitor at his house, and every year that I knew him I learned to regard and respect him increasingly.

Looking back over these fourteen years, and reviewing my impressions of his personality, I must put first the physical aspect of the man. He seemed older than he was, and even more ascetic, for he looked as if, like the cardinal in *Lothair,* he lived on biscuits and soda-water; whereas he had a hearty appetite for his mid-day meal, and, in his own words, "enjoyed his tea." Still, he carried the irreducible minimum of flesh on his bones, and his hollow cheeks and shrunken jaws threw his massive forehead into striking prominence. His line of features was absolutely faultless in its statuesque regularity, but his face was saved from the insipidity of too great perfection by the imperious – rather ruthless – lines of his mouth and the penetrating lustre of his deep-set eyes. His dress – a black cassock edged and buttoned with crimson, with a crimson skullcap and biretta, and a pectoral cross of gold – enhanced the picturesqueness of his aspect, and as he entered the anteroom where one awaited his approach, the most Protestant knee instinctively bent.

His dignity was astonishing. The position of a Cardinal, with a princely rank recognized abroad, but officially ignored in England, was a difficult one to carry off, but his exquisite tact enabled him to sustain it to perfection. He never put himself forward; never asserted his rank ; never exposed himself to rebuffs; still, he always contrived to be the most conspicuous figure in any company which he entered; and whether one greeted him with the homage due to a Prince of the Church or merely with the respect which no one refuses to a courtly old gentleman, his manner was equally easy, natural, and unembarrassed. The fact that the Cardinal's name, after due consideration, was inserted in the Royal Commission on the Housing of the Poor immediately after that of the Prince of Wales and before Lord Salisbury's was the formal recognition of a social precedence which his adroitness and judgment had already made his own.

To imagine that Cardinal Manning regarded station or dignity, or even power, as treasures to be valued in themselves would be ridiculously to misconceive the man. He had two supreme and absorbing objects in life – if, indeed, they may not be more properly spoken of as one – the glory of God and the salvation of men. These were, in his intellect and conscience, identified with the victory of the Roman Church. To these all else was subordinated; by its relation to these all else was weighed and calculated. His ecclesiastical dignity, and the secular recognition of it, were valuable as means to htgh ends. They attracted public notice to his person and mission ; they secured him a wider hearing ; they gave him access to circles which, perhaps, would otherwise have been closed. Hence, and for no other reason, they were valuable.

It is always to be borne in mind that Manning was essentially a man of the world, though he was much more than that. Be it far from me to disparage the ordinary type of Roman ecclesiastic, who is bred in a seminary, and perhaps spends his lifetime in a religious community. That peculiar training produces, often enough, a character of saintliness and unworldly grace on which one can only " look," to use a phrase of Mr. Gladstone's, " as men look up at the stars." But it was a very different process that had made Cardinal Manning what he was. He had touched life at many points. A wealthy home, four years at Harrow, Balliol in its palmiest clays, a good degree, a College Fellowship, political and secular ambitions of no common kind, apprenticeship to the practical work of a Government office, a marriage brightly but all too briefly happy, the charge of a country parish, and an early initiation into the duties of ecclesiastical rulership; all these experiences had made Henry Manning, by the time of his momentous change, an accomplished man of the world.

His subsequent career, though, of course, it super- added certain characteristics of its own, never obliterated or even concealed the marks left by those earlier phases, and the octogenarian Cardinal was a beautifully mannered, well-informed, sagacious old gentleman, who, but for his dress, might have passed for a Cabinet Minister, an eminent judge, or a great county magnate.

His mental alertness was remarkable. He seemed to read everything that came out, and to know all that was going on. He probed the secrets of character with a glance, and was particularly sharp on pretentiousness and self-importance. A well-known publicist, who perhaps thinks of himself rather more highly than he ought to think, once ventured to tell the Cardinal that he knew nothing about the subject of a painful agitation which pervaded London in the summer of 1885. " I have been hearing confessions in London for thirty years, and I fancy more people have confided their secrets to me than to you, Mr. ," was the Cardinal's reply.

Once, when his burning sympathy with suffering and his profound contempt for Political Economy had led him, in his own words, to " poke fun at the Dismal Science," the *Times* lectured him in its most superior manner, and said that the venerable prelate seemed to mistake cause and effect. "That," said the Cardinal to me, "is the sort of criticism that an undergraduate makes, and thinks himself very clever. But I am told that in the present day the *Times* is chiefly written by undergraduates."

I once asked him what he thought of a high dignitary of the English Church, who had gone a certain way in a public movement, and then had been frightened back by clamor. His reply was the single word *"infirmus,"* accompanied by that peculiar sniff which every one whoever conversed with him must remember as adding so much to the piquancy of his terse judgments. When he was asked his opinion of a famous biography in which a son had disclosed, with too absolute frankness, his father's innermost thoughts and feelings, the Cardinal replied: " I think that has committed the sin of Ham."

His sense of humor was peculiarly keen, and though it was habitually kept under control, it was sometimes used to point a moral with admirable effect.

" What are you going to do in life ?" he asked a rather flippant undergraduate at Oxford.

" Oh, I'm going to take Holy Orders," was the airy reply.

"Take care you get them, my son."

Though he was intolerant of bumptiousness, the Cardinal liked young men. He often had some about him, and in speaking to them the friendliness of his manner was touched with fatherliness in a truly attractive fashion. And as with young men, so with children. Surely nothing could be prettier than this answer to a little girl in New York who had addressed some of her domestic experiences to "Cardinal Manning, England":

" My Dear Child, – You ask me whether I am glad to receive letters from little children. I am always glad, for they write kindly and give no trouble. I wish all my letters were like them. Give my blessing to your father, and tell him that our good Master will reward him a hundredfold for all he has lost for the sake of his faith. Tell him that when he comes over to England he must come to see me. And mind you bring your violin, for I love music, but seldom have any time to hear it. The next three or four years of your life are very precious. They are like the ploughing-time and the sowing-time of the year. You are learning to know God, the Holy Trinity, the Incarnation, the presence and voice of the Holy Ghost in the Church of Jesus Christ. Learn all these things solidly, and you will love the Blessed Sacrament and our Blessed Mother with all your heart. And now you will pray for me that I may make a good end of a long life, which cannot be far off. And may God guide you, and guard yon in innocence and in fidelity through this evil, evil world ! And may His blessing be on your home and all belonging to you ! Believe me always a true friend,

" Henry Edward, " Card. Abp. of Westminster."

The Cardinal had, I should say, rather a contempt for women. He exercised a great influence over them, but I question if he rated their intellectual and moral qualities as highly as he ought, and their "rights" he held in utter detestation. General society, though in his later days he saw little of it except at the Athenaeum, he thoroughly enjoyed. Like most old people, he was fond of talking about old days, and as he had known hosts of important and interesting men, had a tenacious memory, and spoke the most finished English, it was a pleasure to listen to his reminiscences. He wrote as well as he talked. His pointed and lucid style gave to his printed performances a semblance of cogency which they did not really possess; and his letters – even his shortest notes – were as exquisite in wording as in penmanship. As he grew older he became increasingly sensible of the charms of " Auld Lang Syne," and he delighted to renew his acquaintance with the scenes and associations of his youth.

On July 15, 1888, being the first day of the Eton and Harrow Match at Lord's, a few Old Harrovians of different generations met at a Harrow dinner. The Cardinal, who had just turned eighty, was invited. He declinedto dine, on the ground that he never dined out, but he would on no account forego the opportunity of meeting the members of his old school, and he recalled with pride that he had been for two years in the Harrow Eleven. He appeared as soon as dinner was over, gallantly faced the cloud of cigar-smoke, was in his very best vein of anecdote and reminiscence, and stayed till the party broke up.

The Cardinal's friendships were not, I believe, numerous, but his affection for Mr. Gladstone is well known. It dated from Oxford. Through Manning and Hope-Scott the influence of the Catholic revival reached the young member for Newark, and they were the godfathers of his eldest son. After their secession to Rome in 1851 this profound friendship fell into abeyance. As far as Manning was concerned, it was renewed when, in 1868, Mr. Gladstone took in hand to disestablish the Irish Church.

It was broken again by the controversy about *Vaticanism* in 1875; and a few years ago was happily revived by the good offices of a common friend. " Gladstone is a very fine fellow," said the Cardinal to me in 1890. "He is not vindictive. You may fight him as hard as you like, and when the fight is over you will find that it has left no rancor behind it."

This affection for Mr. Gladstone was a personal matter, quite independent of politics; but in political matters also they had much in common. " Yon know," wrote the Cardinal to Mrs. Gladstone on her Golden Wedding, "how nearly I have agreed in William's political career, especially in his Irish policy of the last twenty years." He accepted the principle of Home Rule, though he thought badly of the Bill of 1886, and predicted its failure from the day when it was brought in. The exclusion of the Irish members was in his eyes a fatal blot, as tending rather to separation than to that Imperial federation which washis political ideal. But the Cardinal always held his politics in subordination to his religion, and at the General Election of 1885 his vigorous intervention on behalf of denominational education, which he considered to be imperilled by the Radical policy, considerably embarrassed the Liberal cause in those districts of London where there is a Roman Catholic vote.

It is necessary to say a word about Cardinal Manning's method of religious propagandism. He excelled in the art of driving a nail where it would go. He never worried his acquaintance with controversy, never introduced religious topics unseasonably, never cast his pearls before nnappreciative animals. But when he saw a chance, an opening, a sympathetic tendency, or a weak spot, he fastened on it with unerring instinct. His line was rather admonitory than persuasive. When he thought that the person whom he was addressing had an inkling of the truth, but was held back from avowing it by cowardice or indecision, he would utter the most startling warnings about the danger of dallying with grace.

"I promise you to become a Catholic when I am twenty-one," said a young lady whom he was trying to convert.

" But can you promise to live so long ?" was the searching rejoinder.

In Manning's belief, the Roman Church was the one oracle of truth and the one ark of salvation; and his was the faith which would compass sea and land, sacrifice all that it possessed, and give its body to be burned, if it might by any means bring one more soul to safety. If he could win a single human being to see the truth and act on it, he was supremely happy. To make the Church of Rome attractive, to enlarge her borders, to win recruits for her, was therefore his constant effort. He had an ulterior eye to it in all his public works – hiszealous teetotalism, his advocacy of the claims of labor, his sympathy with the cause of Home Rule; and the same principle which animated him in these large schemes of philanthropy and public policy made itself felt in the minutest details of daily life and personal dealing. Where he saw the possibility of making a convert, or even of dissipating prejudice and inclining a single Protestant more favorably towards Rome, he left no stone unturned to secure this all - important end. Hence it came that he was constantly, and not wholly without reason, depicted as a man whom in religious things it was impossible to trust; with whom the end justified the means; and whose every act and word, where the interests of his Church were involved, must be watched with the most jealous suspicion.

All this was grossly overstated. Whatever else Cardinal Manning was, he was an English gentleman of the old school, with a nice sense of honor and propriety. But still, under a mass of calumny and exaggeration there lay this substratum of truth – that he who wills the end wills the means; and that where the interests of a sacred cause are at stake, an enthusiastic adherent will sometimes use methods to which, in enterprises of less pith and moment, recourse could not possibly be had.

Manning had what has been called " the ambition of distinctiveness." He felt that he had a special mission which no other man could so adequately fulfil, and this was to establish and popularize in England his own robust faith in the cause of the Papacy as identical with the cause of God. There never lived a stronger Papal- ist. He was more Ultramontane than the Ultramon- tanes. Everything Roman was to him divine. Italian architecture, Italian vestments, the Italian mode of pronouncing ecclesiastical Latin were dear to him, because they visibly and audibly implied the all-pervading presence and power of Rome. Rightly or wrongly, he conceived that English Romanism, as it was when he joined the Roman Church, was practically Gallicanism ; that it minimized the Papal supremacy, was disloyal to the Temporal Power, and was prone to accommodate itself to its Protestant and secular environment. Against this time-serving spirit he set his face like a flint. He believed that he had been divinely appointed to Papalize England. The cause of the Pope was the cause of God; Manning was the person who could best serve the Pope's cause, and therefore all forces which opposed him were in effect opposing the Divine Will. This seems to have been his simple and sufficient creed, and certainly it had the merit of supplying a clear rule of action. It made itself felt in his hostility to the Religious Orders, and especially the Society of Jesus. Religious Orders are extra-episcopal. The Jesuits are scarcely subject to the Pope himself. Certainly neither the Orders nor the Society would, or could, be subject to Manning. A power independent of, or hostile to, his authority was inimical to religion, and must, as a religious duty, he checked, and, if possible, destroyed. Exactly the same principle animated his dealings with Cardinal Newman. Rightly or wrongly, Manning thought Newman a halfhearted Papalist. He dreaded alike his way of putting tiiings and his practical policy. Newman's favorite scheme of establishing a Roman Catholic college at Oxford Manning regarded as fraught with peril to the faith of the rising generation. The scheme must, therefore, be crushed and its author snubbed.

I must in candor add that these differences of opinion between the two Cardinals were mixed with, and embittered by, a sense of personal dislike. When Newman died there appeared in a monthly magazine a series of very unflattering sketches by one who had known himwell. I ventured to ask Cardinal Manning if he had seen these sketches. He replied that he had, and thought them very shocking; the writer must have a very unenviable mind, etc.; and then, having thus sacrificed to propriety, after a moment's pause he added: " But if you ask me if they are like poor Newman, I am bound to say – *a photograph."*

It was, I suppose, matter of common knowledge that Manning's early and conspicuous ascendency in the counsels of the Papacy rested largely on the intimacy of his personal relations with Pius IX. But it was news to most of us that (if his biographer is right) he wished to succeed Antonelli as Secretary of State in 1876, and to transfer the scene of his activities from Westminster to Rome ; and that he attributed the Pope's disregard of his wishes to mental decrepitude. The point, if true, is an important one, for his accession to the Secretaryship of State, and permanent residence in Rome, could not have failed to affect the development of events when, two years later, the Papal throne became vacant by the death of Pius IX. But *Deo aliter visum.* It was ordained that he should pass the evening of his days in England, and that he should outlive his intimacy at the Vatican and his influence on the general policy of the Church of Rome. With the accession of Leo XIII. a new order began, and Newman's elevation to the sacred purple seemed to affix the sanction of Infallibility to principles, views, and methods against which Manning had waged a Thirty Years' War. Henceforward he felt himself a stranger at the Vatican, and powerless beyond the limits of his own jurisdiction.

Perhaps this restriction of exterior activities in the ecclesiastical sphere drove the venerable Cardinal to find a vent for his untiring energies in those various efforts of social reform in which, during the last ten years ofhis life, he played so conspicuous a part. If this be so, though Rome may have lost, England was unquestionably a gainer. It was during those ten years that I was honored by his friendship. The storms, the struggles, the ambitions, the intrigues which had filled so large a part of his middle life lay far behind. He was revered, useful, and I think contented, in his present life, and looked forward with serene confidence to the final, and not distant, issue. Thrice happy is the man who, in spite of increasing infirmity and the loss of much that once made life enjoyable, thus

"Finds comfort in himself and in his cause,
And, while the mortal mist is gathering, draws
His breath in confidence of Heaven's applause." LOHD HOUGHTOIT

It is narrated of an ancient Fellow of All Souls' that, lamenting the changes which had transformed his College from a nest of aristocratic idlers into a society of accomplished scholars, he exclaimed : " Hang it all, sir, we were *sui generis."* What the unreformed Fellows of All Souls' were among the common run of Oxford dons, that, it may truly (and with better syntax) be said, the late Lord Houghton was among his fellow- citizens. Of all the men I have ever known he was, I think, the most completely *sui generis.* His temperament and turn of mind were, as far as I know, quite unlike anything that obtained among his predecessors and contemporaries ; nor do I see them reproduced among the men who have come after him. His peculiarities were not external. His appearance accorded with his position. He looked very much what one would have expected in a country gentleman of large means and prosperous circumstances. His early portraits show that he was very like all the other young gentlemen of fashion whom D'Orsay drew, with their long hair, high collars, and stupendous neckcloths. The admirably faithful work of Mr. Lehmann will enable all posterity to know exactly what he looked in his later years, with his loose-fitting clothes, comfortable figure, and air of genial gravity. Externally all was normal. His peculiarities were those of mental habit, temperament, and taste. As far as I know, he had not a drop of foreign blood in his veins, yet his nature was essentially un-English.

A country gentleman who frankly preferred living in London, and a Yorkshireman who detested sport, made a sufficiently strange phenomenon ; but in Lord Houghton the astonished world beheld as well a politician who wrote poetry, a railway director who lived in literature, a *libre-penseur* who championed the Tractarians, a sentimentalist who talked like a cynic, and a philosopher who had elevated conviviality to the dignity of an exact science. Here, indeed, was a "living oxymoron" – a combination of inconsistent and incongruous qualities which to the typical John Bull – Lord Palmerston's "Fat man with a white hat in the twopenny omnibus" – was a sealed and hopeless mystery.

Something of this unlikeness to his fellow-Englishmen was due, no doubt, to the fact that Lord Houghton, the only son of a gifted, eccentric, and indulgent father, was brought up at home. The glorification of the Public School has been ridiculously overdone. But it argues no blind faith in that strange system of unnatural restraints and scarcely more reasonable indulgences to share Gibbon's opinion that the training of a Public School is the best adapted to the common run of Englishmen.

"It made us what we were, sir," said Major Bagstock to Mr. Dombey; "we were iron, sir, and it forged us." The average English boy being what he is by nature – "a soaring human boy," as Mr. Chadband called him – a Public School simply makes him more so. It confirms alike his characteristic faults and his peculiar virtues, and turns him out after five or six years that altogether lovely and gracious product – the Average Englishman. This may be readily conceded; but, after all, the pleasantness of the world as a place of residence, and the growing good of the human race, do not depend exclusively on the Average Englishman ; and something may be said for the system of training which has produced (not only all famous foreigners, for they, of course, are a negligible quantity), but such exceptional Englishmen as William Pitt, and Thomas Macaulay, and John Keble, and Samuel Wilberforce, and Richard Monckton Milnes.

From an opulent and cultivated home young Milnes passed to the most famous college in the world, and found himself under the tuition of Whewell and Thirl- wall, and in the companionship of Alfred Tennyson and Julius Hare, Charles Buller and John Sterling – a highhearted brotherhood who made their deep mark on the spiritual and intellectual life of their own generation and of that which succeeded it.

After Cambridge came foreign travel, on a scale and plan quite outside the beaten track of the conventional "grand tour" as our fathers knew it. From the Continent Richard Milnes brought back a gayety of spirit, a frankness of bearing, a lightness of touch which were quite un-English, and " a taste for French novels, French cookery, and French wines " with which Miss Crawley would have sympathized. In 1837 he entered Parliament as a " Liberal Conservative " for the Borough of Ponte- fract, over which his father exercised considerable influence, and he immediately became a conspicuous figure in the social life of London. A few years later his position and character were drawn by the hand of a master in a passage which will well bear yet one more reproduction :

"Mr. Vavasour was a social favorite ; a poet, and a real poet, and a troubadour, as well as a Member of Parliament ; travelled, sweet-tempered, and good-hearted; amusing and clever. With catholic sympathies and an eclectic turn of mind, Mr. Vavasour saw something good in everybody and everything, which is certainly amiable, and perhaps just, but disqualifies a man in some degree for the business of life, which

requires for its conduct a certain degree of prejudice. Mr. Vavasour's breakfasts were renowned. Whatever your creed, class, or country – one might almost add your character – you were a welcome guest at his matutinal meal, provided you were celebrated. That qualification, however, was rigidly enforced. A real philosopher, alike from his genial disposition and from the influence of his rich and various information, Vavasour moved amid the strife, sympathizing with every one ; and perhaps, after all, the philanthropy which was his boast was not untinged by a dash of humor, of which rare and charming quality he possessed no inconsiderable portion. Vavasour liked to know everybody who was known, and to see everything which ought to be seen. His life was a gyration of energetic curiosity; an insatiable whirl of social celebrity. There was not a congregation of sages and philosophers in any part of Europe which he did not attend as a brother. He was present at the camp of Kalish in his yeomanry uniform, and assisted at the festivals of Barcelona in an Andalusian jacket. He was everywhere, and at everything ; he had gone down in a diving-bell and gone up in a balloon. As for his acquaintances, he was welcomed in every land; his universal sympathies seemed omnipotent. Emperor and King, Jacobin and Carbonaro, alike cherished him. He was the steward of Polish balls, and the vindicator of Russian humanity; he dined with Louis Philippe, and gave dinners to Louis Blanc."

Lord Beaconsfield's penetration in reading character and skill in delineating it were never, I think, displayed to better advantage than in the foregoing passage. Divested of its intentional and humorous exaggerations, it is not a caricature, but a portrait. It exhibits with singular fidelity the qualities which made Lord Houghton, tothe end of his long life, at once unique and lovable. We recognize the overflowing sympathy, the keen interest in life, the vivid faculty of enjoyment, the absolute freedom from national prejudice, the love of seeing and of being seen.

During the Chartist riots of 1848 Matthew Arnold wrote to his mother : " Tell Miss Martineau it is said here that Monckton Milnes refused to be sworn in a special constable, that he might be free to assume the post of President of the Republic at a moment's notice." And those who knew Lord Houghton best suspect that he himself originated the joke at his own expense. The assured ease of young Milnes's social manner, even among complete strangers, so unlike the morbid self-repression and proud humility of the typical Englishman, won for him the nickname of " The Cool of the Evening." His wholly un-Euglish tolerance, and constant effort to put himself in the place of others whom the world condemned, procured for him from Carlyle (who genuinely loved him) the title of " President of the Heaven-aud- Hell - Amalgamation Company." Bishop Wilberforce wrote, describing a dinner-party in 1847 : " Carlyle was very great. Monckton Milnes drew him out. Milnes began the young man's cant of the present day – the barbarity and wickedness of capital punishment; that, after all, we could not be sure others were wicked, etc. Carlyle broke out on him with: ' None of your Heaven-and- Hell-Amalgamation Companies for me. We *do* know what is wickedness. *I* know wicked men, men whom I *would not live with ;* men whom under some conceivable circumstances I would kill or they should kill me. No, Milnes, there's no truth or greatness in all that. It's just poor, miserable littleness.'"

Lord Houghton's faculty of enjoyment was peculiarly keen. He warmed both hands, and indeed all his nature, before the fire of life. "All impulses of soul and sense

" affected him with agreeable emotions; no pleasure of body or spirit came amiss to him. And in nothing was he more characteristically nn-English than in the frank manifestation of his enjoyment, bubbling over with an infections jollity, and never, even when touched by years and illness, taking his pleasures after that melancholy manner of our nation to which it is a point of literary honor not more directly to allude. Equally un-English was his frank openness of speech and bearing. His address was pre-eminently what old-fashioned people called "forthcoming." It was strikingly – even amusingly – free from that frigid dignity and arrogant reserve for which, as a nation, we are so justly famed. I never saw him kiss a guest on both cheeks, but if I had I should not have felt the least surprised.

What would have surprised me would have been if the guest (whatever his difference of age or station) had not felt immediately and completely at home, or if Lord Houghton had not seemed and spoken as if they had known one another from the days of short frocks and skipping-ropes. There never lived so perfect a host. His sympathy was genius, and his hospitality a fine art. He was peculiarly sensitive to the claims of "Auld Lang Syne," and when a young man came up from Oxford or Cambridge to begin life in London he was certain to find that Lord Houghton had travelled on the Continent with his father, or had danced with his mother, or had made love to his aunt, and was eagerly on the look-out for an opportunity of showing gracious and valuable kindness to the son of his ancient friends.

When I first lived in London Lord Houghton was occupying a house in Arlington Street made famous by the fact that Hogarth drew its interior and decorations in his pictures of " Mariage a la Mode." And nowhere did the social neophyte receive a warmer welcome, or find himself amid a more eclectic and representative society. Queens of fashion, professional beauties, authors and authoresses, ambassadors, philosophers, discoverers, actors – every one who was famous or even notorious, who had been anywhere or had done anything, from a successful speech in Parliament to a hazardous leap at the Aquarium – jostled one another on the wide staircase and in the gravely ornate drawing-rooms. And amid the motley crowd the genial host was omnipresent, with a warm greeting and a twinkling smile for each successive guest – a good story, a happy quotation, the last morsel of piquant gossip, the newest theory of ethics or of politics.

Lord Houghton's humor had a quality which was quite its own. Nothing was sacred to it – neither age, nor sex, nor subject was spared; but it was essentially good-natured. It was the property of a famous spear to heal the wounds which itself had made; the shafts of Lord Houghton's fun needed no healing virtue, for they made no wound. When that saintly friend of temperance and all good causes, Mr. Cowper Temple, was raised to the peerage as Lord Mount Temple, Lord Houghton went about saying : "You know that the precedent for Billy Cowper's title is in *Don Juan* –

"'And Lord Mount Coffee-house, the Irish peer,
Who killed himself for love, with drink, last year.'"

When a very impecunious youth, who could barely afford to pay for his cab-fares, lost a pound to him at whist, Lord Houghton said, as he pocketed the coin, "Ah! my dear boy, the *great* Lord Hertford, whom foolish people called the *wicked* Lord Hertford – Thackeray's Steyne and Dizzy's Monmouth – used to say, ' There is no pleasure in winning money from a man who does not feel it.'How true that was !" And when he saw a young friend at a club supping *on pate defoie gras* and champagne, he said encouragingly, " That's quite right. All the pleasant things in life are unwholesome, or expensive, or wrong." And amid these rather grim morsels of experimental philosophy he would interject certain *obiter dicta* which came straight from the unspoiled goodness of a really kind heart.

"All men are improved by prosperity," he used to say. Envy, hatred, and malice had no place in his nature. It was a positive enjoyment to him to see other people happy, and a friend's success was as gratifying as his own. His life, though in most respects singularly happy, had not been without its disappointments. At one time he had nursed political ambitions, and his peculiar knowledge of foreign affairs had seemed to indicate a special line of activity and success. But things went differently. He always professed to regard his peerage as "a Second Class in the School of Life," and himself as a political failure. Yet no tinge of sourness, or jealousy, or cynical disbelief in his more successful contemporaries ever marred the geniality of his political conversation.

As years advanced he became not (as the manner of most men is) less Liberal, but more so ; keener in sympathy with all popular causes ; livelier in his indignation against monopoly and injustice. Thirty years ago, in the struggle for the Reform Bill of 1866, his character and position were happily hit off by Sir George Trevelyan in a description of a walk down Piccadilly : –

" There on warm midsummer Sundays Fryston's Bard is wont to
wend,
Whom the Ridings trust and honor, Freedom's staunch and jovial friend:
Loved where shrewd hard-handed craftsmen cluster round the
northern kilns – He whom men style Baron Houghton, but the Gods call Dicky
Milnes."

And eighteen years later there was a whimsical pathos in the phrase in which he announced his fatal illness to a friend: "Yes, I am going to join the Majority – and yon know I have always preferred Minorities."

It would be foreign to my purpose to criticize Lord Houghton as a poet. My object in these papers is merely to record the characteristic traits of eminent men who have honored me with their friendship, and among those there is none for whose memory I cherish a warmer sentiment of affectionate gratitude than for him whose likeness I have now tried to sketch. His was the most precious of combinations – a genius and a heart. An estimate of his literary gifts and performances lies altogether outside my scope, but the political circumstances of the present hour impel me to conclude this paper with a quotation which, even if it stood alone, would, I think, justify Lord Beaconsfield's judgment quoted above – that "he was a poet, and a true poet." Here is the lyrical cry which, writing in 1843, he puts into the mouth of Greece : –

" And if to his old Asian seat,
From this usurped, unnatural throne,
The Turk is driven, 'tis surely meet
That we again should hold our own ;
Be but Byzantium's native sign
Of Cross on Crescent once unfurled,

And Greece shall guard by right divine
The portals of the Eastern world."

The Turks adopted the sign of the Crescent from Byzantium after the Conquest: the Cross above the Crescent is found on many ruins of the Grecian city – among others, on the Genoese castle on the Bosphorus.

3

SECTION 3

VI

RELIGION AND MORALITY

In these papers I have been trying to recall some notable people through whom I have been brought into contact with the social life of the past. I now propose to give the impressions which they conveyed to me of the moral, material, and political condition of England just at the moment when the old order was yielding place to new, and modern society was emerging from the birth- throes of the French Revolution. All testimony seems to me to point to the fact that towards the close of the last century, Religion was almost extinct in the highest and lowest classes of English society. The poor were sunk in ignorance and barbarism, and the aristocracy was honeycombed by profligacy. Morality, discarded alike by high and low, took refuge in the great Middle Class, then, as now, largely influenced by Evangelical Dissent. A dissolute Heir - Apparent presided over a social system in which not merely religion but decency was habitually disregarded. The Princes of the Blood were notorious for a feedom of life and manners which would be ludicrous if it were not shocking.

Here I may cite an unpublished diary of Lord Robert Seymour (son of the first Marquis of Hertford), who was born in 1748 and died in 1831. He was a man of fashion and a Member of Parliament; and these are some of the incidents which he notes in 1788:

" The Prince of Wales declares there is not an honestWoman in London, excepting Ly. Parker and Ly. Westmoreland, and those are so stupid he can make nothing of them, they are scarcely fit to blow their own Noses."

"At Mrs. Vaneck's assembly last week, the Prince of Wales, very much to the honor of his polite and elegant Behavior, measured the breadth of Mrs. V. behind with his Handkerchief, and shew'd the measurement to most of the Company."

" Another Trait of the P. of Wales' Respectful Conduct is that at an assembly he beckoned to the poor old Dutchess of Bedford across a large Room, and, when she had taken the trouble of crossing the Room, he very abruptly told her he had nothiug to say to her."

" The P. of W. called on Miss Vaueck last week with two of his Equerries. On coming into the Room he exclaimed, ' I *must* do it; I *must* do it.' Miss V. asked him what it was that he was obliged to do, when he winked at St. Leger and the other *accomplice,* who lay'd Miss V. on the Floor, and the P. possitively wipped her. The occasion of this extraordinary behavior was occasioned by a Bett wcb. I suppose he had made in one of his mad Fits. The next day, however, he wrote her a penitential Letter, and she now receives him on the same footing as ever."

"The Prince of Wales very much affronted the D. of Orleans and his natural Brother, L'Abbe de la Fai, at Newmarket, L'Abbe declaring it possible to charm a Fish out of the Water, which being disputed occasioned a Bett; and the Abbe stooped down over the water to tickle the Fish with a little switch. Fearing, however, the Prince sd. play him some Trick, he declared he hoped the P. wd. not use him unfairly by throwing him into the water. The P. answer'd him that he wd. not upon his Honor. The Abbe had no sooner began the operation by leaning over a little Bridge when the P. took holdof his Heels and threw him into the Water, which was rather deep. The Abbe, much enraged, the moment he got himself out run at the P. with g'. violence, a Horsewhip in his Hand, saying he thought very meanly of a P. who cou'd not keep his word. The P. flew fr. him, and getting to the Inn locked himself in one of the Rooms."

"Prince of Wales, Mrs. FitzHerbert, the Duke and Dutchess of Cumberland, and Miss Pigott, Mrs. F.'s companion, went a Party to Windsor during the absence of *The Family* fm. Windsor; and going to see a cold Bath Miss P. expressed a great wish to bathe this hot weather. The D. of 0. very imprudently pushed her in, and the Dut. of C. having the presence of mind to throw out the Rope saved her when in such a disagreeable State from fear and surprise as to be near sinking. Mrs. F. went into convulsion Fits, and the Dut. fainted away, and the scene proved ridiculous in the extreme, as Report says the Duke called out to Miss P. that he was instantly coming to her in the water, and continued undressing himself. Poor Miss P/s clothes entirely laid upon the water, and made her appear an awkward figure. They afterwards pushed in one of the Prince's attendants."

So much for High Life at the close of the last century. It is more difficult to realize that we are separated only by some sixty years from a time when the Lord Chancellor and a brother of the Sovereign conducted a business-like correspondence on the question whether the Chancellor had or had not turned the Prince out of the house for insulting his wife. The journals, newspapers, and memoirs of the time throw (especially for those who can read between the lines) a startling light on that hereditary principle which plays so important a part in our political system. All the ancillary vices flourished with a rank luxuriance. Hard drinking was the indispensable accomplishment of a fine gentleman, and great estates were constantly changing owners at the gamingtable.

The fifth Duke of Bedford (who had the temerity to attack Burke's pension, and thereby drew down upon himself the most splendid repartee in literature) was a bosom friend of Fox, and lived in a like-minded society. One night at Newmarket he lost a colossal sum at hazard, and jumping up in a passion, he swore that the dice were loaded, put them in his pocket, and went to bed. Next morning he examined the dice in the presence of his boon companions, found that they were not loaded, and had to apologize and pay. Some years afterwards one of the party was lying on his death-bed, and he sent for the duke. " I have sent for you to tell you that you were right. The dice *were* loaded. We waited till you were asleep, went to your bedroom, took them out of your waistcoat pocket, replaced them with unloaded ones, and retired."

"But suppose I had woke and caught you doing it?" "Well, we were desperate men – *and we had pistols."* Anecdotes of the same type might be multiplied endlessly, and would serve to confirm the strong impression which all contemporary evidence leaves upon the mind – that the closing years of the last century witnessed the *nadir* of English virtue. The national conscience was in truth asleep, and it had a rude awakening. " I have heard persons of great weight and authority," writes Mr. Gladstone, "such as Mr. Grenville, and also, I think, Archbishop Howley, ascribe the beginnings of a reviving seriousness in the upper classes of lay society to a reaction against the horrors and impieties of the first French Revolution in its later stages." And this reviving seriousness was by no means confined to Nonconformist circles. In the last century the religions activities of the timeproceeded largely (though not exclusively) from persons who, from one cause or another, were separated from the Established Church. Much theological learning and controversial skill, with the old traditions of Anglican divinity, had been drawn aside from the highway of the Establishment into the secluded byways of the Nonjurors. Whitefield and the Wesleys, and that grim but grand old Mother in Israel, Selina Countess of Huntingdon, found their evangelistic energies fatally cramped by episcopal authority, and, quite against their natural inclinations, were forced to act through independent organizations of their own making. But at the beginning of this century things took a different turn.

The distinguishing mark of the religious revival which issued from the French Revolntion was that it lived and moved and had its being within the precincts of the Church of England. Of that Church, as it existed at the close of the last century and the beginning of this, the characteristic feature had been a quiet worldliness. The typical clergyman, as drawn, for instance, in Crabbe's poems and Miss Austen's novels, is a well-bred, respectable, and kindly person, playing an agreeable part in the social life of his neighborhood, and doing a secular work of solid value, but equally removed from the sacerdotal pretensions of the Caroline divines and from the awakening fervor of the Evangelical preachers. The professors of a more spiritual or a more aggressive religion were at once disliked and despised. Sydney Smith was never tired of poking fun at the "sanctified village of Clap- ham" and its "serious" inhabitants, at missionary effort and revivalist enthusiasm. When Lady Louisa Lennox was engaged to a prominent Evangelical and Liberal – Mr. Tighe, of Woodstock – her mother, the Duchess of Richmond, said : " Poor Louisa is going to make a shocking marriage – a man called *Tiggy,* my dear, a Saint anda Radical." When Lord Melbourne had accidentally found himself the unwilling hearer of a rousing Evangelical sermon about sin and its consequences, he exclaimed in much disgust as he left the church : "Things have come to a pretty pass when religion is allowed to invade the sphere of private 'life !"

Arthur Young tells us that a daughter of the first Lord Carrington said to a visitor: " My papa used to have prayers in his family; *but none since he has been a Peer."* A venerable Canon of Windsor, who was a younger son of a great family, told me that his old nurse, when she was putting him and his little brothers to bed, used to say : "If you're very good little boys, and go to bed without giving trouble, you needn't say your prayers to-night." When the late Lord Mount Temple was a youth, he wished to take Holy Orders; and the project so horrified his parents that, after holding a family council, they plunged him into fashionable society in the hope of distracting his mind from religion, and accomplished their end by making him join the Blues.

The quiet woiidliness which characterized the English Church as a whole was unpleasantly varied here and there by instances of grave and monstrous scandal. The system of Pluralities left isolated parishes in a condition of practical heathenism. Even bare morality was not always observed. In solitary places clerical drunkenness was common. On Saturday afternoon the parson would return from the nearest town "market-merry." He consorted freely with the farmers, shared their habits, and spoke their language.

I have known a lady to whom a country clergyman said, pointing to the darkened windows where a corpse lay awaiting burial, " There's a stiff 'un in that house." I have known a country gentleman in Shropshire who had seen his own vicar drop the chalice at the Holy Communion because he was too drnnk to hold it. I know a corner of Bedfordshire where, within the recollection of persons living thirty years ago, three clerical neighbors used to meet for dinner at oue another's parsonages in turn. One winter afternoon a corpse was brought for burial to the village church. The vicar of the place came from his dinner so drunk that he could not read the service, although his sister supported him with one hand and held the lantern with the other. He retired beaten, and both his guests made the same attempt with no better success. So the corpse was left in the church, and the vicar buried it next day when he had recovered from his debauch.

While the prevailing tone of quiet worldliness was thus broken, here and there, by horrid scandals, in other places it was conspicuously relieved by splendid instances of piety and self-devotion, such as George Eliot drew in the character of Edgar Tryan of Milby. But the innovating clergy of the Evangelical persuasion had to force their way through " the teeth of clenched antagonisms." The bishops, as a rule, were opposed to enthusiasm, and the bishops of that day were, in virtue of their wealth, their secular importance, and their professional cohesive- ness, a formidable force in the life of the Church.

In the "good old days" of Erastian Clmrchmanship, before the Catholic revival had begun to breathe new life into ancient forms, a bishop was enthroned by proxy f Sydney Smith, rebuking Archbishop Howley for his undue readiness to surrender cathedral property to the Ecclesiastical Commission, pointed out that his conduct was inconsistent with having sworn at his enthronement that he would not alienate the possessions of the Church of Canterbury. " The oath," he goes on, "may be less present to the Archbishop's memory from the fact of his not having taken the oath in person, but by the

medium of a gentleman sent down by the coach to take it for him – a practice which, though I believe it to have been long established in the Church, surprised me, I confess, not a little. A proxy to vote, if you please – a proxy to consent to arrangements of estates, if wanted ; but a proxy sent down in the Canterbury fly to take the Creator to witness that the Archbishop, detained in town by business or pleasure, will never violate that foundation of piety over which he presides – all this seems to me an act of the most extraordinary indolence ever recorded in history." In this judgment the least ritualistic of laymen will heartily concur. But from Archbishop Howley to Archbishop Temple is a far cry, and the latest enthronement in Canterbury Cathedral must have made clear to the most casual eye the enormous transformation which sixty years have wrought alike in the inner temper and the outward aspects of the Church of England.

Once Dr. Liddon, walking with me down the hall of Christ Church, pointed to the portrait of an extremely bloated and sensual-looking prelate on the wall, and said, with that peculiar kind of mincing precision which added so much to the point of his sarcasms: "How singular, dear friend, to reflect that *that person* was chosen, in the providential order, to connect Mr. Keble with the Apostles !" And certainly this connecting link bore little resemblance to either end of the chain. The considerations which governed the selection of a bishop in those good old days were indeed not a little singular. Perhaps he was chosen because he was a sprig of good family, like Archbishop Cornwallis, whose junketings at Lambeth drew down npon him the ire of Lady Huntingdon and the threats of George III., and whose sole qualification for the clerical office was that when an undergraduate he had suffered from a stroke of palsy which partially crippled him, but " did not, however, prevent him from holding a hand at cards."

Perhaps he had been, like Bishop Sumner, "bearleader" to a great man's son, and had won the gratitude of a powerful patron by extricating young hopeful from a matrimonial scrape. Perhaps, like Marsh or Vafi Mil- dert, he was a controversial pamphleteer who had tossed a Calvinist or gored an Evangelical. Or, perhaps, he was, like Blomfield and Monk, a "Greek Play Bishop," who had annotated . Eschylus or composed a Sapphic Ode on a Royal marriage. "Young Crumpet is sent to school; takes to his books ; spends the best years of his life in making Latin verses; knows that the *Crum* in Crumpet is long and the *pet* short; goes to the university ; gets a prize for an Essay on the Dispersion of the Jews; takes Orders ; becomes a bishop's chaplain ; has a young nobleman for his pupil; publishes a useless classic and a Serious Call to the Unconverted ; and then goes through the Elysian transitions of Prebendary, Dean, Prelate, and the long train of purple, profit, and power."

Few – and very few – are the adducible instances in which, in the. reigns of George III., George IV., and William IV., a bishop was appointed for evangelistic zeal or pastoral efficiency.

But, on whatever principle chosen, the bishop, once duly consecrated and enthroned, was a formidable person, and surrounded by a dignity scarcely less than royal. "Nobody likes our bishop," says Parson Lingon in *Felix Holt.* " He's all Greek and greediness, and too proud to dine with his own father." People still living can remember the days when the Archbishop of Canterbury was preceded by servants bearing flambeaux when he walked across from Lambeth Chapel to what were called "Mrs. Howley's Lodgings." When the Archbishop dined out he was treated with princely honors, and no one left theparty till His Grace had made his bow. Once a week he dined in state in the great hall of Lambeth, presiding over a company of self-invited guests – strange perversion of the old archiepiscopal charity to travellers and the poor – while, as Sydney Smith said, "the domestics of the prelacy stood, with swords and bag-wigs, round pig and turkey and venison, to defend, as it were, the orthodox gastronome from the fierce Uiritarian, the fell Baptist, and all the famished children of dissent." When Sir John Coleridge, father of the late Lord Chief Justice, was a young man at the Bar, he wished to obtain a small legal post in the Archbishop's prerogative court. An influential friend undertook to forward his application to the Archbishop. " But remember," he said, " in writing your letter, that His Grace can only be approached on gilt-edged paper." Archbishop Harcourt never went from Bishopthorpe to York Minster except attended by his chaplains, in a coach and six, while Lady Anne was made to follow in a pair-horse carriage, to show her that her position was not the same thing among women that her husband's was among men. At Durham, which was worth $40,000 a year, the Bishop, as Prince Palatine, exercised a secular jurisdiction, both civil and criminal, and the commission at the assizes ran in the name of "Our Lord the Bishop." At Ely, Bishop Sparke gave so many of his best livings to his family that it was locally said that you could find your way across the Fens on a dark night by the number of little Sparkes along the road ; and when this good prelate secured a residentiary canonry for his eldest son, the event was so much a matter of course that he did not deem it worthy of special notice; but when he secured a second canonry for his second son, he was so filled with pious gratitude that, as a thanksgiving offering, he gave a ball at the Palace of Ely to all the county of Cambridge. " And I think," said BishopWoodford, in telling me the story, "that the achievement and the way of celebrating it were equally remarkable."

This grand tradition of mingled splendor and profit ran down, in due degree, through all ranks of the hierarchy. The poorer bishoprics were commonly held in conjunction with a rich deanery or prebend, and not seldom with some important living; so that the most impecunious successor of the Apostles could manage to have four horses to his carriage and his daily bottle of Madeira. Not so splendid as a palace, but quite as comfortable, was a first-class deanery. A "Golden Stall" at Durham or St. Paul's made its occupant a rich man. And even the rectors of the more opulent parishes contrived to "live," as the phrase went, "very much like gentlemen."

The old Prince Bishops are as extinct as the dodo. The Ecclesiastical Commission has made an end of them. Bishop Sumner, of Winchester, who died in 1874, was the last of his race. But the dignified country clergyman, who combined private means with a rich living, did his county business in person, and performed his religious duties by deputy, survived into very recent times. I have known a fine old specimen of this class – a man who never entered his church on a week-day, nor wore a white neckcloth except on Sunday; who was an active magistrate, a keen sportsman, an acknowledged authority on horticulture and farming; and who boasted that he had never written a sermon in his life, but could alter one with any man in England – which, in truth, he did so effectively that the author would never have recognized his own handiwork. When the neighboring parsons first tried to get up a periodical " clerical meeting " for the study of theology, he responded genially to the suggestion : " Oh yes; I think it sounds a capitalthing, and I suppose we shall finish up with a rubber and a bit of supper."

The reverence in which a rector of this type was held, and the difference, not merely of degree, but of kind, which was supposed to separate him from the inferior order of curates, were amusingly exemplified in the case of an old friend of mine. Returning to his parish after his autumn holiday, and noticing a woman at her cottage door with a baby in her arms, he asked, "Has that child been baptized ?" "Well, sir," replied the curtseying mother, "I shouldn't like to say as much as that; but your young man came and *did what he could."*

Lost in these entrancing recollections of Anglicanism as it once was, but will never be again, I have wandered far from my theme. I began by saying that all one has read, all one has heard, all one has been able to collect by study or by conversation, points to the close of the last century as the low-water mark of English religion and morality. The first thirty years of this century witnessed a great revival, due chiefly to the Evangelical movement, not only, as in the last century, on lines outside the Establishment, but in the very heart and core of the Church of England. The movement, though little countenanced by ecclesiastical authority, changed the whole tone of religious thought and life in England; it recalled men to serious ideas of faith and duty; it curbed profligacy, it made decency fashionable, it revived the external usages of piety, and it prepared the way for that later movement which, issuing from Oxford in 1833, has so momentously transfigured the outward aspect of the Church of England.

" I do not mean to say," wrote Mr. Gladstone in 1879, "that the founders of the Oxford School announced, or even that they knew, to how large an extent they were to be pupils and continuators of the Evangelical work, besides being something else. . . . Their distinctive speech was of Church and priesthood, of sacraments and services, as the vesture under the varied folds of which the form of the Divine Redeemer was to be exhibited to the world in a way capable of, and suited for, transmission by a collective body from generation to generation. It may well have happened that, in straining to secure for their ideas what they thought their due place, some at least may have forgotten or disparaged that personal and experimental life of the human soul with God which profits by all ordinances, but is tied to none, dwelling ever, through all its varying moods, in the inner courts of the sanctuary whereof the walls are not built with hands. The only matter, however, with which I am now concerned is to record the fact that the pith and life of the Evangelical teaching, as it consists in the reintroduction of Christ our Lord to be the woof and warp of preaching, was the great gift of the movement to the teaching Church, and has now penetrated and possessed it on a scale so general that it may be considered as pervading the whole mass." VII

SOCIAL EQUALIZATION

It was a characteristic saying of Talleyrand that no one conld conceive how pleasant a thing life was capable of being who had not belonged to the French aristocracy before the Revolution. There were, no doubt, in the case of that great man's congeners some legal and constitutional prerogatives which rendered their condition supremely enviable; but so far as splendor, state- liness, and exclusive privilege are elements of a pleasant life, he might have extended his remark to England. Similar conditions of social existence here and in France were similarly and simultaneously transformed by the same tremendous upheaval which marked the final disappearance of the feudal spirit and the birth of the modern world.

The old order passed away, and the face of human society was made new. The law-abiding and temperate genius of the Anglo-Saxon race saved England from the excesses, the horrors, and the dramatic incidents which marked this period of transition in France; but, though more quietly effected, the change in England was not less marked, less momentous, or less permanent than on the Continent. I have spoken in a former paper of the religious revival which was the most striking result in England of the Revolution in France. To-day I shall say a word about another result, or group of results, which may be summarized as Social Equalization.

The barriers between ranks and classes were to a large extent broken down. The prescriptive privileges of aristocracy were reduced. The ceremoniousness of social demeanor was diminished. Great men were content with less elaboration and display in their retinues, equipages, and mode of living. Dress lost its richness of ornament and its distinctive characteristics. Young men of fashion no longer bedizened themselves in velvet, brocade, and gold lace. Knights of the Garter no longer displayed the Blue Ribbon in Parliament. Officers no longer went into society with uniform and sword. Bishops laid aside their wigs ; dignified clergy discarded the cassock. Colored coats, silk stockings, lace ruffles, and hair-powder survived only in the footmen's liveries. When the Reform Bill of 1832 received the Royal Assent, the Lord Bathurst of the period, who had been a member of the Dnke of Wellington's Cabinet, solemnly cut off his pigtail, saying: " Ichabod, for the glory is departed"; and to the first Reformed Parliament only one pigtail was returned (it pertained to Mr. Sheppard, M. P. for Frome) – an impressive symbol of social transformation.

The lines of demarcation between the peerage and the untitled classes were partially obliterated. How clear and rigid those lines had been it is difficult for us to conceive. In *Humphrey Clinker* the nobleman refuses to fight a duel with the squire on the ground of their social inequality. Mr. Wilberforce declined a peerage because it would exclude his sons from intimacy with private gentlemen, clergymen, and mercantile families. I have stated in a previous paper that Lord Bathurst, who was born in 1791, told me that at his private school he and the other sons of peers sate together on a privileged bench apart from the rest of the boys. A typical aristocrat was the first Marquis of Abercorn. He diedin 1818, but he is still revered in Ulster under the name of "The Owld Marquis." This admirable nobleman always went out shooting in his Blue Ribbon, and required his housemaids to wear white kid-gloves when they made his bed. Before he married his first cousin, Miss Cecil Hamilton, he induced the Prince Regent to confer Oq her the titular rank of an Earl's daughter, that he might not marry beneath his position ; and, when he discovered that she contemplated eloping, he sent a message begging her to take the family-coach, as it ought never to be said that Lady Abercorn left her husband's roof in a hack-chaise. By such endearing traits do the truly great live in the hearts of posterity.

In the earlier part of this century Dr. Arnold inveighed with characteristic vigor against " the insolences of our aristocracy, the scandalous exemption of the peers from all ignominious punishments short of death, and the insolent practice of allowing peers to vote in criminal trials on their honor, while other men vote on their oath." But generally the claims of rank and birth were admitted with a childlike cheerfulness. The high function of government was the birthright of the few. The people, according to episcopal showing, had nothing to do with the laws but to obey them. The ingenious author of *Russell's Modern Europe* states in his preface to that immortal work that his object in adopting the form of a Series of Letters from a Nobleman to his Son is " to give more Weight to the Moral and Political Maxims, and to entitle the author to offer, without seeming to dictate to the World, such reflections on Life and Manners as are supposed more immediately to belong to the higher orders in Society." Nor were the privileges of rank held to pertain merely to temporal concerns. When Selina Countess of Huntingdon asked the Duchess of Buckingham to accompany her to a sermon of Whitefield's, the Duchess replied : "Ithank your ladyship for the information concerning the Methodist preachers; their doctrines are most repulsive, and strongly tinctured with impertinence and disrespect towards their superiors, in perpetually endeavoring to level all ranks and do away with all distinctions. It is monstrous to be told you have a heart as sinful as the common wretches that crawl on the earth ; and I cannot but wonder that your ladyship should relish any sentiments so much at variance with high rank and good breeding."

The exclusive and almost feudal character of the English peerage was destroyed, finally and of set purpose, by Pitt when he declared that every man who had an estate of ten thousand a year had a right to be a peer. In Lord Beaconsfield's words: " He created a plebeian aristocracy and blended it with the patrician oligarchy. He made peers of second-rate squires and fat graziers. He caught them in the alleys of Lombard Street, and clutched them from the counting-houses of Cornhill." This democratization of the peerage was accompanied by great modifications of pomp and stateliness in the daily life of the peers. In the last century the Duke and Duchess of Atholl were always served at their own table before their guests, in recognition of their royal rank as Sovereigns of the Isle of Man ; and the Duke and Duchess of Argyll observed the same courteous usage for no better reason than because they liked it. The " Household Book " of Aluwick Castle records the extraordinary amplitude and complexity of the domestic hierarchy which ministered to the Duke and Duchess of Northumberland ; and at Arundel and Belvoir, and Trent- ham and Wentworth, the magnates of the peerage lived in a state little less than regal. Seneschals and gentlemen-ushers, ladies-in-waiting and pages-of-the-presenceadorned noble as well as royal households. The private chaplain of a great Whig duke, within the recollection of people whom I have known, used to preface his sermon with a prayer for the nobility, and " especially for the noble duke to whom I am indebted for my scarf" – the badge of chaplaincy – accompanying the words by a profound bow towards His Grace's pew. The last" running footman" pertained to "Old Q." – the notorious Duke of Queensberry, who died in 1810. Horace Wai- pole describes how, when a guest playing cards at Wo- burn Abbey dropped a silver piece on the floor, and said, " Oh, never mind ; let the Groom of the Chambers have it," the Duchess replied, "Let the carpet-sweeper have it; the Groom of the Chambers never takes anything but gold."

These grotesque splendors of domestic living, the almost regal magnificence of private entertainment, and the luxurious habits that were the distinguishing features of this epoch, went out with the last century. Dr. Johnson, who died in 1784, had already noted their decline. There was a general approach towards external equalization of ranks, and that approach was accompanied by a general diffusion of material enjoyments and by a gradual acknowledgment of those rights to which the masses laid claim.

The luxury of the last century was prodigal rather than refined. The art of Brillat-Savarin had not arrived at that perfection which it afterwards attained, and which has so characterized the customs of society down to our own day. There lies before me as I write a tavern-bill for a dinner for seven persons in the year 1751. I reproduce the items verbally and literally, and it will be at once perceived that the bill of fare here recorded is worth studying as a record of gastronomical exertion on a heroic scale:

Bread and Beer.
Potage de Tortue.
Calipash.
Calipees.
Un Pate de Jambon de Bayone.
Potage Julien Verd.
Two Turbots to remove the Soops.
Haunch of Venison.
Palaits de Mouton.
Selle de Mouton.
Sulade.
Saucisses au Ecrevisses.
Boudin Blanc a le Reine.
Petits Pates a l'Espaniol.
Coteletts a la Cardinal.
Selle d'Agneau glace aux Coco mbres.
Saumon a la Chambord.
Fillets de Saules Royales.
Une bisque de Lait de Maquer- eaux.
Un Lambert aux Innocents.
Des Perdrix Sauce Vin de Champaign.
Poulets a le Russiene.
Ris de Veau en Arlequin.
Quee d'Agneau a la Montaban.

Dix Cailles.
Un Lapreau.
Un Phesant.
Dix Ortolans.
Une Tourte de Cerises.
Artichaux a le Provensalle.
Choufleurs au flour.
Cretes de Cocq en Bonets.
Amorte de Jesuits.
Salade.
Chicken.
Ice Cream and Fruits.
Fruit of various sorts, forced.
Fruit from Market.
Butter and Cheese.
Claret.
Champaign.
Burgundy.
Hock.
White wine.
Madeira.
Sack.
Cape. '
Cyprus.
Neuilly.
Usquebaugh.
Spa and Bristol Waters.
Oranges and Lemons.
Coffee and Tea.
Lemonade.

The total charge for this dinner for seven amounted to $81 11s. *Qd.,* and a footnote informs the curious reader that there was also "A turtle sent as a Present to the Company, and dress'd in a very high *Gout* after the West Indian Manner." Old cookery-books, such as the immortal work of Mrs. Glasse, Dr. Kitchener's *Cook's Oracle,* and the anonymous but admirable *Culina,* all concur in their testimony to the enormous amount of animal food which went to make an ordinary meal, and the amazingvariety of irreconcilable ingredients which were combined to form a single dish. Lord Beaconsfield, whose knowledge of this recondite branch of English literature was curiously minute, thus describes – no doubt from authentic sources – a family dinner at the end of the last century :

" The ample tureen of *potage royal* had a boned duck swimming in its centre. At the other end of the table scowled in death the grim countenance of a huge roast pike, flanked on one side by a leg of mutton *d la daube,* and on the other by the tempting delicacies of Bombarded Veal. To these succeeded that masterpiece of the culinary art, a grand Battalia Pie, in which the bodies of chickens, pigeons, and rabbits were embalmed in spices, cocks' combs, and savory balls, and well bedewed with one of those rich sauces of claret, anchovy, and sweet herbs in which our grandfathers delighted, and which was technically termed a Lear. A Florentine tourte or tansy, an old English custard, a more refined blamango, and a riband jelly of many colors offered a pleasant relief after these vaster inventions, and the repast closed with a dish of oyster-loaves and a pomepetone of larks."

As the old order yielded place to the new, this enormous profusion of rich food became by degrees less fashionable, though its terrible traditions endured, through the days of Soyer and Francatelli, almost to our own time. But gradually refinement began to supersede profusion. Simultaneously all forms of luxury spread from the aristocracy to the plutocracy; while the middle and lower classes attained a degree of solid comfort which would a few years before have been impossible. Under Pitt's administration wealth increased rapidly. Great fortunes were amassed through the improvement of agricultural methods and the application of machinery to manufacture. The Indian Nabobs, as they were called, became a recognized and powerful element in society, and their habits of "Asiatic luxury" are represented by Chatham, Burke, Voltaire, and Home Tooke as producing a marked effect upon the social life of the time. Lord Robert Seymour notes in his diary for 1788 that a fashionable lady gave $100 a year to the cook who superintended her suppers ; that at a sale of bric-a-brac 230 guineas were paid for a mirror ; and that, at a ball given by the Knights of the Bath at the Pantheon, the decorations cost upwards of $3000. The general consumption of French and Portuguese wines in place of beer, which had till recently been the beverage even of the affluent, was regarded by grave writers as a most alarming sign of the times, and the cause of a great increase of drunkenness among the upper classes. The habits and manners prevalent in London spread into the country. As the distinction between the nobility, who, roughly speaking, had been the frequenters of the capital, and the minor gentry, who had lived almost entirely on their own estates, gradually disappeared, the distinction between town and country life sensibly diminished.

The enormous increase in the facilities for travelling and for the interchange of information contributed to the same result; and grave men lamented the growing addiction of the provincial ladies to the card- table, the theatre, the assembly, the masquerade, and – singular juxtaposition – the Circulating Library. The process of social assimilation, while it spread from town to country, and from nobility to gentry, reached down from the gentry to the merchants, and from the merchants to the tradesmen. The merchant had his villa three or four miles away from his place of business, and lived at Clapham or Dnlwich in a degree and kind of luxury which had a few years before been the monopoly of the aristocracy. The tradesman no longer inhabitedthe rooms over his shop, but a mansion in Bloomsbury or Soho. Where, fifty years before, one fire in the kitchen served the whole family, and one dish of meat appeared on the table, now a footman waited at the banquet of imported luxuries, and small beer and punch had made way for Burgundy and Madeira.

But the subject expands before us, and it is time to close. Now I propose to inquire how far this Social Equalization was accompanied by Social Amelioration.

4

SECTION 4

VIII

SOCIAL AMELIORATION

In my last chapter I endeavored to illustrate that process of Social Equalization which, issuing from the French Revolution, so conspicuously marked the close of the eighteenth century and the beginning of the nineteenth. I concluded by saying that I would next inquire how far that Social Equalization was accompanied here in England by Social Amelioration. At this point it is necessary to look back a little, and to clear our minds of the delusion that an age of splendor is necessarily an age of refinement. We have seen something of the regal state and prodigal luxury which surrounded the English aristocracy in the middle of the last century. Yet at no period of our national history – unless, perhaps, during the orgies of the Restoration – were aristocratic morals at so low an ebb. Edmund Burke, in a passage which is as ethically questionable as it is rhetorically beautiful, taught that vice loses half its evil when it loses all its grossness. But in the English society of the last century grossness was as conspicuous as vice itself, and it infected not only the region of morals, but also that of manners.

Sir Walter Scott has described how, in his youth, refined gentlewomen read aloud to their families the most startling passages of the most outrageous authors. I have been told by one who heard it from an eye-witness that a great Whig duchess, who figures brilliantly in thesocial and political memoirs of the last century, turning to the footman -who was waiting on her at dinner, exclaimed, "I wish to God that you wouldn't keep rubbing your great greasy belly against the back of my chair." Men and women of the highest fashion swore like troopers; the Princes of the highest Blood Royal, who carried down into the middle of this century the courtly habits of the last, setting the example. Mr. Gladstone told me the following anecdote, which he had from the Lord Pembroke of the period, who was present at the scene.

In the early days of the first Reformed Parliament the Whig Government were contemplating a reform of the law of Church Rates. Success was certain in the House of Commons, but the Tory peers, headed by the Duke of Cumberland, determined to defeat the Bill in the House of Lords. A meeting of the party was held, when it appeared that, in the balanced state of parties, the Tory peers could not effect their purpose unless they could rally the bishops to their aid. The question was, What would the Archbishop of Canterbury do ? He was Dr. Howley, the mildest and most apostolic of men, and the most averse from strife and contention. It was impossible to be certain of his action, and the Duke of Cumberland posted off to Lambeth to ascertain it. Returning in hot haste to the caucus, he burst into the room exclaiming, " It's all right, my lords; the Archbishop says he will be damned to hell if he doesn't throw the Bill out." The Duke of Wellington's " Twopenny Damn " has become proverbial; and Sydney Smith neatly rebuked a similar propensity in Lord Melbourne by saying, " Let us assume everybody and everything to be damned, and come to the point." The Miss Berrys, who had been the correspondents of Horace Walpole, and who carried down to the fifties the most refined traditions of the social life of the last century, habitually "damned" the teakettle if it burned their fingers, and called their male friends by their surnames – "Come, Milnes, will you have a cup of tea ?" " Now, Macaulay, we have had enough of that subject."

So much, then, for the refinement of the upper classes in the last century. Did the Social Equalization of which we have spoken bring with it anything in the way of Social Amelioration ? A philosophical orator of my time at the Oxford Union, now a valued member of the House of Lords, once said in a debate on national intemperance that he had made a careful study of the subject, and, with much show of scientific analysis, he thus announced the result of his researches: "The causes of national intemperance are three: first, the adulteration of liquor; second, the love of drink; and, third, the desire for more. Knowing my incapacity to rival this masterpiece of exact thinking, I have not thought it necessary in these papers to enlarge on the national habit of excessive drinking in the late years of the last cen- tury. The grossness and the universality of the vice are too well known to need elaborating. All oral tradition, all contemporary literature, all satiric art tell the same horrid tale; and the number of bottles which a single toper would consume at a sitting not only, in Burke's phrase, " outraged economy," but " staggered credibility."

In this respect, no doubt, the turn of the century witnessed some social amelioration among the upper classes of society. There was a change, if not in quantity, at least in quality. Where port and Madeira had been the staple drinks, corrected by libations of brandy, less potent beverages became fashionable. The late Mr. Thomson Hankey, formerly M. P. for Peterborough, told me that he remembered his father coming home fromthe city one day and saying to his mother, "My dear, I have ordered a dozen bottles of a new white wine. It is called sherry, and I am told the Prince Regent drinks nothing else." The late Lord Derby told me that the cellar - books at Knowsley and St. James's Square had been carefully kept for a hundred years, and that – contrary to what every one wonld have supposed – the number of bottles drunk in a year had not diminished. The alteration was in the alcoholic strength of the wines consumed. Burgundy, port, and Madeira had made way for light claret, champagne, and hock. That, even under these changed conditions of potency, the actual number of bottles consumed showed no diminution, was accounted for by the fact that at balls and evening parties a great deal more champagne was drunk than formerly, and that luncheon in a large house had now become practically an earlier dinner.

The growth of these subsidiary meals has been a curious feature of the present century. We exclaim with horror at such preposterous bills of fare as that which I quoted in iny last paper, but it should be remembered, in justice to our fathers, that dinner was the only substantial meal of the day. Holland House was regarded in the first half of this century as the very ark and sanctuary of refined luxury, and Macaulay tells us that the viands at a breakfast - party there were tea and coffee, eggs, rolls, and butter. The fashion of going to the Highlands for shooting, which began in this century, popularized in England certain northern habits of feeding, and a morning meal at which game and cold meat appeared was known in England as a "Scotch breakfast." Apparently it had made some way by 1840, for the *Ingoldsby Legends,* published in that year, thus describe the morning meal of the ill - fated Sir Thomas:

" It seems he had taken a light breakfast – bacon,
An egg, with a little broiled haddock; at most
A round and a half of some hot butter'd toast;
With a slice of cold sirloin from yesterday's roast."

Luncheon, or " nuncheon " as some very ancient friends of mine always called it, was the merest mouthful. Men went out shooting with a sandwich in their pocket; the ladies who sat at home had some cold chicken and wine and water brought into the drawing-room on a tray.

Miss Austen in her novels always dismisses the midday meal under the cursory appellation of "cold meat." The celebrated Dr. Kitchener, the sympathetic author of the *Cook's Oracle,* writing in 1825, says: "Your luncheon may consist of a bit of roasted poultry, a basin of beef tea, or eggs poached, or boiled in the shell; fish plainly dressed, or a sandwich; stale bread; and half a pint of good home - brewed beer, or toast and water, with about one-fourth or one-third part of its measure of wine." And this prescription would no doubt have worn an aspect of liberal concession to the demands of the patient's appetite. It is difficult, by any effort of a morbid imagination, to realize a time when there was no five-o'clock tea; and yet that most sacred of our national institutions was only invented by the Duchess of Bedford who died in 1857, and whose name should surely be enrolled in the Positivist Calendar as a benefactress of the human race. No wonder that by seven o'clock our fathers, and even our mothers, were ready to tackle a dinner of solid properties; and even to supplement it with the amazing supper (which Dr. Kitchener prescribes for "those who dine very late") of "gruel, or a little bread and cheese, or pounded cheese, and a glass of beer."

This is a long digression from the subject of excessive drinking, with which, however, it is not remotely connected; and both in respect of drunkenness and of gluttony the habits of English society in the years which immediately succeeded the French Revolution showed a marked amelioration. To a company of enthusiastic Wordsworthians who were deploring their master's confession that he got drunk at Cambridge, Mr. Shorthouse, the accomplished author of *John Inglesant,* soothingly remarked, that in all probability "Wordsworth's standard of intoxication was miserably low."

Simultaneously with the restriction of excess there was seen a corresponding increase in refinement of taste and manners. Some of the more brutal forms of so-called sport, such as bull-baiting and cock-fighting, became less fashionable. The more civilized forms, such as foxhunting and racing, increased in favor. ./Esthetic culture was more generally diffused. The stage was at the height of its glory. Music was a favorite form of public recreation. Great prices were given for works of art. The study of physical science, or "natural philosophy" as it was called, became popular. Public libraries and local " book-societies " sprang up, and there was a wide demand for encyclopedias and similar vehicles for the diffusion of general knowledge. The love of natural beauty was beginning to move the hearts of men, and it found expression at once in an entirely new school of landscape-painting, and in a more romantic and natural form of poetry.

But against these marked instances of social amelioration must be set some darker traits of national life. The public conscience had not yet revolted against violence and brutality. The prize-ring, patronized by Royalty, was at its zenith. Humanitarians and philanthropists were as yet an obscure and ridiculed sect. The slave - trade, though menaced, was still undisturbed. Under a system scarcely distinguishable from slavery, pauper childrenwere bound over to the owners of factories and subjected to the utmost rigor of enforced labor. The treatment of the insane was darkened by incredible barbarities. As late as 1828 Lord Shaftesbury found that the lunatics in Bedlam were chained to their straw beds, and left from Saturday to Monday without attendance, and with only bread and water within their reach, while the keepers were enjoying themselves. Discipline in the services, in workhouses, and in schools was of the most brutal type. Our prisons were unreformed. Our penal code was inconceivably sanguinary and savage. In 1770 there were one hundred and sixty capital offences on the Statute-book, and by the beginning of this century the number had greatly increased. To steal five shillings' worth of goods from a shop was punishable by death. A girl of twenty-two was hanged for receiving a piece of woollen stuff from the man who had stolen it.

In 1789 a woman was burned at the stake for coining. People still living have seen the skeletons of pirates and highwaymen hanging in chains. I have heard that the children of the Bluecoat School at Hertford were always taken to see the executions there; and as late as 1820 the dead bodies of the Cato Street conspirators were decapitated in front of Newgate, and the Westminster boys had a special holiday to enable them to see the sight, which was thus described by an eye-witness, the late

Lord de Ros : " The executioner and his assistant cut down one of the corpses from the gallows, and placed it in the coffin, but with the head hanging over on the block. The man with the knife instantly severed the head from the body, and the executioner, receiving it in his hands, held it up, saying, in a loud voice, 'This is the head of a traitor.' He then dropped it into the coffin, which, being removed, another was brought forward, and they proceeded to cut down the next body and to go through the same ghastly operation. It was observed that the mob, which was very large, gazed in silence at the hanging of the conspirators, and showed not the least sympathy; but when each head was cut off and held up a loud and deep groan of horror burst from all sides, which was not soon forgotten by those who heard it." Duelling was the recognized mode of settling all personal disputes, and no attempt was made to enforce the law which, theoretically, treated the killing of a man in a duel as wilful murder; but, on the other hand, debt was punished with what often was imprisonment for life. A woman died in the County Jail at Exeter after forty- five years' incarceration for a debt of $19. Crime was rampant. Daring burglaries, accompanied by every circumstance of violence, took place nightly. Highwaymen infested the suburban roads, and not seldom plied their calling in the capital itself. The iron post at the end of the narrow footway between the gardens of Devonshire House and Lansdowne House is said by tradition to have been placed there after a Knight of the Road had eluded the officers of justice by galloping down the stone steps and along the nagged path. I have told in a former paper how Sir Hamilton Seymour was "stopped" in his father's travelling carriage near the bottom of Grosvenor Place. Young gentlemen of broken fortunes, and tradesmen whose business had grown slack, swelled the ranks of these desperadoes. It was even said that an Irish prelate – Dr. Twysden, Bishop of Raphoe – whose incurable love of adventure had drawn him to "the road," received the penalty of his uncanonical diversion in the shape of a bullet from a traveller whom he had stopped on Honnslow Heath. The Lord Mayor was made to stand and deliver on Turnham Green. Stars and " Georges " were snipped of$ ambassadors and peers as they entered St. James's Palace.

It is superfluous to multiply illustrations. Enough has been said to show that the circumscription of aristocratic privilege and the diffusion of material luxury did not precipitate the millennium. Social Equalization was not synonymous with Social Amelioration. Some improvement, indeed, in the tone and habit of society we have seen at the turn of the century; but it was little more than a beginning I proceed to trace its development, and to indicate its source.

5

SECTION 5

IX

THE EVANGELICAL INFLUENCE

I Have indicated the closing years of the last century as the period at which the moral and social life of England touched its lowest point. In support of this view I have cited the evidence of contemporary literature and biography, of people whom I have known, and of documents which I have examined. I have quoted Mr. Gladstone's testimony that "persons of great weight and authority" whom he knew in his youth ascribed the beginnings of a reviving seriousness in the upper classes of lay society to a reaction against the horrors and impieties of the French Revolution in its later stages. I closed my last chapter by saying that some improvement in our national habits was discernible by the beginning of the present century, and that I should next attempt to trace the development and to indicate the source of that improvement.

Mr. Lecky justly remarks that "it is difficult to measure the change which must have passed over the public mind since the days when the lunatics in Bedlam were constantly spoken of as one of the sights of London ; when the maintenance of the African slave-trade was a foremost object of English commercial policy; when men and even women were publicly whipped through the streets; when skulls lined the top of Temple Bar and rotting corpses huug on gibbets along the Edgware Road; when persons exposed in the pillory not unfrequently died through the ill-usage of the mob; and when the procession every six weeks of condemned criminals to Tyburn was one of the great festivals of London."

Difficult, indeed, it is to measure so great a change, and it is not wholly easy to ascertain with precision its various and concurrent causes, and to attribute to each its proper potency. But we shall certainly not be wrong if, among those causes, we assign a prominent place to the Evangelical revival of religion. It would be a mistake to claim for the Evangelical movement the whole credit of our social reform and philanthropic work. Even in the darkest times of spiritual torpor and general profligacy Eugland could show a creditable amount of practical benevolence. The public charities of London were large and excellent. The first Foundling Hospital was established in 1739 ; the first Magdalen Hospital in 1769. In 1795 it was estimated that the annual expenditure on charity-schools, asylums, hospitals, and similar institutions in London was $750,000.

Mr. Lecky, whose study of these social phenomena is exhaustive, imagines that the habit of unostentatious charity, which seems indigenous to England, was powerfully stimulated by the philosophy of Shaftesbury and Voltaire, by Rousseau's sentiment and Fielding's fiction. This theory may have something to say for itself, and indeed it is antecedently plausible; but I can hardly believe that purely literary influences counted for so very much in the sphere of practice. I doubt if any considerable number of Englishmen were effectively swayed by that humanitarian philosophy of France which in the actions of its maturity so awfully belied the promise of its youth. We are, I think, on surer ground when, admitting a national bias towards material benevolence, and not denying some stimulus from literature and philosophy, weassigu to the Evangelical revival the main credit of our social regeneration.

The life of John Wesley, practically coterminous with the last century, witnessed both the lowest point of our moral degradation and also the earliest promise of our moral restoration. He cannot, indeed, be reckoned the founder of the Evangelical school; that title belongs rather to George Whitefield. But his influence, combined with that of his brother Charles, acting on such men as Newton and Cecil, and Venn and Scott, of Aston Sandford; on Selina Lady Huntingdon and Mrs. Hannah More; on Howard and Clarkson and William Wilber- force, made a deep mark on the Established Church, gave new and permanent life to English Nonconformity, and sensibly affected the character and aspect of secular society.

Wesley himself had received the governing impulse of his life from Law's *Serious Call* and *Christian Perfection,* and he had been a member of one of those religious societies (or guilds, as they would now be called) with which the piety of Bishop Beveridge and Dr. Horneck had enriched the Church of England. These societies were, of course, distinctly Anglican in origin and character, and were stamped with the High Church theology. They constituted, so to say, a church within the Church, and, though they raised the level of personal piety among their members to a very high point, they did not widely affect the general tone and character of national religion. The Evangelical leaders, relying on less exclusively ecclesiastical methods, diffused their influence over a much wider area, and, under the impulse of their teaching, drunkenness, indecency, and profanity were sensibly abated. The reaction from the rampant wickedness of the last century drove men into strict and even puritanical courses.

Lord Robert Seymour wrote on the 20th March, 1788:"Tho" Good Friday, Mrs. Sawbridge has an assembly this evening; tells her invited friends they really are only to play for a watch which she has had some time on her hands and wishes to dispose of."

" ' Really, I declare 'pon my honor it's true' (said Ly. Bridget Talmash to the Dutchess of Bolton) ' that a great many people now go to chapel. I saw a vast number of carriages at Portman Chapel last Sunday.' The Dut. told her she always went to chapel on Sunday, and in the country read prayers in the hall to her family."

But now there began a marked abstention from fashionable forms of recreation, such as dancing, card-playing, and the drama. Sunday was observed with a Judaical rigor. A more frequent attendance on public worship was accompanied by the revival of family prayers and grace before meat. Manuals of private devotion were multiplied. Religious literature of all kinds was published in great quantity. A higher standard of morals was generally professed. Marriage was gradually restored in public estimation to its proper place, not merely as a civil bond or social festival, but as a chief solemnity of the Christian religion.

There was no more significant sign of the times than this alteration, for in the last century some of the gravest of our social offences had clustered round the institution of marriage, which was almost as much dishonored in the observance as in the breach. In the first half of that century the irregular and clandestine weddings, celebrated without banns or license in the Fleet Prison, had been one of the crying scandals of the middle and lower classes ; and in the second half, the nocturnal flittings to Gretna Green of young couples who could afford such a Pilgrimage of Passion lowered the conception of marriage. It was through the elopement of Miss Child – heiress of the opulent banker at Temple Bar – from herfather's house in Berkeley Square (now Lord Rosebery's) that the ownership of the great banking business passed eventually to the present Lord Jersey, and the annals of almost every aristocratic family contain the record of similar escapades.

The Evangelical movement, not content with permeating England, sought to expand itself all over the Empire. The Society for the Propagation of the Gospel and the Society for Promoting Christian Knowledge had been essentially Anglican institutions ; and similar societies, but less ecclesiastical in character, now sprang up in great numbers. The London Missionary Society was founded in 1795, the Church Missionary Society in 1799, the Re- ligious Tract Society in the same year, and the British and Foreign Bible Society three years later. All these were distinctly creations of the Evangelical movement, as were also the Societies for the Reformation of Manners and for the Better Observance of the Lord's Day. Religious education found in the Evangelical party its most active friends. The Sunday School Society was founded in 1785. Two years later it was educating two hundred thousand children. Its most earnest champions were Rowland Hill and Mrs. Hannah More ; but it is worthy of note that this excellent lady, justly honored as a pioneer of elementary education, confined her curriculum to the Bible and the Catechism, and " such coarse works as may fit the children for servants. *I allow of no writing for the poor."*

To the Society of Friends – a body not historically or theologically Evangelical – belongs the credit of having first awoke and tried to rouse others to a sense of the horrors and iniquities involved in the slave-trade; but the adhesion of William Wilberforce and his friends at Clapham identified the movement for emancipation with the Evangelical party. Never were the enthusiasm, theactivity, the uncompromising devotion to principle which marked the Evangelicals turned to better account. Their very narrowness gave intensity and concentration to their work, and their victory, though deferred, was complete. It has been truly said that when the English nation had been thoroughly convinced that slavery was a curse which must be got rid of at any cost, we cheerfully paid down as the price of its abolition twenty millions in cash, and threw the prosperity of our West Indian colonies into the bargain. Yet we only spent on it one-tenth of what it cost us to lose America, and one-fiftieth of what we spent in avenging the execution of Louis XVI.

In spite of all these conspicuous and beneficent advances in the direction of humanity, a great deal of severity, and what appears to us as brutality, remained embedded in our social system. I have spoken in previous papers of the methods of discipline enforced in the services, in jails, in workhouses, and in schools. A very similar spirit prevailed even in the home. Children were shut up in dark closets, starved, and flogged. Lord Shaftes- bury's father used to knock him down, and recommended his tutor at Harrow to follow the same regimen. Archdeacon Denison describes in his autobiography how he and his brothers were thrashed by their tutor when they were youths of sixteen and had left Eton. *The FaircMld Family* – that quaint picture of Evangelical life and manners – depicts a religious father punishing his quarrelsome children by taking them to see a murderer hanging in chains, and chastising every peccadillo of infancy with a severity which makes one long to flog Mr. Fairchild.

But still, in spite of all these checks and drawbacks and evil survivals, the tide of human!tarianism flowed on, and gradually altered the aspect of English life. The bloody penal code was mitigated. Prisons and workhouses were reformed. The discipline of school and ofhome was tempered by the infusion of mercy and reason into the iron regimen of terror. And this general diminution of brutality was not the only form of social amelioration. It was accompanied by a gradual but perceptible increase in decency, refinement, and material prosperity. Splendor diminished, and luxury remained the monopoly of the rich; but comfort – that peculiarly English treasure – was more generally diffused. In that diffusion the Evangelicals had their full share. Thackeray's admirable description of Mrs. Hobson Xewcome's villa is drawn from the life: "In Egypt itself there were not more savory fleshpots than those at Clapham. Her mansion was long the resort of the most favored among the religious world. The most eloquent expounders, the most gifted missionaries, the most interesting converts from foreign islands were to be found at her sumptuous table, spread with the produce of her magnificent gardens ... a great shining mahogany table, covered with grapes, pineapples, plum-cake, port wine, and Madeira, and surrounded by stout men in black, with baggy white neckcloths, who took little Tommy on their knees and questioned him as to his right understanding of the place whither naughty boys were bound."

Again, in his paper on *Dinners* the same great master of a fascinating subject speaks the words of truth and soberness when he says : " The inferior clergy dine very much and well. I don't know when I have been better entertained, as far as creature comforts go, than by men of very Low Church principles ; and one of the very best repasts that ever I saw in my life was at Darlington, given by a Quaker." The same admirable tradition of material comfort allied with Evangelical opinion extended into my own time. The characteristic weakness of Mr. Stiggins has no place in my recollection ; but Mr. C'hadband I have frequently met in Evangelical circles, both insideand outside the Establishment. Debarred by the strictness of their principles from such amusements as dancing, cards, and theatres, the Evangelicals took their pleasure in eating and drinking. They abounded in hospitality ; and when they were not entertaining or being entertained, occupied their evenings with systematic reading, which gave their religious compositions a sound basis of general culture. Austerity, gloom, and Pharisaism had no place among the better class of Evangelicals. Wilberforce, pronounced by Madame de Stae'l to be the most agreeable man in England, was of " a most gay and genial disposition"; "lived in perpetual sunshine, and shed its radiance all around him." Legh Richmond was " exceedingly good company." Robinson, of Leicester, was "a capital conversationalist, very lively and bright." Alexander Knox found that Mrs. Hannah More " far exceeded his expectations in pleasant manners and interesting conversation."

The increasing taste for solid comfort and easy living which accompanied the development of humanitarian- ism, and in which, as we have just seen, the Evangelicals had their full share, was evidenced to the eye by the changes in domestic architecture. There was less pretension in exteriors and elevations, but more regard to convenience and propriety within. The space was not all sacrificed to reception-rooms. Bedrooms were multiplied and enlarged ; and fireplaces were introduced into every room, transforming the arctic "powdering-closet" into a habitable dressing-room. The diminution of the Window Tax made light and ventilation possible. Personal cleanliness became fashionable, and the means of attaining it were cultivated. The whole art or science of domestic sanitation – rudimentary enough in its beginnings – belongs to this century. The system which went before it was too primitively abominable to bear elaborat-edescription. Sir Robert Rawlinson, the sanitary expert, who was called in to inspect Windsor Castle after the Prince Consort's death, reported that, within the Queen's reign, " cesspools full of putrid refuse and drains of the worst description existed beneath the basements. . . . Twenty of these cesspools were removed from the upper ward, and twenty - eight from the middle and lower wards. . . . Means of ventilation by windows in Windsor Castle were very defective. Even in the royal apartments the upper portions of the windows were fixed. Lower casements alone could be opened, so that by far the largest amount of air spaces in the rooms contained vitiated air, comparatively stagnant." When this was the condition of our Royal Palaces, no wonder that the typhoid-germ, like Solomon's spider, laid "hold with her hands, and was in kings' palaces." And well might Sir George Trevelyan, in his ardent youth, exclaim :

" We must revere our sires; they were a famous nice of men. For every glass of port we drink, they nothing thought of

ten. They lived above the foulest drains, they breathed the closest

air, They had their yearly twinge of gout, but little seemed to

care. But, though they burned their coals at home, nor fetched their ice from Wenham, They played the man before Quebec and stormed the lines at Blenheim.

When sailors lived on mouldy bread and lumps of rusty pork, No Frenchman dared to show his nose between the Downs and

Cork. But now that Jack gets beef and greens and next his skin wears flannel, The ' Standard' says we've not a ship in plight to hold the Channel."

So much for Social Amelioration.

6

SECTION 6

POLITICS

These chapters are founded on contact with some very aged people whom, many years ago, it was my privilege to question about the scenes and events of their youth. From that contact one naturally derived certain clear impressions concerning the condition of England during the latter part of the last century and the earlier part of this. Of our religious, moral, and social condition at that time I have already spoken. Now I approach our political condition, and that was to a great extent the product of the French Revolution. Some historians, indeed, when dealing with that inexhaustible theme, have wrought cause and effect into a circular chain, and have reckoned among the circumstances which prepared the way for the French Revolution the fact that Voltaire in his youth spent three years in England, and mastered the philosophy of Bacon, Newton, and Locke, the Deism of the English Free-thinkers, and the English theory of political liberty. That these doctrines, recommended by Voltaire's mordant genius and matchless style, and circulating in a community prepared by tyranny to receive them, acted as a powerful solvent on the intellectual basis of French society, is indeed likely enough. But to pursue the theme would carry us too far back into the last century. In dealing with the recollections of persons whom one's self has known, we must dismiss from view the causes of theFrench Revolution. Our business is with its effect on political thought and action in England.

About half-way through this century it became the fashion to make out that the effect of the Revolution on England had been exaggerated. Satirists made fun of our traditional Gallophobia. In that admirable skit on philosophical history, the introduction to the *Book of Snobs,* Thackeray first illustrates his theme by a reference to the French Revolution, and then adds (in sarcastic brackets): "Which the reader will be pleased to have introduced so early." Lord Beaconsfield, quizzing John "Wilson Croker in *Coningsby,* says: " He bored his audience with too much history, especially the French Revolution, which he fancied was his forte, so that the people at last, whenever he made any allusion to the subject, were almost as much terrified as if they had seen the guillotine." In spite of these gibes, historians have of late years returned to the earlier and truer view, and have deliberately reaffirmed the tremendous effect of the Revolution 011 English politics. The philosophical Mr. Lecky says that it influenced English history in the later years of the last century more powerfully than any other event; that it gave a completely new direction to the statesmanship of Pitt; that it instantaneously shattered, and rendered ineffectual for a whole generation, one of the two great parties in the State; and that it determined for a like period the character and complexion of our foreign policy.

All contemporary Europe – all subsequent time – quivered with the shock and sickened at the carnage; but I have gathered that it was not till the capture of the Bastille that the events which were taking place in France attracted any general or lively interest in England. The strifes of rival politicians, the illness of George III., and the consequent questions as to the Regency, engrossedthe public mind, and what little interest was felt in foreign affairs was directed much more to the possible designs of Russia than to the actual condition of Prance. The capture of the Bastille, however, was an event so startling and so dramatic that it instantly arrested the public attention of England, and the events which immediately followed in rapid and striking succession raised interest into excitement, and excitement into passion. Men who had been accustomed from their childhood to regard the Monarchy of France as the type of a splendid, powerful, and enduring polity now saw a National Army constituted in complete independence of the Crown; a Representative Body assuming absolute power and denying the King's right to dissolve; the King himself borne in ignominious triumph to the palace of the Municipality ; the summary abrogation of the whole feudal system, which a year before had seemed endowed with perpetual vigor; an insurrection of the peasantry against their territorial tyrants, accompanied by every horror of pillage, arson, and bloodshed; the beautiful and stately Queen flying, half naked, for her life, amid the slaughter of her sentinels and courtiers ; and the King himself virtually a prisoner in the very Court which, up to that moment, had seemed the ark and sanctuary of absolute government. All over England these events produced their immediate and natural effect. Enemies of religious establishments took courage from the downfall of ecclesiastical institutions in France. Enemies of monarchy rejoiced in the formal and public degradation of a monarch. Those who had long been conscientiously working for Parliamentary reform saw with glee their principles expressed in the most uncompromising terms in the French Declaration of Rights, and practically applied in the constitution of the Sovereign Body of France. These convinced and constitutional reformers foundnew and strange allies. Serious advocates of Republican institutions, mere lovers of change and excitement, secret sympathizers with lawlessness and violence, sedentary theorists, reckless adventurers, and local busybodies associated themselves in the endeavor to popularize the French Revolution in England and to imbue the English mind with congenial sentiments. The movement had leaders of greater mark. The Duke of Norfolk and the Duke of Richmond, Lord Lansdowne and Lord Stanhope, held language about the Sovereignty of the People such as filled the reverent and orderly mind of Burke with indignant astonishment. In Dr. Priestley the revolutionary party had an eminent man of science and a polemical writer of rare power. Dr. Price was a rhetorician whom any cause would have gladly enlisted as its champion. The Revolution Society, founded to commemorate the capture of the Bastille, corresponded with the leaders of the Revolution, and promised its alliance in a revolutionary compact. And, to add a touch of comedy to these more serious demonstrations, the young Duke of Bedford and other leaders of fashion discarded hair-powder, and wore their hair cut short in what was understood to be the Republican mode of Paris.

Amid all this hurly-"burly Pitt maintained a stately and cautious reserve. Probably he foresaw his opportunity in the inevitable disruption of his opponents; and if so, his foresight was soon realized by events. On the capture of the Bastille, Fox exclaimed : " How much the greatest event it is that ever happened in the world ! and how much the best!" At the same time Burke was writing to an intimate friend : " The old Parisian ferocity has broken out in a shocking manner. It is true that this may be no more than a sudden explosion. If so, no indication can be taken from it; but if it should be character rather than accident, then that people are not fitfor liberty, and must have a strong hand like that of their former masters to coerce them." This contrast between the judgments of the two great Whigs was continuously and rapidly heightened. Fox threw himself into the revolutionary cause with all the ardor which he had displayed on behalf of American independence. Burke opposed with characteristic vehemence the French attempt to build up a theoretical Constitution on the ruins of religion, history, and authority; and any fresh act of cruelty or oppression which accompanied the process stirred in him that tremendous indignation against violence and injustice of which Warren Hastings had learned by stern experience the intensity and the volume. The *Reflections on the French Revolution* and the *Appeal from the Neiv to the Old Whigs* expressed in the most splendid English which was ever written the dire apprehensions that darkened their author's receptive and impassioned mind. " A voice like the Apocalypse sounded over England, and even echoed in all the Courts of Europe. Burke poured the vials of his hoarded vengeance into the agitated heart of Christendom, and stimulated the panic of a world by the wild pictures of his inspired imagination."

Meanwhile the Whig party was rent in twain. The Duke of Portland, Lord Fitzwilliam, the Duke of Devonshire, Lord John Cavendish, and Sir George Elliot adhered to Burke. Fox as stoutly opposed him, and was reinforced by Sheridan, Francis, Erskine, and Grey. The pathetic issue of the dispute, in Burke's formal repudiation of Fox's friendship, has taken its place among those historic Partings of Friends which have modified the course of human society. As far as can now be judged, the bulk of the country was with Burke, and the execution of Louis XVI. was followed by an astonishing outbreak of popular feeling. The theatres were closed. The whole population wore mourning. The streets rang with the cry, " War with France I" The very pulpits re-echoed the summons. Fox himself was constrained to declare to the electors of Westminster that there was no one outside France who did not consider this sad catastrophe "as a most revolting act of cruelty and injustice."

But it was too late. The horror and indignation of England were not to be allayed by soothing words of decorous sympathy from men who had applauded the earlier stages of the tragedy, though they wept at its culmination. The warlike spirit of the race was aroused, and it spoke in the cry, "No peace with the regicides !" Pitt clearly discerned the feeling of the country, and promptly gave effect to it. He dismissed Chauvelin, who informally represented the Revolutionary Government in London, and he demanded from Parliament an immediate augmentation of the forces.

On January 20, 1793, France declared war against the King of England. The great struggle had begun, and that declaration was a new starting-point in the political history of England. English parties entered into new combinations. English politics assumed a new complexion. Pitt's imperial mind maintained its ascendency, but the drift of his policy was entirely changed. All the schemes of Parliamentary, financial, and commercial reform in which he had been immersed yielded place to the stern expedients of a Minister fighting for his life against revolution abroad and sedition at home. For though, as I said just now, popular sentiment was stirred by the King's execution into vehement hostility to France, still the progress of the war was attended by domestic consequences which considerably modified this sentiment. Hostility gave way to passive acquiescence, and acquiescence to active sympathy.

Among the causes which produced this change were the immense increase of national burdens; the sudden agglomeration of a lawless population in the manufacturing towns which the war called into being ; the growing difficulties in Ireland, where revolutionary theories found ready learners ; the absolute abandonment of all attempts at social and political improvement; the dogged determination of those in authority to remedy no grievance however patent, and to correct no abuse however indefensible.

The wise and temperate reforms for which the times were ripe, and which the civil genius of Pitt pre-eminently qualified him to effect, were not only suspended, but finally abandoned under the influence of an insane reaction. The besotted resistance to all change stimulated the desire for it. Physical distress co-operated with political discontent to produce a state of popular disaffection such as the whole preceding century had never seen. The severest measures of coercion and repression only, and scarcely, restrained the populace from open and desperate insurrection, and thirty years of this experience brought England to the verge of a civil catastrophe.

Patriotism was lost in partisanship. Political faction ran to an incredible excess. The whole community was divided into two hostile camps. Broadly speaking, the cause of France was espoused, with different degrees of fervor, by all lovers of civil and religious freedom at home. To the Whigs the humiliation of Pitt was a more cherished object than the defeat of Napoleon. Fox wrote to a friend : " The triumph of the French Government over the English does, in fact, afford me a degree of pleasure which it is very difficult to disguise "; and I have gathered that this was the prevalent temper of Whiggery during the long and desperate struggle withRepnblican and Imperial Prance. What Byron called " The crowning carnage, Waterloo," brought no abatement of political rancor. The question of France, indeed, was eliminated from the contest, but its elimination enabled English Liberals to concentrate their hostility on the Tory Government without incurring the reproach of unpatriotic sympathy with the enemies of England.

In the great fight between Tory and Whig, Government and Opposition, Authority and Freedom, there was no quarter. Neither age nor sex was spared. No department of national life was untouched by the fury of the contest. The Royal Family was divided. The Duke of Cumberland was one of the most dogged and unscrupulous leaders of the Tory party ; the Duke of Sussex toasted the memory of Charles James Fox, and at a public dinner joined in singing " The Trumpet of Liberty," of which the chorus ran :

" Fall, tyrants, fall 1
These are the days of liberty ;
Fall, tyrants, fall!"

The Established Church was on the side of authority; the Dissenters stood for freedom. "Our opponents," said Lord John Russell, in one of his earliest speeches – " our opponents deafen us with their cry of ' Church and King.' Shall I tell you what they mean by it ? They mean a Church without the Gospel and a King above the law." An old Radical electioneerer, describing the activity of the country clergy on the Tory side, said : " In every village we have the Black Recruiting- Sergeant against us." Even within sacred walls the echoes of the fight were heard. The State Holy-days – Gunpowder Treason, Charles the Martyr, the Restoration, and the Accession – gave suitable occasion for sermons of the most polemical vehemence. Even the two Collectsfor the King at the beginning of the Communion Service were regarded as respectively Tory and Whig. The first, with its bold assertion of the Divine Right of Sovereignty, was that which commended itself to every loyal clergyman on his promotion; and unfavorable conclusions were drawn with regard to the civil sentiments of the man who preferred the colorless alternative. As in the Church, so in our educational system. Oxford, with its Caroline and Jacobite traditions, was the Tory University; Cambridge, the nursing mother of Whigs; Eton was supposed to cherish a sentiment of romantic affection for the Stuarts ; Harrow was profoundly Hanoverian. Even the drama was involved in political antipathies, and the most powerful adherents of Kean and Kemble were found respectively among the leaders of Whig and Tory society. The vigor, heartiness, and sincerity of this political hatred put to shame the more tepid convictions of our degenerate days. The first Earl of Leicester, better known as " Coke of Norfolk," told my father that when he was a child his grandfather took him on his knee and said, " Now, remember, Tom, as long as you live, never trust a Tory"; and he used to say, "I never have, and, by God, I never will." The little daughter of a great Whig statesman, accustomed from her cradle to hear language of this sort, asked her mother, "Mamma, are Tories born wicked, or do they grow wicked afterwards ?" and her mother judiciously replied, "They are born wicked, and grow worse." I well remember in my youth an eccentric old maiden lady – Miss Harriett Fanny Cuyler – who had spent a long and interesting life in the innermost circles of aristocratic Whiggery, and she never would enter a four - wheel cab until she had extorted from the driver his personal assurance that he never had cases of infectious disease in his cab, that he was not a Puseyite, and was a Whig.

I am bound to say that this vehement prejudice was not unnatural in a generation that remembered, either personally or by immediate tradition, the iron coercion which Pitt exercised in his later days, and which his successors continued. The barbarous executions for high- treason remain a blot on the fair fame of the nineteenth century. Scarcely less horrible were the trials for sedition, which sent an English clergyman to transportation for life because he had signed a petition in favor of Parliamentary reform.

"The good old Code, like Argus, had a hundred watchful eyes, And each old English peasant had his good old English spies, To tempt his starving discontent with good old English lies, Then call the British yeomanry to stop his peevish cries."

At Woburn, a market-town forty miles from London, under the very shadow of a great Whig house, no political meeting could be held for fear of Pitt's spies, who dropped down from London by the night coach and returned to lay information against popular speakers ; and when the politicians of the place desired to express their sentiments, they had to repair secretly to an adjacent village off the coach-road, where they were harangued under cover of night by the young sons of the Duke of Bedford.

The ferocity, the venality, the profligate expenditure, the delirious excitement of contested elections have made an indelible mark on our political history. In 1780 King George III. personally canvassed the borough of Windsor against the Whig candidate, Admiral Kep- pel, and propitiated a silk mercer by calling at his shop and saying: " The Queen wants a gown – wants a gown. No Keppel. No Keppel." It is pleasant to reflect that the friends of freedom were not an inch behind the upholders of tyranny in the vigor and adroitness of theirelectioneering methods. The contest for the City of Westminster in 1788 is thus described in the manuscript diary of Lord Robert Seymour:

"The Riotts at the Westr. Election are carried such lengths the Military obliged to be called into the assistance of Ld. Hood's party. Several Persons have been killed by Ld. J. Townsend's Butchers who cleave them to the Ground with their Cleavers – Mr. Fox very narrowly escaped being killed by a Bayonet wch. w'd certainly have been fatal had not a poor Black saved him fm. the blow. Mr. Macnamara's Life is despaired of – & several others have died in the difft. Hospitals. Next Thursday decides the business.

"July 25. – Lord John Townsend likely to get the Election – what has chiefly contributed to Ld. Hood's losing it is that Mr. Pulteney is his Friend – Mr. P. can command 15,000 Votes – & as he is universally disliked by his Tenants they are unanimous in voting against him – wch. for Ld. II. proves a very unfortunate circumstance. The Duke of Bedford sent $10,000 towards the Expenses of the Opposition.

"It is thought that Lord Hood will not attempt a Scrutiny. One of Ld. Hood's votes was discovered to be a carrot-scraper in St. James's Market who sleeps in a little Kennel about the Size of a Hen Coup.

"Augt. 5th – The Election decided in favor of Ld. J. T., who was chaired – and attend'd by a Procession of a mile in length. On his Head was a Crown of Laurel. C. Fox follow'd him in a Landau & 6 Horses cover'd in Favors & Lawrels. The appearance this Procession made was equal in splendor to the public Entry of an Embassador."

A by-election was impending in Yorkshire, and Pitt, paying a social visit to the famous Mrs. B. – one of the Whig Queens of the West Riding – said, banteringly,"Well, the election is all right for us. Ten thousand guineas for the use of our side go down to Yorkshire tonight by a sure hand." " The devil they do !" responded Mrs. B., and that night the bearer of the precious burden was stopped by a highwayman on the Great North Road, and the ten thousand guineas procured the return of the Whig candidate. The electioneering methods, less adventurous but not more scrupulous, of a rather later day have been depicted in *Pickwick,* and *Middle- march,* and *Coningsby,* and *My Novel,* with all the suggestive fun of a painting by Hogarth.

And so, with startling incidents and culpable expedients and varying fortunes, the great struggle for political freedom was conducted through the first thirty years of the present century, and it has been my interesting fortune to know some of the toughest of the combatants both among the leaders and in the rank-and-file. And from all of them alike – and not only from them, but from all who remembered the time – I have gathered the impression that all through their earlier life the hidden fires of revolution were smouldering under English society, and that again and again an actual outbreak was only averted by some happy stroke of fortune. At the Election of 1868 an old laborer in the agricultural Borough of Woodstock told a Liberal canvasser from Oxford that in his youth arms had been stored in his father's cottage so as to be in readiness for the outbreak which was to take place if Lord Grey's Reform Bill was finally defeated. A Whig nobleman, of great experience and calm judgment, told me that if our Gracious Queen had died before she succeeded to the throne, and thereby Ernest Duke of Cumberland had become King on the death of William IV., no earthly power could have averted a revolution. " I have no hesitation in saying," I heard Mr. Gladstone say, "that if the repeal of theCorn Laws had been defeated, or even retarded, we should have had a revolution." Charles Kingsley and his fellow-workers for Social Reform expected a Revolution in April, 1848.

But, after all, these testimonies belong to the region of conjecture. Let me close this paper by a narrative of fact, derived from the late Lord de Ros, an eye-witness of the events which he narrated. Arthur Thistlewood, one of the Cato Street conspirators, was a young Englishman who had been in Paris in the time of Robespierre's ascendency, and had there imbibed revolutionary sentiments. He served for a short time as an officer in the English army, and after quitting the service he made himself notorious by trying to organize a political riot in London, for which he was tried and acquitted. He subsequently collected round him a secret society, chiefly recruited from the class of disaffected citizens, and proceeded to arrange a plan by which he hoped to paralyze Government and establish a reign of Terror in London.

One evening, in the winter of 1819-20, a full-dress ball was given by the Spanish Ambassador in Portland Place, and was attended by the Prince Regent, the Royal Dukes, the Duke of Wellington, the Ministers of State, and the leaders of fashion and society. "About one o'clock, just before supper, a sort of order was circulated among the junior officers to draw towards the head of the stairs, though no one knew for what reason, except that an unusual crowd had assembled in the street. The appearance of Lavender and one or two well-known Bow Street officers in the entrance-hall also gave rise to surmises of some impending riot. While the officers were whispering to one another as to what was expected to happen, a great noise was heard in the street, the crowd dispersed with loud cries in all directions, and a squadron of the 3d Life Guards arrived with drawn swords at a gallop from their barracks (then situate in King Street), and rapidly formed in front of the Ambassador's house. Lavender and the Bow Street officers now withdrew ; the officers who had gathered about the stair-head were desired to return to the ballroom.

" The alarm, whatever it might have been, appeared to be over, and before the company broke up the Life Guards had been withdrawn to their barracks. Inside the Ambassador's house all had remained so quiet that very few of the ladies present were aware till next day that anything unusual had happened, but it became known after a short time that the Duke of Wellington had received information of an intended attack upon the house, which the precautions taken had probably prevented ; and upon the trial of Thistlewood and his gang (for the Cato Street Conspiracy) it came out, among other evidence of the various wild schemes they had formed, that Thistlewood had certainly entertained the project, at the time of this ball, to attack the Spanish Ambassador's house, and destroy the Regent and other Royal personages, as well as the Ministers, who were sure to be, most of them, present on the occasion."

For details of the Cato Street Conspiracy the curious reader is referred to the *Annual Register* for 1820, and it is strange to reflect that these explosions of revolutionary rage occurred well within the recollection of old friends of mine, now living, among whom I hope it is not invidious to mention Lady Georgiana Grey and Mr. Charles Villiers.

7

SECTION 7

XI

PARLIAMENTARY ORATORY

In my last chapter I endeavored to give some account of the political condition of England during the closing years of the eighteenth and the earlier part of the nineteenth century. Closely connected with the subject of politics is that of Parliamentary Oratory, and for a right estimate of oratory personal impressions (such as those on which throughout these chapters I have relied) are peculiarly valuable. They serve both to correct and to confirm. It is impossible to form from the perusal of a printed speech anything but the vaguest and often the most erroneous notion of the effect which it produced upon its hearers. But from the testimony of contemporaries one can often gain the clew to what is otherwise unintelligible. One learns what were the special attributes of bearing, voice, or gesture, the circumstances of delivery, or even the antecedent conditions of character and reputation, which perhaps doomed some magnificent peroration to ludicrous failure, or, on the contrary, "ordained strength " out of stammering lips and disjointed sentences. Testimony of this kind the circumstances of my life have given me in great abundance. My chain of tradition links me to the days of the giants.

Almost all the old people whose opinions and experience I have recorded were connected, either personally or through their nearest relations, with one or other of the Houses of Parliament. Not a few of them were conspicnous actors on the stage of political life. Lord Robert Seymour, from whose diary I have quoted, died in 1831, after a long life spent in the House of Commons, which he entered in 1771, and of which for twenty-three years he was a fellow-member with Edmund Burke. Let me linger for a moment on that illustrious name.

In originality, erudition, and accomplishments Burke had no rival among Parliamentary speakers. His prose is, as we read it now, the most fascinating, the most musical, in the English language. It bears on every page the divine lineaments of genius. Yet an orator requires something more than mere force of words. He must feel, while he speaks, the pulse of his audience, and instinctively regulate every sentence by reference to their feelings. All contemporary evidence shows that in this kind of oratorical tact Burke was eminently deficient. His nickname, "The Dinner-bell of the House of Commons," speaks for his effect on the mind of the average M. P. "In vain," said Moore, "did Burke's genius put forth its superb plumage, glittering all over with the hundred eyes of fancy. The gait of the bird was heavy and awkward, and its voice seemed rather to scare than attract."

Macaulay has done full justice to the extraordinary blaze of brilliancy which on supreme occasions threw these minor defects into the shade. Even now the old oak rafters of Westminster Hall seem to echo that superlative peroration which taught Mrs. Siddons a higher flight of tragedy than her own, and made the accused proconsul feel himself for the moment the guiltiest of men. Mr. Gladstone avers that Burke was directly responsible for the war with France, for " Pitt could not have resisted him." For the more refined, the more cultivated, the more speculative intellects he had – and has – an almost supernatural charm. His style is, without any exception, the richest, the most picturesque, the most inspired andinspiring in the language. In its glories and its terrors it resembles the Apocalypse. Mr. Morley, in the most striking of all his critical essays, has truly said that the natural ardor which impelled Burke to clothe his judgments in glowing and exaggerated phrase is one secret of his power over us, because it kindles in those who are capable of that generous infection a respondent interest and sympathy. " He has the sacred gift of inspiring men to care for high things, and to make their lives at once rich and austere." Such a gift is rare indeed. We feel no emotion of revolt when Mackintosh speaks of Shakespeare and Burke in the same breath as being, both of them, above mere talent. We do not dissent when Macaulay, after reading Burke's works over again, exclaims: "How admirable! The greatest man since Milton *I"*

No sane critic would dream of comparing the genius of Pitt with that of Burke. Yet where Burke failed Pitt succeeded. Burke's speeches, indeed, are a part of our national literature ; Pitt was, in spite of grave and undeniable faults, the greatest Minister that ever governed England. Foremost among the gifts by which he acquired his supreme ascendency must be placed his power of parliamentary speaking. He was not, as his father was, an orator in that highest sense of oratory which implies something of inspiration, of genius, of passionate and poetic rapture ; but he was a public speaker of extraordinary merit. He had while still a youth what Coleridge aptly termed "a premature and unnatural dexterity in the combination of words," and this developed into a "power of pouring forth with endless facility perfectly modulated sentences of perfectly chosen language, which as far surpassed the reach of a normal intellect as the feats of an acrobat exceed the capacities of a normal body." It was eloquence particularly well calculated tosway a popular assembly which yet had none of the characteristics of a mob. A sonorous voice; a figure and bearing which, though stiff and ungainly, were singularly dignified; an inexhaustible copiousness of grandiloquent phrase ; a peculiar vein of sarcasm which froze like ice and cut like steel – these were some of the characteristics of the oratory which from 1782 to 1806 at once awed and fascinated the House of Commons.

" I never want a word, but Mr. Pitt always has at command the right word." This was the generous tribute of Pitt's most eminent rival, Charles James Fox. Never were great opponents in public life more exactly designed by nature to be contrasts to one another. While every tone of Pitt's voice and every muscle of his countenance expressed with unmistakable distinctness the cold and stately composure of his character, every particle of Fox's mental and physical formation bore witness to his fiery and passionate enthusiasm. "What is that fat gentleman in such a passion about ?" was the artless query of the late Lord Eversley, who, as Mr. Speaker Shaw-Le- fevre, so long presided over the House of Commons, and who as a child had been taken to the gallery to hear Mr. Fox. While Pitt was the embodied representative of Order, his rival was the Apostle and Evangelist of Liberty. If the master passion of Pitt's mind was enthusiasm for his country, Fox was swayed by the still nobler enthusiasm of Humanity. His style of oratory was the exact reflex of his mind. He was unequalled in passionate argument, in impromptu reply, in ready and spontaneous declamation. His style was unstudied to a fault. Though he was so intimately acquainted with the great models of classical antiquity, his oratory owed little to the contact, and nothing to the formal arts of rhetoric – everything to inborn genius and the greatness of the causes which he espoused. It would be difficult to point to a single publie question of his time on which his voice did not sound with rousing effect, and whenever that voice was heard it was on behalf of freedom, humanity, and the sacred brotherhood of nations.

I pass on to the orator of whose masterpiece Fox said that "eloquent indeed it was; so much so that all he had ever heard, all he had ever read, dwindled into nothing and vanished like vapor before the sun." In sparkling brilliancy and pointed wit, in all the livelier graces of declamation and delivery, Sheridan surpassed all his contemporaries. When he concluded his speech on the charge against Warren Hastings of plundering the Begums of Oude, the peers and strangers joined with the House in a tumult of applause, and could not be restrained from clapping their hands in ecstasy. The House adjourned in order to recover its self-possession. Pitt declared that this speech surpassed all the eloquence of ancient and modern times, and possessed everything that genius or art could furnish to agitate or control the human mind. And yet, while Sheridan's supreme efforts met with this startling success, his deficiencies in statesmanship and character prevented him from commanding that position in the House and in the Government which his oratorical gift, if not thus handicapped, must have secured for its possessor.

As a speaker in his own sphere Lord Erskine was not inferior to the greatest of his contemporaries. He excelled in fire, force, and passion. Lord Brougham finely described "that noble figure every look of whose countenance is expressive, every motion of whose form graceful ; an eye that sparkles and pierces and almost assures victory, while it' speaks audience ere the tongue.'" Yet, as is so often the case, the unequalled advocate found himself in the House of Commons less conspicuously successful than he had been at the Bar. The forensic manner of speech, in which he was a head and shoulders higher than any of his legal contemporaries, is, after all, distinct from parliamentary eloquence.

The same disqualification attached to the oratory of Lord Brougham, whose speech at the bar of the House of Lords in defence of Queen Caroline had made so deep an impression. His extraordinary fierceness and even violence of nature pervaded his whole physical as well as intellectual being. When he spoke he was on springs and quicksilver, and poured forth sarcasm, invective, argument, and declamation in a promiscuous and headlong flood. Yet all contemporary evidence shows that his grandest efforts were dogged by the inevitable fate of the man who, not content with excellence in one or two departments, aims at the highest point in all. In reading his speeches, while one admires the versatility, one is haunted by that fatal sense of superficiality which gave rise to the caustic saying that if the Lord Chancellor only knew a little law he would know something about everything.

Pitt died in 1806, but he lived long enough to hear the splendid eloquence of Grattan, rich in imagination, metaphor, and epigram ; and to open the doors of the official hierarchy to George Canning. Trained by Pitt, and in many gifts and graces his superior, Canning first displayed his full greatness after the death of his illustrious master. For twenty years he was the most accomplished debater in the House of Commons, and yet he never succeeded in winning the full confidence of the nation, nor, except in foreign affairs, in leaving his mark upon our national policy. "The English are afraid of genius," and when genius is displayed in the person of a social adventurer, however brilliant and delightful, it is doubly alarming. We can judge of Canning's speeches more exactly than of those of his predecessors, for by the timethat he had become famous the art of parliamentary reporting had attained almost to its present perfection ; and there are none which more amply repay critical study.

Second only to Bnrke in the grandeur and richness of his imagery, he far excelled him in readiness, in tact, and in those adventitious advantages which go so far to make an orator. Mr. Gladstone still recalls the " light and music" of the eloquence with which he fascinated Liverpool seventy years ago. Scarcely any one has contributed so many beautiful thoughts and happy phrases to the common stock of public speech. All contemporary observers testify to the effect produced by the proud strength of his declaration on foreign policy : "I called the New World into existence in order to redress the balance of the Old." And the language does not contain *a* more magnificent or perfect image than that in which he likens a strong nation at peace to a great man-of-war lying calm and motionless till the moment for action comes, when " it puts forth all its beauty and its bravery, collects its scattered elements of strength, and awakens its dormant thunder."

Lord John Russell entered the House of Commons in 1813, and left it in 18C1. He used to say that in his early days there were a dozen men there who could make a finer speech than any one now living; "but," he used to add, "there were not another dozen who could understand what they were talking about." I asked him who was, on the whole, the best speaker he ever heard. He answered "Lord Plunket,"and subsequently gave as his reason this – that while Pluuket had his national Irish gifts of fluency, brilliant imagination, and ready wit very highly developed, they were all adjuncts to his strong, cool, inflexible argument. This, it will be readily observed, is a very rare and a very striking combination, and goes far to account for the transcendent success which Plunket attained at the Bar and in the House, and alike in the Irish and the English Parliament. Lord Brougham said of him that his eloquence was a continuous flow of "clear statement, close reasoning, felicitous illustration, all confined strictly to the subject in hand ; every portion, without any exception, furthering the process of conviction"; and I do not know a more impressive passage of sombre passion than the peroration of his first speech against the Act of Union : " For my own part, I will resist it to the last gasp of my existence, and with the last drop of my blood ; and when I feel the hour of my dissolution approaching I will, like the father of Hannibal, take my children to the altar and swear them to eternal hostility against the invaders of their country's freedom."

Before the death of Pitt another great man had risen to eminence, though the main achievement of his life associates him with 1832. Lord Grey was distinguished by a stately and massive eloquence which exactly suited his high purpose and earnest gravity of nature, while its effect was enormously enhanced by his handsome presence and kingly bearing. Though the leader of the popular cause, he was an aristocrat in nature, and pre-eminently qualified for the great part which, during twenty years, he played in that essentially aristocratic assembly – the unreformed House of Commons. In a subsequent paper I hope to say a little about parliamentary orators of a rather more recent date; and here it may not be uninteresting to compare the House of Commons as we have seen it and known it, modified by successive extensions of the suffrage, with what it was before Grey and Russell destroyed forever its exclusive character.

The following description is taken from Lord Beacons- field, who is drawing a character derived in part fromSir Francis Burdett (1770-1840) and in part from George Byng, who was M. P. for Middlesex for fifty-six years, and died in 1847 : " He was the father of the House, though it was difficult to believe that from his appearance. He was tall, and had kept his distinguished figure; a handsome man, with a musical voice, and a countenance now benignant, though very bright, and once haughty. He still retained the same fashion of costume in which he had ridden up to Westminster more than half a century ago to support his dear friend Charles Fox – real top-boots and a blue coat and buff waistcoat. He had a large estate, and had refused an earldom. Knowing E., he came and sate by him one day in the House, and asked him, good-naturedly, how he liked his new life. ' It is very different from what it was when I was your age. Up to Easter we rarely had a regular debate, never a party division ; very few people came up indeed. But there was a good deal of speaking on all subjects before dinner. We had the privilege then of speaking on the presentation of petitions at any length, and we seldom spoke on any other occasion. After Easter there was always at least one great party fight. This was a mighty affair, talked of for weeks before it came off, and then rarely an adjourned debate. We were gentlemen, used to sit up late, and should have been sitting up somewhere else had we not been in the House of Commons. After this party fight the House for the rest of the session was a mere club. . . . The House of Commons was very much like what the House of Lords is now. Yon went home to dine, and then came back for an important division. . . . Twenty years ago no man would think of coming down to the House except in evening dress. I remember, so late as Mr. Canning, the Minister always came down in silk stockings and pantaloons or knee-breeches. All these things change, andquoting Virgil will be the next thing to disappear. In the last Parliament we often had Latin quotations, but never from a member with a new constituency. I have heard Greek quoted here, but that was long ago, and a great mistake. The House was quite alarmed. Charles Fox used to say as to quotation: " No Greek; as much Latin as you like; and never French under any circumstances. *No* English poet unless he has completed his century."' These were, like some other good rules, the unwritten orders of the House of Commons." XII

PARLIAMENTARY ORATORY

I Concluded my last chapter with a quotation from Lord Beaconsfield, describing parliamentary speaking as it was when he entered the House of Commons in 1837. Of that particular form of speaking perhaps the greatest master was Sir Robert Peel. He was deficient in those gifts of imagination and romance which are essential to the highest oratory. He utterly lacked – possibly he would have despised – that almost prophetic rapture which we recognize in Burke and Chatham and Erskine. His manner was frigid and pompous, and his rhetorical devices were mechanical. Every parliamentary sketch of the time satirizes his habit of turning round towards his supporters at given periods to ask for their applause; his trick of emphasizing his points by perpetually striking the box before him; and his inveterate propensity to indulge in hackneyed quotation. But when we have said this we have said all that can be urged in his disparagement. As a parliamentary speaker of the second, and perhaps most useful, class he has never been excelled. Firmly, though dispassionately, persuaded of certain political and economic doctrines, he brought to the task of promoting them unfailing tact, prompt courage, intimate acquaintaiice with the foibles of his hearers, unconquerable patience and perseverance, and an inexhaustible supply of sonorous phrases and rounded periods. Nor was his success confined to the House of Commons. As a speaker on public platforms, in the heyday of the ten-pound householder and the middle-class franchise, he was peculiarly in his element. He had beyond most men the art of " making a platitude endurable by making it pompous." He excelled in demonstrating the material advantages of a moderate and cautious conservatism, and he could draw at will and with effect upon a prodigious fund of constitutional commonplaces. If we measure the merit of a parliamentary speaker by his practical influence, we must allow that Peel was pre-eminently great.

In the foremost rank of orators a place must certainly be assigned to O'Connell. He was not at his best in the House of Commons. His coarseness, violence, and cunning were seen to the worst advantage in what was still an assemblage of gentlemen. His powers of ridicule, sarcasm, and invective, his dramatic and sensational predilections, required another scene for their effective display. But few men have ever been so richly endowed by nature with the original, the incommunicable, the inspired qualifications which go to make an orator. He was magnificently built, and blessed with a voice which, by all contemporary testimony, was one of the most thrilling, flexible, and melodious that ever vibrated through a popular assembly. "From grave to gay, from lively to severe," he flew without delay or difficulty. The raciest wit gave point to the most irrelevant personalities, and cogency to the most illogical syllogisms; the most daring perversions of truth and justice were driven home by appeals to the emotions which the coldest natures conld scarcely withstand. "The passions of his audience were playthings in his hand." Lord Lytton thus describes the effect of the great oratorical power of the leader of the Repeal agitation and the champion of Catholic emancipation:

" Once to my sight the giant thus was given :
Wall'd by wide air, and roof'd by boundless heaven,
Beneath his feet the human ocean lay,
And wave on wave flow'd into space away.
Methought no clarion could have sent its sound
Even to the centre of the hosts around ;
But, as I thought, rose the sonorous swell,
As from some church tower swings the silvery bell.
Aloft and clear, from airy tide to tide
It glided, easy as a bird may glide;
To the last verge of that vast audience sent,
It play'd with each wild passion as it went;
Now stirr'd the uproar, now the murmur still'd,
And sobs or laughter answcr'd as it will'd.
Then did I know what spells of infinite choice,
To rouse or lull, hath the sweet human voice;
Then did I seem to seize the sudden clue
To that grand troublous Life Antique – to view,
Under the rockstand of Demosthenes,
Mutable Athens heave her uoisy seas."

A remarkable contrast, as far as outward characteristics went, was offered by the other great orator of the same time. Sheil was very small and of mean presence, with a singularly fidgety manner, a shrill voice, and a delivery unintelligibly rapid. But in sheer beauty of elaborated diction not O'Connell nor any one else could surpass him. There are few finer speeches in the language than that in which he took Lord Lyndhurst to task for applying the word "alien" to the Irish in a speech on municipal reform :

"Aliens ! Good God ! was Arthur Duke of Wellington in the House of Lords, and did he not start up and exclaim : 'Hold ! I have seen the aliens do their duty'? ... I appeal to the gallant soldier before me, from whose opinions I differ, but who bears, I know, a generous heart in an intrepid bosom, tell me, for you needs must remember – on that day when the destinies of mankind were trembling in the balance – while death fell in showers – tell me if for an instant, when to hesitate for an instant was to be lost, the 'aliens' blenched. . . . On the field of Waterloo the blood of England, of Scotland, and of Ireland flowed in the same stream and drenched the same field. When the chill morning dawned their dead lay cold and stark together; in the same deep pit their bodies were deposited; the green corn of spring is now breaking from their commingled dust; the dew falls from heaven npon this union in the grave. Partakers in every peril, in the glory shall we not be permitted to participate ? And shall we be told as a requital that we are 'aliens' from the noble country for whose salvation our life-blood was poured out ?"x

By the time which we are now considering there had risen to eminence a man who, if he could not be ranked with the great orators of the beginning of the century, yet inherited their best traditions and came very near to rivalling their fame. I refer to the great Lord Derby. His eloquence was of the most impetuous kind, corresponding to the sensitive fierceness of the man, and had gained for him the nickname of "The Rupert of Debate." Lord Beaconsfield, speaking in the last year of his life to Mr. Matthew Arnold, said that the task of carrying Mr. Forster's Coercion Bill of 1881 through the House of Commons " needed such a man as Lord Derby was in his youth – a man full of nerve, dash, fire, and resource, who carried the House irresistibly along with him" – no mean tribute from a consummate judge. Among Lord Derby's ancillary qualifications were his musical voice, his fine English style, and his facility in apt and novel quotation, as when he applied Meg Mer- rilies's threnody over the ruins of Derncleugh to the destruction of the Irish Church Establishment. I turn to Lord Lytton again for a description :

"One after one, the Lords of Time advance;
Here Stanley meets – how Stanley scorns ! – the glance.
The brilliant chief, irregularly great,
Frank, haughty, rash, the Rupert of Debate;
Nor gout nor toil his freshness can destroy,
And time still leaves all Eton in the boy.
First in the class, and keenest in the ring,
He saps like Gladstone, and he fights like Spring!
Yet who not listens, with delighted smile,
To the pure Saxon of that silver style;
In the clear style a heart as clear is seen,
Prompt to the rash, revolving from the mean."

I turn now to Lord Derby's most eminent rival – Lord Russell. Writing in 1844, Lord Beaconsfield thus describes him: " He is not a natural orator, and labors nnder physical deficiencies which even a Demosthenic impulse could scarcely overcome. But he is experienced in debate, quick in reply, fertile in resource, takes large views, and frequently compensates for a dry and hesitating manner by the expression of those noble truths that flash across the fancy and rise spontaneously to the lip of men of poetic temperament when addressing popular assemblies." Twenty years earlier Moore had described Lord John Russell's public speaking in a peculiarly happy image:

"An eloquence, not like those rills from a height
Which sparkle and foam and in vapor are o'er;
But a current that works out its way into light

Through the filtering recesses of thought and of lore."

Cobden, when they were opposed to one another in the earlier days of the struggle for Free Trade, described him as *"a,* cunning little fox," and avowed that he dreaded his dexterity in parliamentary debate more than that of any other opponent.

In 1834 Lord John made his memorable declaration in favor of a liberal policy with reference to the Irish Church Establishment, and, in his own words, "The speech made a great impression ; the cheering was loud and general; and Stanley expressed his sense of it in a well-known note to Sir James Graham: 'Johnny has upset the coach.'" The phrase was perpetuated by Lord Lytton, to whom I must go once again for a perfectly apt description of the Whig leader, both in his defects of manner and in his essential greatness :

"Next cool, and all unconscious of reproach,
Comes the calm Johnny who ' upset the coach,"
How formed to lead, if not too proud to please !
His fame would fire you, but his manners freeze,
Like or dislike, he does not care a jot;
He wants your vote, but your affections not.
Yet human hearts need sun as well as oats;
So cold a climate plays the deuce with votes.
But see our hero when the steam is on,
And languid Johnny glows to Glorious John !
When Hampden's thought, by Falkland's muses drest,
Lights the pale cheek and swells the generous breast;
When the pent heat expands the quickening soul,
And foremost in the race the wheels of genius roll."

As the general idea of these papers has been a concatenation of Links with the Past, I must say a word about Lord Palmerston, who was born in 1784, entered Parliament in 1807, and was still leading the House of Commons when I first attended its debates. A man who, when turned seventy, could speak from the " dusk of a summer evening to the dawn of a summer morning" in defence of his foreign policy, and carry the vindication of it by a majority of forty-six, was certainly no common performer on the parliamentary stage; and yet Lord Palmerston had very slender claims to the title of an orator. His style was not only devoid of ornamentand rhetorical device, but it was slipshod and untidy in the last degree. He eked out his sentences with "hum" and "hah"; he cleared his throat, and flourished his pocket-handkerchief, and sucked his orange; he rounded his periods with "You know what I mean" and "All that kind of thing," and seemed actually to revel in au anticlimax – "I think the hon. member's proposal an outrageous violation of constitutional propriety, a daring departure from traditional policy, and, in short, a great mistake."

It taxed all the skill of the reporters' gallery to trim his speeches into decent form ; and yet no one was listened to with keener interest, no one was so much dreaded as an opponent, and no one ever approached him in the art of putting a plausible face upon a doubtful policy and making the worse appear the better cause. Palmerston's parliamentary success perfectly illustrates the judgment of Demosthenes, that "it is not the orator's language that matters, nor the tone of his voice; but what matters is that he should have the same predilections as the majority, and should entertain the same likes and dislikes as his country." If those are the requisites of public speaking, Palmerston was supreme.

The most conspicuous of all Links with the Past in the matter of Parliamentary Oratory is obviously Mr. Gladstone. Like the younger Pitt, he had a "premature and unnatural dexterity in the combination of words." He was trained under the immediate influence of Canning, who was his father's friend. When he was sixteen his style was already formed. I quote from the records of the Eton Debating Society for 1826 :

"Thus much, sir, I have said, as conceiving myself bound in fairness not to regard the names under which men have hidden their designs so much as the designs themselves. I am well aware that my prejudices andmy predilections have long been enlisted on the side of Toryism – (cheers) – and that in a cause like this I am not likely to be influenced unfairly against men bearing that name and professing to act on the principles which I have always been accustomed to revere. But the good of my country must stand on a higher ground than distinctions like these. In common fairness and in common candor, I feel myself compelled to give my decisive verdict against the conduct of men whose measures I firmly believe to have been hostile to British interests, destructive of British glory, and subversive of the splendid and I trust lasting, fabric of the British Constitution."

Mr. Gladstone entered Parliament when he was not quite twenty-three, at the General Election of 1832, and it is evident from a perusal of his early speeches in the House of Commons, imperfectly reported in the third person, and from contemporary evidence, that, when due allowance is made for growth and development, his manner of oratory was then the same as it is to-day. Then, as afterwards, he was only too fluent. His style was copious, redundant, and involved, and his speeches were garnished, after the manner of his time, with IIo- ratian and Virgilian tags. His voice was always clear, flexible, and musical, though his utterance was marked, even more strongly than now, by a Lancastrian " burr." His gesture was varied and animated, though not violent. He turned his face and body from side to side, and often wheeled right round to face his own party as he appealed for their cheers.

" Did you ever feel nervous in public speaking ?" asked the late Lord Coleridge.

" In opening a subject, often," answered Mr. Gladstone ; " *in reply, never.*"

It was a characteristic saying, for, in truth, he was a born debater, never so happy as when coping on the spur of the moment with the arguments and appeals which an opponent had spent perhaps days in elaborating beforehand. Again, in the art of elucidating figures he was unequalled. He was the first Chancellor of the Exchequer who ever made the Budget interesting. " He talked shop," it was said, "like a tenth muse." He could apply all the resources of a glowing rhetoric to the most prosaic questions of cost and profit; could make beer romantic and sugar serious. He could sweep the widest horizon of the financial future, and yet stoop to bestow the minutest attention on the microcosm of penny stamps and the monetary merits of half-farthings. And yet, extraordinary as were these feats of intellectual athletics, Mr. Gladstone's unapproached supremacy as an orator was not really seen until he touched the moral elements involved in some great political issue. Then, indeed, he spoke like a prophet and a man inspired. His whole physical formation seemed to become "fusile" with the fire of his ethical passion, and his eloquence flowed like a stream of molten lava, carrying all before it in its irresistible rush, glorious as well as terrible, and fertilizing while it subdued. Mr. Gladstone's departure from the House of Commons closed a splendid tradition, and Parliamentary Oratory as our fathers understood it may now be reckoned among the lost arts.

8

SECTION 8

XIII

CONTERSATION

We have agreed that Parliamentary Oratory, as our fathers understood that phrase, is a lost art. Must Conversation be included in the same category ? To answer with positiveness is difficult; but this much may be readily conceded – that a belief in the decadence of conversation is natural to those who have specially cultivated Links with the Past; who grew up in the traditions of Luttrell and Mackintosh, and Lord Alvanley and Samuel Rogers; who have felt Sydney Smith's irresistible fun, and known the overwhelming fulness of Lord Macaulay. It is not unreasonable even in that later generation which can still recall the frank but high-bred gay- ety of the great Lord Derby, the rollicking good-humor and animal spirits of Bishop Wilberforce, the saturnine epigrams of Lord Beaconsfleld, the versatility and choice diction of Lord Honghton, the many-sided yet concentrated malice which supplied the stock-in-trade of Abraham Hayward. More recent losses have been heavier still. Nine years ago died Mr. Matthew Arnold, who possessed the various elements which make good conversation – urbanity, liveliness, quick sympathy, keen interest in the world's works and ways, the happiest choice of words, and a natural and never - failing humor, as genial as it was pungent. It was his good fortune that he knew how to be a man of the world without being frivolous, and a man of letters without being pedantic.

Eight years ago I was asked to discuss the Art of Conversation in one of the monthly reviews, and I could then illustrate it by such living instances as Lord Gran- ville, Sir Robert Peel, Lord Coleridge, Lord Bowen, Mr. Browning, and Mr. Lowell. Each of those distinguished men had a conversational gift which was peculiarly his own. Each talked like himself, and like no one else; each made his distinct and individual contribution to the social agreeableness of London. If in now endeavoring to recall their characteristic gifts I use words which I have used before, my excuse must be that the contemporary record of a personal impression cannot with advantage be retouched after the lapse of years.

Lord Granville's most notable quality was a humorous urbanity. As a story-teller he was unsurpassed.- He had been everywhere and had known every one. He was quick to seize a point, and extraordinarily apt in anecdote and illustration. His fine taste appreciated whatever was best in life, in conversation, in literature, even when (as in his selection of the preface to the *Sanctus* as his favorite piece of English prose) it was gathered from fields in which he had not habitually roamed. A man whose career had been so full of vivid and varied interests must often have felt acutely bored by the trivial round of social conversation. But if he could not rise – who can? – to the apostolic virtue of suffering bores gladly, at any rate he endured their onslaughts as unflinchingly as he bore the gout. A smiling countenance and an unfailing courtesy concealed the torment which was none the less keen because it was unexpressed. He could always feel, or at least could show, a gracious interest in what interested his company, and he possessed in supreme perfection the happy knack of putting those to whom he spoke in good conceit with themselves.

The late Sir Robert Peel was, both mentally and physically, one of the most picturesque figures in society. Alike in his character and in his aspect, the Creole blood which he had inherited from his maternal descent triumphed over the robust and serviceable commonplace which was the characteristic quality of the Peels. Lord Beaconsfield described "a still gallant figure, scrupulously attired ; a blue frock-coat, with a ribboned buttonhole ; a well - turned boot; hat a little too hidalgoish, but quite new. There was something respectable and substantial about him, notwithstanding his mustaches and a carriage too debonair for his years." The description, for whomsover intended, is a lifelike portrait of Sir Robert Peel. His most salient feature as a talker was his lovely voice – deep, flexible, melodious. Mr. Gladstone – no mean judge of such matters – pronounced it the finest organ he ever heard in Parliament; but, with all due submission to so high an authority, I should have said that it was a voice better adapted to the drawing-room than to the House of Commons. In a large space a higher note and a clearer tone tell better, but in the close quarters of social intercourse one appreciates the sympathetic qualities of a rich barytone. And Sir Robert's voice, admirable in itself, was the vehicle of conversation quite worthy of it. He could talk of art and sport, and politics and books ; he had a great memory, varied information, lively interest in the world and its doings, and a full-bodied humor which recalled the social tone of the last century.

His vein of personal raillery was rather robust than refined. Nothing has been heard in our time quite like his criticism of Sir Edgar Boehm in the House of Commons, or his joke about Mr. Justice Chitty at the election for Oxford in 1880. But his humor (to quote his own words) " had an English ring," and much must be pardoned to a man who, in this portentous age of reticence and pose, was wholly free from solemnity, and when he heard or saw what was ludicrous was not afraid to laugh at it. Sir Robert Peel was an excellent hand at what our fathers called banter and we call chaff. A prig or a pedant was his favorite butt, and the performance was rendered all the more effective by his elaborate assumption of the *grand seigneur's* manner. The victim was dimly conscious that he was being laughed at, but comically uncertain about the best means of reprisal. Sydney Smith described Sir James Mackintosh as "abating and dissolving pompous gentlemen with the most successful ridicule." Whoever performs that process is a social benefactor, and the greatest master of it whom I have ever known was Sir Robert Peel.

The Judges live so entirely in their own narrow and rather technical circle that their social abilities are lost to the world. It is a pity, for several of them are men well fitted by their talents and accomplishments to take a leading part in society. The late Lord Coleridge was pre-eminently a case in point. Personally, I had an almost fanatical admiration for his genius, and in many of the qualities which make an agreeable talker he was unsurpassed. Every one who ever heard him at the Bar or on the Bench must recall that silvery voice and that perfect elocution which prompted a competent judge of such matters to say : " I should enjoy listening to Coleridge even if he only read out a page of *Bradshaw."* To these gifts were added an immense store of varied knowledge, a genuine enthusiasm for whatever is beautiful in literature or art, an inexhaustible copiousness of anecdote, and a happy knack of exact yet not offensive mimicry. It is always pleasant to see a man in great station who, in the intercourse of society, is perfectly untrammelled by pomp and form, can make a joke and enjoy it, and is not too cautious to garnish his conversation with personalities or to season it with sarcasm. Perhaps Lord Coleridge's gibes were a little out of place on "the Royal Bench of British Themis," but at a dinner-table they were delightful, and they derived a double zest from the exquisite precision and finish of the English in which they were conveyed.

Another judge who excelled in conversation was the late Lord Bowen. Those who knew him intimately would say that he was the best talker in London. In spite of the burden of learning which he carried and his marvellous rapidity and grasp of mind, his social demeanor was quiet and unobtrusive almost to the point of affectation. His manner was singularly suave and winning, and his smile resembled that of the much-quoted Chinaman who played but did not understand the game of euchre. This singular gentleness of speech gave a special piquancy to his keen and delicate satire, his readiness in repartee, and his subtle irony. No one ever met Lord Bowen without wishing to meet him again ; no one ever made his acquaintance without desiring his friendship. The meritorious but disappointing memoir of him just published only illustrates afresh the impossibility of transplanting to the printed page the rarefied humor of so delicate a spirit. Had he been more widely known, the traditions of his table-talk would probably have taken their place with the best recollections of

English conversation. His admirers can only regret that gifts so rich and so rare should have been buried in judicial dining- rooms or squandered on the dismal orgies of the Cosmopolitan Club, where dull men sit round a meagre fire, in a large, draughty, and half-lit room, drinking lemon- squash and talking for talking's sake – the most melancholy of occupations.

The society of London between 1870 and 1890 contained no more striking or interesting figure than that ofRobert Browning. No one meeting him for the first time and unfurnished with a clew would have guessed his vocation. He might have been a diplomatist, a statesman, a discoverer, or a man of science. But whatever was his calling, one felt sure that it must be something essentially practical. Of the disordered appearance, the unconventional demeanor, the rapt and mystic air which we assume to be characteristic of the poet he had absolutely none. And his conversation corresponded to his appearance. It abounded in vigor, in fire, in vivacity. It was genuinely interesting, and often strikingly eloquent, yet all the time it was entirely free from mystery, vagueness, and jargon. It was the crisp, emphatic, and powerful discourse of a man of the world who was incomparably better informed than the mass of his congeners. Mr. Browning was the readiest, the blithest, and the most forcible of talkers, and when he dealt in criticism the edge of his sword was mercilessly whetted against pretension and vanity. The inflection of his voice, the flash of his eye, the pose of his head, the action of his hand, all lent their special emphasis to the condemnation. " I like religion to be treated seriously," he exclaimed with reference to a theological novel of great renown, "and I don't want to know what this curate or that curate thought about it. *No, I don't."* Surely the secret thoughts of many hearts found utterance in that emphatic cry.

Here I must venture to insert a personal reminiscence. Mr. Browning had honored me with his company at dinner, and an unduly fervent admirer had button-holed him throughout a long evening, plying him with questions about what he meant by this line, and whom he intended by that character. It was more than flesh and blood could stand, and at last the master extricated himself from the grasp of the disciple, exclaiming with the most airy grace, "But, my clear fellow, this is too bad. *I*am monopolizing *you."* Now and then, at rather rare intervals, when time and place, and company and surroundings, were altogether suitable, Mr. Browning would consent to appear in his true character and to delight his hearers by speaking of his art. Then the higher and rarer qualities of his genius came into play. He kindled with responsive fire at a beautiful thought, and burned with contagious enthusiasm over a phrase which struck his fancy. Yet all the while the poetic rapture was underlain by a groundwork of robust sense. Rant, and gush, and affectation were abhorrent to his nature, and even in his grandest flights of fancy he was always intelligible.

The late Mr. Lowell must certainly be reckoned among the famous talkers of his time. During the years that he represented the United States in London his trim sentences, his airy omniscience, his minute and circumstantial way of laying down literary law, were the inevitable ornaments of serious dinners and cultured tea-tables. My first encounter with Mr. Lowell took place many years before he entered on his diplomatic career. It was in 1872, when I chanced to meet him in a company of tourists at Durham Castle. Though I was a devotee of the *Biglow Papers,* I did not know their distinguished author even by sight; and I was intensely amused by the air of easy mastery, the calm and almost fatherly patronage, with which this cultivated American overrode the indignant showwoman; pointed out, for the general benefit of the admiring tourists, the gaps and lapses in her artistic, architectural, and archaeological knowledge; and made mullion and portcullis, and armor and tapestry the pegs for a series of neat discourses on medieval history, domestic decoration, and the science of fortification.

Which things are an allegory. We, as a nation, take this calm assurance of foreigners at its own valuation. We consent to be told that we do not know our own poets, cannot pronounce our own language, and have no well- educated women. But after a time this process palls. We question the divine right of the superiority thus imposed on us. We ask on what foundation these high claims rest, and we discover all at once that we have paid a great deal of deference where very little was deserved. By processes such as these I came to find, in years long subsequent to the encounter at Durham, that Mr. Lowell, though an accomplished politician, a brilliant writer, and an admirable after-dinner speaker, was, conversationally considered, an inaccurate man with an accurate manner. But, after all, inaccuracy is by no means the worst of conversational faults, and when he was in the vein Mr. Lowell could be exceedingly good company. He liked talking, and talked not only much but very well. He had a genuine vein of wit and great dexterity in phrase- making ; and on due occasion would produce from the rich stores of his own experience some of the most vivid and striking incidents, both civil and military, of that tremendous struggle for human freedom with which his name and fame must be always and most honorably associated.

9

SECTION 9

XIV

r CONVERSATION

Brave men have lived since as well as before Agamemnon, and those who know the present society of London may not unreasonably ask whether, even granting the heavy losses which I enumerated in my last paper, the Art of Conversation is really extinct. Are the talkers of to-day in truth so immeasurably inferior to the great men who preceded them ? Before we can answer these questions, even tentatively, we must try to define our idea of good conversation, and this can best be done by rigidly ruling out what is bad. To begin with, all affectation, unreality, and straining after effect are intolerable ; scarcely less so are rhetoric, declamation, and whatever tends towards speech-making. Mimicry is a very dangerous trick, rare in perfection, and contemptible when imperfect. An apt story well told is delicious, but there was sound philosophy in Mr. Pinto's view that "when a man fell into his anecdotage it was a sign for him to retire from the world." One touch of ill-nature makes the whole world kin, and a spice of malice tickles the intellectual palate ; but a conversation which is mainly malicious is entirely dull. Constant joking is a weariness to the flesh ; but, on the other hand, a sustained seriousness of discourse is fatally apt to recall the conversation between the Hon. Elijah Pogram and the Three Literary Ladies – "How Pogram got out of his depth instantly, and how the Three L. L.'s were never in theirs, is a pieceof history not worth recording. Suffice it that, being all four out of their depths and all unable to swim, they splashed up words in all directions, and floundered about famously. On the whole, it was considered to have been the severest mental exercise ever heard in the National Hotel, and the whole company observed that their heads ached with the effort – as well they might."

A talker who monopolizes the conversation is by common consent insufferable, and a man who regulates his choice of topics by reference to what interests not his hearers but himself has yet to learn the alphabet of the art. Conversation is like lawn - tennis, and requires alacrity in return at least as much as vigor in service. A happy phrase, an unexpected collocation of words, a habitual precision in the choice of terms, are rare and shining ornaments of conversation, but they do not for an instant supply the place of lively and interesting matter, and an excessive care for them is apt to tell unfavorably on the substance of discourse.

" I might as well attempt to gather up the foam of the sea as to convey an idea of the extraordinary lauguage in which he clothed his description. There were at least five words in every sentence that must have been very much astonished at the use they were put to, and yet no others apparently could so well have expressed his idea. He talked like a racehorse approaching the winning-post – every muscle in action, and the utmost energy of expression flung out into every burst." This is a contemporary description of Lord Beaconsfield's conversation in those distant days when, as a young man about town, he was talking and dressing his way into social fame. Though written in admiration, it seems to me to describe the most intolerable performance that could ever have afflicted society. *He talked like a racehorseapproaching the winning -post.* Could the wit of man devise a more appalling image ?

Mr. Matthew Arnold once said to me : "People think that I can teach them style. What stuff it all is ! Have something to say, and say it as clearly as you can. That is the only secret of style." This dictum applies, I think, at least as well to conversation as to literature. The one thing needful is to have something to say. The way of saying it may best be left to take care of itself. A young man about town once remarked to me, in the tone of one who utters an accepted truism : " It is so much more interesting to talk about people than things." The sentiment was highly characteristic of the mental calibre and associations of the speaker; and certainly the habitual talk – for it is not conversation – of that section of society which calls itself " smart" seems to touch the lowest depth of spiteful and sordid dulness. But still, when the mischiefs of habitual personality have been admitted to the uttermost, there remains something to be said on the other side. We are not inhabitants of Jupiter or Saturn, but human beings to whom nothing that is human is wholly alien. And if in the pursuit of high abstractions and improving themes we imitate too closely Wordsworth's avoidance of Personal Talk, our dinner-table will run much risk of becoming as dull as the poet's own fireside.

Granting, then, that to have something to say which is worth hearing is the substance of good conversation, we must reckon among its accidents and ornaments a manner which knows how to be easy and free without being free - and - easy ; a habitual deference to the tastes and even the prejudices of other people ; a hearty desire to be, or at least to seem, interested in their concerns; and a constant recollection that even the most patient hearers may sometimes wish to be speakers. Above all else, the agreeable talker cultivates gentleness and delicacy of speech, avoids aggressive and overwhelming displays, and remembers the tortured cry of the neurotic bard :

" Vociferated logic kills me quite ;
A noisy man is always in the right –
I twirl my thumbs, fall back into my chair,
Fix on the wainscot a distressful stare;
And when I hope his blunders all are out,
Reply discreetly, ' To be sure – no doubt 1'"

If these, or something like these, are the attributes of good conversation, in whom do we find them best exemplified ? Who best understands the Art of Conversation ? Who, in a word, are our best talkers ? I hope that I shall not be considered ungallant if I say nothing about the part borne in conversation by ladies. Really, it is a sacred awe that makes me mute. London is happy in the possession of not a few hostesses, excellently accomplished, and not more accomplished than gracious, of whom it is no flattery to say that to know them is a liberal education. But, as Lord Beaconsfield observes in a more than usually grotesque passage of *Lothair,* "We must not profane the mysteries of Bona Dea." We will not "peep and botanize" on sacred soil, nor submit our most refined delights to the impertinences of critical analysis.

In considering the Art of Conversation I obey a natural instinct when I think first of Mr. Charles Villiers, M. P. His venerable age alone would entitle him to this pre-eminence, for he was born in 1802, and though he has now retired from general society, he was for seventy years one of the best talkers in London. Born of a family which combined high rank with intellectual distinction, his parentage was a passport to all that was best in social and political life. It argues no political bias tomaintain that in the first quarter of this century Toryism afforded its neophytes no educational opportunities equal to those which a young Whig enjoyed at Bowood and Panshanger and Holland House. There the best traditions of the last century were constantly reinforced by accessions of fresh intellect. The charmed circle was indeed essentially, but it was not exclusively, aristocratic; genius held the key, and there was a *carriere ouverte aux talents.*

Thus it came to pass that the society of Lord Lans- downe and Lord Holland and Lord Melbourne was also the society of Brougham, and Mackintosh, and Macau- lay, and Sydney Smith. It presented every variety of accomplishment and experience and social charm, and offered to a man beginning life the best conceivable education in the art of making oneself agreeable. For that art Mr. Villiers had a natural genius, and his lifelong association with the Whigs superadded a technical training in social art. But this, though much, was by no means all. I hold it to be an axiom that a man who is only a member of society can never be so agreeable as one who is something else as well. And Mr. Villiers, though " a man about town," a story-teller, and a diner- out of high renown, has had seventy years' experience of practical business and Parliamentary life. Thus the resources of his knowledge have been perpetually enlarged, and, learning much, he has forgotten nothing. The stores of his memory are full of treasures, new and old. He has taken part in the making of history, and can estimate the great men of the present day by a comparison with the political immortals.

That this comparison is not always favorable to some exalted reputations of the present hour is indeed sufficiently notorious to all who have the pleasure of Mr. Villiers's acquaintance; and nowhere is his mastery ofthe art of conversation more conspicuous than in his knack of implying dislike and insinuating contempt without crude abuse or noisy denunciation. He has a delicate sense of fun, a keen eye for incongruities and absurdities, and that genuine cynicism which springs, not from the poor desire to be thought worldly-wise, but from a lifelong acquaintance with the foibles of political men. To these gifts must be added a voice which age has not robbed of its sympathetic qualities, a style of diction and a habit of pronunciation which belong to the last century, and that formal yet facile courtesy which no one less than eighty years old seems capable of even imitating.

I have instanced Mr. Villiers as an eminent talker. I now turn to an eminent man who talks – Mr. Gladstone. An absurd story has long been current among credulous people with rampant prejudices that Mr. Gladstone was habitually uncivil to the Queen. Now, it happens that Mr. Gladstone is the most courteous of mankind. His courtesy is one of his most engaging gifts, and accounts in no small degree for his power of attracting the regard of young men and undistinguished people generally. To all such he is polite to the point of deference, yet never condescending. His manners to all alike – young and old, rich and poor – are the ceremonious manners of the old school, and his demeanor towards ladies is a model of chivalrous propriety. It would therefore have been to the last degree improbable that he should make a departure from his usual habits in the case of a lady who was also his Sovereign. And, as a matter of fact, the story is so ridiculously wide of the mark that it deserves mention only because, in itself false, it is founded on a truth connected with the subject of our present inquiry.

" I," said the Duke of Wellington on a memorable occasion, " have no small talk, and Peel has no manners."Mr. Gladstone has manners, but no small talk. He is so consumed by zeal for great subjects that he leaves out of account the possibility that they may not interest other people. He pays to every one, and not least to ladies, the compliment of assuming that they are on his own intellectual level, engrossed in the subjects which engross him, and furnished with at least as much information as will enable them to follow and to understand him. Hence the genesis of that absurd story about his demeanor to the Queen.

" He speaks to me as if I was a public meeting," is a complaint which is said to have proceeded from illustrious lips. That most successful of all courtiers, the astute Lord Beaconsfield, used to engage her Majesty in conversation about water-color drawing and the third-cousin- ships of German princes. Mr. Gladstone harangues her about the polity of the Hittites, or the harmony between the Athanasian Creed and Homer. The Queen, perplexed and uncomfortable, tries to make a digression – addresses a remark to a daughter, or proffers biscuits to a begging terrier. Mr. Gladstone restrains himself with an effort till the Princess has answered or the dog has sat down, and then promptly resumes: "I was about to say – " Meanwhile the flood has gathered force by delay, and when it bursts forth again it carries all before it.

No image except that of a flood can convey the notion of Mr. Gladstone's table-talk on a subject which interests him keenly – its rapidity, its volume, its splash and dash, its frequent beauty, its striking effects, the amount of varied matter which it brings with it, the hopelessness of trying to withstand it, the unexpectedness of its onrush, the subdued but fertilized condition of the subjected area over which it has passed. The bare mention of a topic which interests Mr. Gladstone opens the floodgates and submerges a province. But the torrent does not wait forthe invitation. If not invited it comes of its own accord; headlong, overwhelming, sweeping all before it, and gathering fresh force from every obstacle which it encounters on its course. Such is Mr. Gladstone's table- talk. For conversation, strictly so called, he has no turn. He asks questions when he wants information, and answers them copiously when asked by others. But of give-and-take, of meeting you half-way, of paying you back in your own conversational coin, he has no notion. He discourses, he lectures, he harangues. But if a subject is started which does not interest him it falls flat. He makes no attempt to return the ball. Although, when he is amused, his amusement is intense and long sustained, his sense of humor is highly capricious. It is impossible for even his most intimate friends to guess beforehand what will amuse him and what will not; and he has a most disconcerting habit of taking a comic story in grim earnest, and arguing some farcical fantasy as if it was a serious proposition of law or logic. Nothing funnier can be imagined than the discomfiture of a storyteller who has fondly thought to tickle the great man's fancy by an anecdote which depends for its point upon some trait of baseness, cynicism, or sharp practice. He finds his tale received in dead silence, looks up wonder- ingly for an explanation, and finds that what was intended to amuse has only disgusted. Mr. Browning once told Mr. Gladstone a highly characteristic story of Dis- raelitish duplicity, and for all reply heard a voice choked with indignation : " Do you call that amusing, Browning? *I call it devilish."* XV

CONVERSATION

More than thirty years have passed since the festive evening described by Sir George Trevelyan in *The Ladies in Parliament :*

"When, over the port of the innermost bin,
The circle of dinfirs was laughing with Phinn ;
When Brookfleld had hit on his happiest vein,
And Harcourt was capping the jokes of Delane."

The sole survivor of that brilliant group now leads the Opposition; but at the time when the lines were written he had not yet entered the House of Commons. As a youth of twenty-five he had astonished the political world by his anonymous letters on *The Morality of Public Men,* in which he denounced, in the style of Junius, the Protectionist revival of 1852, and to which he prefixed the scathing motto:

" Quid Crassos, quid Pompeios evertit ? . . .
Summus nempe locus nulla non arte petitus."

He had fought a plucky but unsuccessful fight at Kirk- caldy; was making his five thousand a year at the Parliamentary Bar; had taught the world international law over the signature of " Historicus," and was already, what he is still, one of the most conspicuous and interesting figures in the society of London. Of Sir WilliamHarcourt's political alliances this is not the place nor am I the person to treat.

"Let the high Muse chant loves Olympian:
We are but mortals, and must sing of Man."

My theme is not Sir William Harcourt the politican, but Sir William Harconrt the man, the member of society – above all, the talker. And, although I have thus deliberately put politics on one side, it is strictly relevant to my purpose to observe that Sir William is essentially and typically a Whig. For Whiggery, rightly understood, is not a political creed, but a social caste. The Whig, like tho poet, is bom, not made. It is as difficult to become a Whig as to become a Jew. Macanlay was probably the only man who, being born outside the privileged enclosure, ever -penetrated to its heart and assimilated its spirit. The Whigs, indeed, as a body have held certain political opinions and pursued certain political tactics which have been analyzed by the hand of a master in Chapters XIX. and XXI. of the unexpurgated *Book of Snobs.* But those opinions and those practices have been mere accidents, though perhaps inseparable accidents, of Whiggery. Its substance has been relationship.

When Lord John Eussell formed his first Administration his opponents alleged that it was mainly composed of his cousins, and one of his younger brothers was charged with the impossible task of rebutting the accusation in a public speech. Mr. Beresford Hope, in one of his novels, made excellent fun of what he called " the sacred circle of the great-grand-motherhood." He showed – what, indeed, the Whigs themselves knew uncommonly well – that from a certain Earl Gower, who flourished in the last century, and was great-great-greatgrandfather of the present Duke of Sutherland, are descended all the Levesons, Gowers, Howards, Cavendishes, Grosvenors, Rnssells, and Harcourts who walk on the face of the earth. Truly a noble and a highly favored progeny. "They *are* our superiors," said Thackeray; "and that's the fact. I am not a Whig myself (perhaps it is as unnecessary to say so as to say I'm not a King Pippin in a golden coach, or King Hudson, or Miss Bur- dett-Coutts). I'm not a Whig; but oh, how I should like to be one !"

From this illustrious stock Sir William Harcourt is descended through his grandmother, Lady Anne Harcourt – born Leveson-Gower, and wife of the last Prince-Archbishop of York (whom, by the way, Sir William strikingly resembles both in figure and in feature). When one meets Sir William Harcourt for the first time in society, perhaps one is first struck by the fact that he is in aspect and bearing a great gentleman of the old school, and then that he is an admirable talker. He is a true Whig in culture as well as in blood. Though his conversation is never pedantic, it rests on a wide and strong basis of generous learning. Even those who most cordially admire his political ability do not always remember that he is an excellent scholar, and graduated as eighth in the First Class of the Classical Tripos in the year when Bishop Lightfoot was Senior Classic. He has the *Corpus Poetarum* and Shakspeare and Pope at his finger-ends, and his intimate acquaintance with the political history of England elicited a characteristic compliment from Lord Beaconsfield. It is his favorite boast that in all his tastes, sentiments, and mental habits he belongs to the eighteenth century, which he glorifies as the golden age of reason, patriotism, and liberal learning. This self-estimate strikes me as perfectly sound, and it requires a very slight effort of the imagination to conceive this well-born young Templar wielding his doughty pen in the Bangorian Controversy, or declaiming on the hustings for Wilkes and Liberty; bandying witticisms with Sheridan, and capping Latin verses with Charles James Pox; or helping to rule England as a member of that "Venetian Oligarchy" on which Lord

Beaconsfield lavished all the vials of his sarcasm. In truth, it is not fanciful to say that whatever was best in the last century – its robust common - sense, its racy humor, its thorough and unaffected learning, its ceremonious courtesy for great occasions, its jolly self-abandonment in social intercourse – is exhibited in the demeanor and conversation of Sir William Harcourt. He is an admirable host, and, to borrow a phrase from Sydney Smith, "receives his friends with that honest joy which warms more than dinner or wine." As a guest, he is a splendid acquisition, always ready to amuse and to be amused, delighting in the rapid cut-and-thrust of personal banter, and bringing out of his treasure things new and old for the amusement and the benefit of a later and less instructed generation.

Extracts from the private conversation of living people, as a rule, I forbear ; but some of Sir William's quotations are so extraordinarily apt that they deserve a permanent place in the annals of table-talk. That famous old country gentleman, the late Sir Rainalcl Knightley (who was the living double of Dickens's Sir Leicester Dedlock), had been expatiating after dinner on the undoubted glories of his famous pedigree. The company was getting a little restive under the recitation, when Sir William was heard to say, in an appreciative aside, " This reminds me of Addison's evening hymn:

" ' And Knightley to the listening earth
Repeats the story of his birth.' "

Surely the force of apt citation can no farther go. When
Lord Tennyson chanced to say in Sir William Harcourt's
hearing that his pipe after breakfast was the most enjoyable of the day, Sir William softy murmured the Tenny- sonian line:

"The earliest pipe of half-awakened birds."

Some historians say that he substituted " bards" for " birds," and the reception accorded by the poet to the parody was not as cordial as its excellence deserved.

Another capital talker is Sir George Trevelyan. He has been, from the necessities of his position, a man of the world and a politician, and he is as ready as Mr. Bertie - Tremaine's guests in *Endymion* to talk of "that heinous subject on which enormous fibs are ever told – the Registration." But, after all, the man of the world and the politician are only respectable parts which he has been bound to assume, and he has played them with assiduity and success; but the true man in Sir George Trevelyan is the man of letters. Whenever he touches a historical or literary theme his whole being seems to undergo a transformation. The real nature flashes out through his twinkling eyes. While he muses the fire burns, and, like the Psalmist, he speaks with his tongue. Dates and details, facts and traditions, cantos of poetry, reams of prose, English and Latin and Greek and French, come tumbling out in headlong but not disorderly array. He jumps at an opening, seizes an allusion, replies with lightning quickness to a conversational challenge, and is ready at a moment's notice to decide any literary or historical controversy in a measured tone of deliberate emphasis which is not wholly free from exaggeration. Like his uncle, Lord Macaulay, Sir George Trevelyan has "his own heightened and telling way of putting things," and those who know him well make allowance for this habit. For the rest, he is delightful company, light-hearted as a boy, full of autobiographical chit-chat about Harrow andTrinity, and India and Holly Lodge, eagerly interested in his friends' concerns, brimming over with enthusiasm, never bored, never flat, never stale. A well-concerted party is a kind of unconscious conspiracy to promote cheerfulness and enjoyment, and in such an undertaking there can be no more serviceable ally than Sir George Trevelyan.

Mr. John Morley's agreeableness in conversation is of a different kind. His leading characteristic is a dignified austerity of demeanor which repels familiarity and tends to keep conversation on a high level; but each time one meets him there is less formality and less restraint, and the grave courtesy which never fails is soon touched with friendliness and frank good-humor in a singularly attractive fashion. He talks, not much, but remarkably well. His sentences are deliberate, clear-cut, often eloquent. He excels in phrase-making. His quotations are apt and novel. His fine taste and varied reading enable him to hold his own in many fields where the merely professional politician is apt to be terribly astray. His kindness to social and literary beginners is one of his most engaging traits. He invariably finds something pleasant to say about the most immature and unpromising efforts, and he has the knack of so handling his own early experience as to make it an encouragement and a stimulus, and not (as the manner of some is) a burden and a bogey. Mr. Morley never obtrudes his own opinions, never introduces debatable matter, never dogmatizes. But he is always ready to pick up the gauntlet, especially if a Tory flings it down; is merciless towards ill-informed assertion, and is the alert and unsparing enemy of what Mr. , Buskin calls " the obscene empires of Mammon and Belial."

Lord Salisbury goes so little into general society that his qualities as a talker are not familiarly known. He ispainfully shy, and at a club or in a large party undergoes the torments of the lost. Yet no one can listen, even casually, to his conversation without appreciating the fine manner, full of both dignity and of courtesy; the utter freedom from pomposity, formality, and self-assertion, and the agreeable dash of genuine cynicism which modifies, though it does not mask, the flavor of his fun. After a visit to Hatfield in 1868, Bishop Wil- berforce wrote in his diary: " Gladstone how struck with Salisbury: 'Never saw a more perfect host.'" And again: "He remarked to me on the great power of charming and pleasant host-ing possessed by Salisbury." And it is the universal testimony of Lord Salis- 'bury's guests, whether at Hatfield or in Arlington Street, that he is seen at his very best in his own house. The combination of such genuine amiability in private life with such calculated brutality in public utterance constitutes a psychological problem which might profitably be made the subject of a Romanes Lecture.

Barring the shyness, from which Mr. Balfour is conspicuously free, there is something of Lord Salisbury's social manner about his accomplished nephew. He has the same courtesy, the same sense of humor, the same freedom from official solemnity. But the characteristics of the elder man are exaggerated in the younger. The cynicism which is natural in Lord Salisbury is affected in Mr. Balfour. He cultivates the art of indifference, and gives himself the airs of a jaded Epicurean who craves only for a new sensation. There is what an Irish member, in a moment of inspiration, called a " toplofti- ness" about his social demeanor which is not a little irritating. He is too anxious to show that he is not as other men are. Among politicians he is a philosopher; among philosophers, a politician. Before that hard-bitten crew whom Burke ridiculed – the "calculators and economists" – he will talk airily of golf and ladies' fashions; and ladies he will seek to impress by the Praise of Vivisection or the Defence of Philosophic Doubt. His social agree- ableness has, indeed, been marred by the fatuous idolatry of a fashionable clique, stimulating the self-consciousness which was his natural foible ; but when he can for a moment forget himself he still is excellent company, for he is genuinely amiable and thoroughly well informed.

SECTION 10

XVI

CONVERSATION

The writer of these chapters has always felt some inward affinity to the character of Lord St. Jerome in *Lothair,* of whom it is recorded that he loved conversation, though he never conversed. "There must be an audience," he would say, "and I am the audience." In my capacity of audience I assign a high place to the agreeableness of Lord Rosebery's conversation. To begin with, he has a delightful voice. It is low, but perfectly distinct, rich and sympathetic in quality, and singularly refined in accent. It is exactly the sort of voice which bespeaks the goodwill of the hearer and recommends what it utters. In a former chapter we agreed that the chief requisite of good conversation is to have something to say which is worth saying; and here Lord Rose- bery is excellently equipped. Last week the newspapers announced with a nourish of rhetorical trumpets that he had just celebrated his fiftieth birthday. Some of the trumpeters, with a laudable intention to be civil, cried, "Is it possible that he can be Bo old?" Others, with subtler art, professed themselves unable to believe that he was so young. Each compliment contained its element of truth. In appearance, air, and tastes Lord Rose- bery is still young. In experience, knowledge, and conduct he is already old. He has had a vivid and a varied

May 7, 1897. experience. He is equally at home on Epsom Downs and in the House of Lords. His life has been full of action, incident, and interest. He has not only collected books, but has read them; and has found time, even amid the engrossing demands of the London County Council, the Turf, and the Foreign Office, not only for study, but – what is much more remarkable – for thought.

So far, then, as substance goes, his conversation is (to use Mr. Gladstone's quaint phrase) " as full of infinitely varied matter as an egg is full of meat"; and in its accidents and ornaments it complies exactly with the conditions laid down in a former paper – a manner which knows how to be easy and free without being free-and- easy ; habitual deference to the tastes and prejudices of other people; a courteous desire to be, or at least to seem, interested in their concerns ; and a recollection that even the most patient hearers (among whom the present writer reckons himself) may sometimes wish to be speakers. To these gifts he adds a keen sense of humor, a habit of close observation, and a sub-acid vein of sarcasm which resembles the dash of Tarragon in a successful salad. In a word, Lord Rosebery is one of the most agreeable talkers of the day; and even if it is true that *il s'ecoute quand il parle,* his friends may reply that it would be strange indeed if one could help listening to what is always so agreeable and often so brilliant.

A genial journalist recently said that Mr. Goschen was now chiefly remembered by the fact that he had once had Sir Alfred Milner for his private secretary. But, whatever may be thought of the First Lord of the Admiralty as a politician and an administrator, I claim for him a high place among agreeable talkers. There are some men who habitually use the same style of speech in public and private life. Happily for his friends, thisis not the case with Mr. Goschen. Nothing can be less agreeable than his public style, whether on the platform or in the House of Commons. Its tawdry staginess, its "Sadler's Wells sarcasm," its constant striving after strong effects, are distressing to good taste. But in private life he is another and a much more agreeable man. He is courteous, genial, perfectly free from affectation, and enters into the discussion of social banalities as eagerly and as brightly as if he had never converted the Three per Cents, or established the ratio between dead millionaires and new iron-clads. His easiness in conversation is perhaps a little marred by a Teutonic tendency to excessive analysis which will not suffer him to rest until he has resolved every subject, and almost every phrase, into its primary elements. But this philosophic temperament has its counterbalancing advantages in a genuine openness of mind, willingness to weigh and measure opposing views, and inaccessibility to intellectual passion. It is true that on the platform the exigencies of his position compel him to indulge in mock- heroics and cut rhetorical capers for which nature never designed him ; but these are for public consumption only, and when he is not playing to the gallery he can discuss his political opponents and their sayings and doings as dispassionately as a microscopist examines a black beetle. Himself a good talker, Mr. Goschen encourages good talk in other people; and in old days, when the Art of Conversation was still seriously cultivated, he used to gather round his table in Portland Place a group of intimate friends who found in '34 port the true well-spring of successful conversation. Among these were Lord Sherbrooke, whose aptness in quotation and dexterity in repartee have never been surpassed in my experience; and Lord Chief

Justice Cockburn, whose "sunny face and voice of music, which lent melody to scorn andsometimes reached the depth of pathos/' were gracefully commemorated by Lord Beaconsfield in his sketch of Hortensins. But this belongs to ancient history, and my business is with the conversation of to-day.

Very distinctly of to-day is the conversation of Mr. Labouchere. Even our country cousins are aware that the Member for Northampton is less an ornament of general society than the oracle of an initiated circle. The smoking-room of the House of Commons is his shrine, and there, poised in an American rocking-chair and delicately toying with a cigarette, he unlocks the varied treasures of his well-stored memory, and throws over the changing scenes of life the mild light of his genial philosophy. It is a chequered experience that has made him what he is. He has known men and cities; has probed in turn the mysteries of the caucus, the green-room, and the Stock Exchange ; has been a diplomatist, a financier, a journalist, and a politician. Under these circumstances, it is perhaps not surprising that his faith – no doubt originally robust – in the purity of human nature and the uprightness of human motive should have undergone some process of degeneration. Still it may be questioned whether, after all that he has seen and done, he is the absolute and all-round cynic that he would seem to be. The palpable endeavor to make out the worst of every one – including himself – gives a certain flavor of unreality to his conversation; but, in spite of this peculiarity, he is an engaging talker. His language is racy and incisive, and he talks as neatly as he writes. His voice is pleasant, and his utterance deliberate and effective. He has a keen eye for absurdities and incongruities, a shrewd insight into affectation and bombast, and an admirable impatience of all the moral and intellectual qualities which constitute the Bore. He is by no means inclined to bow his knee tooslavishly to an exalted reputation, and analyzes with agreeable frankness the personal and political qualities of great and good men, even if they sit on the Front Opposition Bench. As a contributor to enjoyment, as a promoter of fun, as an unmasker of political and social humbug, he is unsurpassed. His performances in debate are no concern of mine, for I am speaking of conversation only ; but most Members of Parliament will agree that he is the best companion that can be found for the last weary half-hour before the division-bell rings, when some eminent nonentity is declaiming his forgone conclusions to an audience whose whole mind is fixed on the chance of finding a disengaged cab in Palace Yard.

Like Mr. Labouchere, Lord Acton has touched life at many points – but not the same ones. He is a theologian, a professor, a man of letters, a member of society ; and his conversation derives a distinct tinge from each of these environments. When, at intervals all too long, he quits his retirement at Cannes or Cambridge, and flits mysteriously across the social scene, his appearance is hailed with devout rejoicing by every one who appreciates manifold learning, a courtly manner, and a delicately sarcastic vein of humor. The distinguishing feature of Lord Acton's conversation is an air of sphinx-like mystery, which suggests that he knows a great deal more than he is willing to impart. Partly by what he says, and even more by what he leaves unsaid, his hearers are made to feel that, if he has not acted conspicuous parts, he has been behind the scenes of many and very different theatres.

He has had relations, neither few nor unimportant, with the Pope and Old Catholics, with Oxford and Lambeth, with the cultivated Whiggery of the great English families, with the philosophic radicalism of Germany, and with those Nationalist complications which, in these laterdays, have drawn official Liberalism into their folds. He has long lived on terms of the closest intimacy with Mr. Gladstone, and may perhaps be bracketed with Canon MacColl and Sir Algernon West as the most absolute and profound Gladstonian outside the family circle of Hawar- den. But he is thoroughly eclectic in his friendships, and when he is in London he flits from Lady Hayter's tea-table to Mr. Goschen's bureau, analyzes at the Athe- nasum the gossip which he has acquired at Brooks's, and by dinner-time is able, if only he is willing, to tell you what the Greek intends and what the Turk ; the secret reasons for Archbishop Temple's appointment, and the subject of Mr. Gladstone's next book ; how long Lord Salisbury will combine the Premiership with the Foreign Office; and the latest theory about the side of Whitehall on which Charles I. was beheaded.

The ranks of our good talkers – none too numerous a body at the best, and sadly thinned by the losses which I described in a former paper – have been opportunely reinforced by the discovery of Mr. Augustine Birrell. For forty-seven years he has walked this earth, but it is only during the last eight – in short, since he entered Parliament – that the admirable qualities of his conversation have been generally recognized. Before that time his delightful *Obiter Dicta* had secured for him a wide circle of friends who had never seen his face, and by these admirers his first appearance on the social scene was awaited with lively interest. What would he be like ? Should we be disillusioned ? Would he talk as pleasantly as he wrote ? Well, in due course he appeared, and the questions were soon answered in a sense as laudatory as his friends or even himself could have desired. It was unanimously voted that his conversation was as agreeable as his writing ; but, oddly enough, its agreeableness was of an entirely different kind. His literary knack ofchatty criticism had required a new word to convey its precise effect. To "birrell" is now a verb as firmly established as to " boycott," and it signifies a style, light, easy, playful, pretty, rather discursive, perhaps a little superficial. Its characteristic note is grace. But when the eponymous hero of the new verb entered the conversational lists it was seen that his predominant quality was strength.

An enthusiastic admirer who sketched him in a novel christened him with the nickname of "The Harmonious Blacksmith," and the collocation of words happily hits off the special quality of his conversation. There is burly strength in his positive opinions, his cogent statement, his remorseless logic, his thorough knowledge of the persons and things that he discusses. In his sledge-hammer blows against humbug and wickedness, intellectual affectation, and moral baseness, he is the Blacksmith all over. In his geniality, his sociability, his genuine love of fun, his frank readiness to amuse or be amused, the epithet "harmonious" is abundantly justified. He cultivates to some extent the airs and tones of the last century, in which his studies have largely lain. He says what he means, and calls a spade a spade, and glories in an old- fashioned prejudice. He is the jolliest of companions and the steadiest of friends, and perhaps the most genuine book-lover in London, where, as a rule, society is too "cultured" to read books, though willing enough to chatter about them.

11

SECTION 11

XVII

CLERGTMEK

Clerus Anglicanus stupor mundi. I believe that this complimentary proverb originally referred to the learning of the English clergy, but it would apply with equal truth to their social agreeableness. When I was writing about the Art of Conversation and the men who excelled in it, I was surprised to find how many of the best sayings that recurred spontaneously to my memory had a clerical origin; and it struck me that a not uninteresting paper might be written about the social agreeable- ness of clergymen. A mere layman may well feel a natural and becoming diffidence in venturing to handle so high a theme.

In a former paper I said something of the secular magnificence which surrounded great prelates in the good old days, when the Archbishop of Canterbury could only be approached on gilt-edged paper; and even the Bishop of impecunious Oxford never appeared in his Cathedral city without four horses p, nd two powdered footmen. In a certain sense, no doubt, these splendid products of established religion conduced to social agreeableness. Like the excellent prelate described in *Friendship's Garland,*they "had thoroughly learned the divine lesson that charity begins at home." They maintained an abundant hospitality ; they celebrated domestic events by balls at the episcopal palace ; they did not disdain (as we gather from the Life of the Hon. and Rev. GeorgeSpencer) the relaxation of a rubber of whist, even on the night before an Ordination, with a candidate for a partner. They dined out, like that well-drawn bishop in *Little Dorrit,* who " was crisp, fresh, cheerful, affable, bland, but so surprisingly innocent"; or like the prelate on whom Thackeray moralized: "My Lord, I was pleased to see good thing after good thing disappear before you; and think that no man ever better became that rounded episcopal apron. How amiable he was! how kind ! He put water into his wine. Let us respect the moderation of the Establishment."

But the agreeableness which I had in my mind when I took upon myself to discourse of agreeable clergymen was not an official but a personal agreeableness. We have been told on high authority that the merriment of parsons is mighty offensive; but the truth of this dictum depends entirely on the topic of the merriment. A clergyman who made light of the religion which he professed to teach, or even joked about the incidents and accompaniments of his sacred calling, would by common consent be intolerable. Decency exacts from priests at least a semblance of piety ; but I entirely deny that there is anything offensive in the "merriment of parsons" when it plays round subjects outside the scope of their professional duties.

Of Sydney Smith Lord Houghton recorded that " he never, except once, knew him to make a jest on any religious subject, and then he immediately withdrew his words, and seemed ashamed that he had uttered them"; and I regard the admirable Sydney as not only the supreme head of all ecclesiastical jesters, but as, on the whole, the greatest humorist whose jokes have come down to us in an authentic and unmutilated form. Almost alone among professional jokers, he made his merriment – rich, natural, fantastic, unbridled as it was – subserve the serious purposes of his life and writing. Each joke was a link in an argument; each sarcasm was a moral lesson.

Peter Plymley's Letters, and those addressed to Archdeacon Singleton, the Essays on *American Taxation* and *Persecuting Bishops,* will probably be read as long as the *Tale of a Tub* or Macaulay's review of Montgomery's Poems; while of detached and isolated jokes – pure freaks of fun clad in literary garb – an incredible number of those which are current in daily converse deduce their birth from this incomparable Canon.

When one is talking of facetious clergymen, it is inevitable to think of Bishop Wilberforce ; but his humor was of an entirely different quality from that of Sydney Smith. To begin with, it is unquotable. It must, I think, have struck every reader of the Bishop's Life, whether in the three huge volumes of the authorized Biography or in the briefer but more characteristic monograph of Dean Burgon, that, though the biographers had themselves tasted and enjoyed to the full the peculiar flavor of his fun, they utterly failed in the attempt to convey it to the reader. Puerile puns, personal banter of a rather homely type, and good stories collected from other people are all that the books disclose. Animal spirits did the rest; and yet, by the concurrent testimony of nearly all who knew him, Bishop Wilberforce was not only one of the most agreeable but one of the most amusing men of his time. We know from one of his own letters that he peculiarly disliked the description which Lord Beaconsfield gave of him in *Lothair,* and, on the principle of *Ce n'est que la verite qui Hesse,* it may be worth while to recall it: " The Bishop was particularly playful on the morrow at breakfast. Though his face beamed with Christian kindness, there was a twinkle in his eye which seemed not entirely superior tomundane self-complacency, even to a sense of earthly merriment. His seraphic raillery elicited sympathetic applause from the ladies, especially from the daughters of the house, who laughed occasionally, even before his angelic jokes were well launched."

Mr. Bright once said, with characteristic downright- ness, "If I was paid what a bishop is paid for doing what a bishop does, I should find abundant cause for merriment in the credulity of *my* countrymen"; and, waiving the theological animus which the saying implies, it is not uncharitable to surmise that a general sense of prosperity, and a strong faculty of enjoying life in all its aspects and phases, had much to do with Bishop Wil- berforce's exuberant and infectious jollity. "A truly emotional spirit," wrote Matthew Arnold, after meeting him in a country house, " he undoubtedly has beneath his outside of society-haunting and men-pleasing, and each of the two lives he leads gives him the more zest for the other."

A scarcely less prominent figure in society than Bishop Wilberf orce, and to many people a much more attractive one, was Dean Stanley. A clergyman to whom the Queen signed herself "Ever yours affectionately" must certainly be regarded as the social head of his profession, and every circumstance of Stanley's nature and antecedents exactly fitted him for the part. lie was in truth a spoiled child of fortune, in a sense more refined and spiritual than the phrase generally conveys. Born of famous ancestry, in a bright and unworldly home ; early filled with the moral and intellectual enthusiasms of Rugby in its best days; steeped in the characteristic culture of Oxford, and advancing, by easy stages of well- deserved promotion, to the most delightful of all offices in the Church of England, his inward nature accorded well with this happy environment. It was in a singulardegree pure, simple, refined, ingenuous. All the grosser and harsher elements of human character seemed to have been omitted from his composition. He was naturally good, naturally graceful, naturally amiable. A sense of humor was, I think, almost the only intellectual gift with which he was not endowed. Lord Beaconsfield spoke of his " picturesque sensibility," and the phrase was happily chosen. He had the keenest sympathy with whatever was graceful in literature; a style full of flexibility and color; a rare faculty of graphic description ; and all-glorified by something of the poet's imagination. His conversation was incessant, teeming with information, and illustrated by familiar acquaintance with all the best that has been thought and said in the world.

Never was a brighter intellect or a more gallant heart housed in a more fragile form. His figure, features, bearing, and accent were the very type of refinement; and as the spare figure, so short yet so full of dignity, marked out by the decanal dress and the red ribbon of the Order of the Bath, threaded its way through the crowded saloons of London society, one felt that the Church, as a civilizing institution, could not be more appropriately represented.

A lady who had been brought up as a Presbyterian, but had conformed to Anglicanism, once said to the present writer : " I dislike the *Episcopal* Church as much as ever, but I love the *Decanal* Church." Her warmest admiration was reserved for that particular Dean, supreme alike in station and in charm, whom I have just now been describing; but there were, at the time of speaking, several other members of the same order who were conspicuous ornaments of the society in which they moved.

There was Dr. Elliot, Dean of Bristol, a yearly visitor to London; handsome, clever, agreeable, highly connected; an administrator, a politician, an admirable talker, and so little trammelled by any ecclesiastical prejudices or habitudes that he might have been the original of Dr. Stanhope in *Barchester Towers.* There was Dr. Liddell, Dean of Christ Church, whose periodical appearances at Court and in society displayed to the admiring gaze of the world the very handsomest and stateliest specimen of the old English gentleman that our time has produced. There was Dr. Church, Dean of St. Paul's, by many competent judges pronounced to be our most accomplished man of letters, yet so modest and so retiring that the world was never suffered to come in contact with him except through his books. And there was Dr. Vaughan, Dean of Llandaff, who concealed under the blandest of manners a remorseless sarcasm and a mordant wit, and who never returned from the comparative publicity of the Athenaeum to the domestic shades of the Temple without leaving behind him some pungent sentence which travelled from month to mouth, and spared neither age nor sex nor friendship nor affinity.

The very highest dignitaries of the Church in London have never, in my experience, contributed very largely to its social life. The garden-parties of Fulham and Lambeth are, indeed, recognized incidents of the London season ; but they present to the critical eye less the aspect of a social gathering than that of a Church Congress combined with a Mothers' Meeting. The overwhelming disparity between the position of host and guests is painfully apparent, and that " drop-down-dead-ative- ness" of manner which Sydney Smith quizzed still characterizes the demeanor of the unbeneficed clergy. Archbishop Tait, whose natural stateliness of aspect and manner was one of the most conspicuous qualifications for his great office, was a dignified and hospitable host; and Archbishop Thomson, reinforced by a beautiful and charming wife, was sometimes spoken of as the Archbishop of Society. Archbishop Benson looked the part to perfection, but did not take much share in general conversation, though I remember one terse saying of his in which the *odium theologicum* supplied the place of wit. A portrait of Cardinal Manning was exhibited at the Royal Academy, and I remarked to the Archbishop on the extraordinary picturesqueness of the Cardinal's appearance. " The dress is very effective," replied the Archbishop, dryly, "but I don't think there is much besides." "Oh, surely it is a fine head?" "No, not a fine head; only *no face."*

Passing down through the ranks of the hierarchy, I shall presently have something to say about two or three metropolitan Canons who are notable figures in society; but before I come to them I must offer a word of affectionate tribute to the memory of Dr. Liddon. Probably there never was a man whose social habit and manner were less like what a mere outsider would have inferred from his physical aspect and public demeanor. Nature had given him the outward semblance of a foreigner and an ascetic ; a lifelong study of ecclesiastical rhetoric had stamped him with a mannerism which belongs peculiarly to the pulpit. But the true inwardness of the man was that of the typical John Bull – hearty, natural, full of humor, utterly free from self-consciousness. He had a healthy appetite, and was not ashamed to gratify it; liked a good glass of wine; was peculiarly fond of sociable company, whether as host or guest; and told an amusing story with incomparable zest and point. His verbal felicity was a marked feature of his conversation. His description of Archbishop Benson (revived, with strange taste, by the *Saturday Review* on the occasion of the Archbishop's death) was a masterpiece of sarcastic character-drawing. The judicious Bishop Davidson and the accomplished Canon Mason were the subjectsof similar pleasantries; and there was substantial truth as well as genuine fun in his letter to a friend written one dark Christmas from Amen Court: " London is just now buried under a dense fog. This is commonly attributed to Dr. Westcott having opened his study-window at Westminster." XVIII

CLERGYMEN'

Of the "Merriment of Parsons" one of the most conspicuous instances was to be found in the Rev. W. H. Brookfield, the "little Frank Whitestock " of Thackeray's *Curate's Walk,* and the subject of Lord Tennyson's characteristic elegy:

" Brooks, for they call'd you so that knew you best-
Old Brooks, who loved so well to mouth my rhymes,
How oft we two have heard St. Mary's chimes !
How oft the Cantab supper, host and guest,
Would echo helpless laughter to your jest!
" You man of humorous-melancholy mark
Dead of some inward agony – is it so?
Our kindlier, trustier Jaques, past away!
I cannot laud this life, it looks so dark:
Ssiac *ijvap* – dream of a shadow, go –
God bless you. I shall join you in a day."

This tribute is as true in substance as it is striking in phrase. I have noticed the same peculiarity about Mr. Brookfield's humor as about Jenny Lind's singing. Those who had once heard it were always eager to talk about it. Ask some elderly man about the early triumphs of the Swedish Nightingale, and notice how he kindles. "Ah ! Jenny Lind ! Yes, there was never anything like that!" And he begins about the *Figlia,* and how she came along the bridge in the *Sonnambula;* and you feel the tenderness in his voice, as of a positive love for her whose voice seems still ringing through him as he talks. I have noticed exactly the same phenomenon when people who knew Mr. Brookfield hear his name mentioned in casual conversation. " Ah ! Brookfield ! Yes ; there never was any one quite like him !" And off they go, with visible pleasure and genuine emotion, to describe the inimitable charm, the touch of genius which brought humorous delight out of the commonest incidents, the tinge of brooding melancholy which threw the flashing fun into such high relief.

Not soon will fade from the memory of any who ever heard it the history of the examination at the ladies' school, where Brookfield, who had thought that he was only expected to examine in languages and literature, found himself required to set a paper in physical science. " What was I to do ? I know nothing about hydrogen or oxygen or any other ' gen.' So I set them a paper in common-sense, or what I called ' Applied Science.' One of my questions was, ' What would you do to cure a cold in the head ?' One young lady answered, 'I should put *my* feet in hot mustard and water till *you* were in a profuse perspiration/ Another said, 'I should put him to bed, give him a soothing drink, and sit by him till he was better.' But, before handing in her paper, she ran her pen through all the ' him's' and ' he's,' and substituted 'her'and 'she.'"

Mr. Brookfield was during the greater part of his life a hard-working servant of the public, and his friends could only obtain his delightful company in the rare and scanty intervals of school-inspecting – a profession of which not even the leisure is leisurely. The type of the French abbe", whose sacerdotal avocations lay completely in the background and who could give the best hours of the days and nights to the pleasures or duties of society, wasbest represented in our day by the Rev. William Harness and the Rev. Henry White. Mr. Harness was a diner- out of the first water; an author and a critic; perhaps the best Shakspearian scholar of his time; and a recognized and even dreaded authority on all matters connected only with the art and literature of the drama. Mr. White, burdened only with the sinecure chaplaincies of the Savoy and the House of Commons, took the Theatre as his parish, mediated with the happiest tact between the Church and the Stage, and pronounced a genial benediction over the famous little suppers in Stratton Street at which an enthusiastic patroness used to entertain Sir Henry Irving when the public labors of the Lyceum were ended for the night.

Canon Malcolm MacColl is an abbe with a difference. No one eats his dinner more sociably or tells a story more aptly ; no one enjoys good society more keenly or is more appreciated in it; but he does not make society a profession. He is conscientiously devoted to the duties of his canonry ; he is an accomplished theologian ; and he is perhaps the most expert and vigorous pamphleteer in England. The Franco-German War, the Athanasian Creed, the Ritualistic prosecutions, the case for Home Rule, and the misdeeds of the Sultan, have in turn produced from his pen pamphlets which have rushed into huge circulations and swollen to the dimensions of solid treatises. Canon MacColl is genuinely and *ex animo* an ecclesiastic ; but he is a politician as well. His inflexible integrity and fine sense of honor have enabled him to play, with credit to himself and advantage to the public, the rather risky part of the Priest in Politics. He has been trusted alike by Lord Salisbury and by Mr. Gladstone ; has conducted negotiations of great pith and moment ; and has been behind the scenes of some historic performances. Yet he has never made an enemy, norbetrayed a secret, nor lowered the honor of his sacred calling.

Miss Mabel Collins, in her vivid story of *The Star Sapphire,* has drawn under a very thin pseudonym a striking portrait of a clergyman who, with his environment, plays a considerable part in the social agreeableness of London at the present moment. Is social agreeableness a hereditary gift ? Nowadays, when everything, good or bad, is referred to heredity, one is inclined to say that it must be ; and though no training could supply the gift where Nature had withheld it, yet a judicious education can. develop a social faculty which ancestry has transmitted. It is recorded, I think, of Madame de Stael, that, after her first conversation with William Wilberforce, she said: " I have always heard that Mr. Wilberforce was the most religious man in England, but I did not know that he was also the wittiest." The agreeableness of the great philanthropist's son – William Wilberforce, Bishop of Oxford and of Winchester – I discussed in my last paper. We may put aside the fulsome dithyrambics of grateful archdeacons and promoted chaplains, and be content to rest the Bishop's reputation for agreeableness on testimony so little interested as that of Matthew Arnold and Archbishop Tait. The Archbishop wrote, after the Bishop's death, of his " social and irresistibly fascinating side, as displayed in his dealings with society"; and in 1864 Mr. Arnold, after listening with only very moderate admiration to one of the Bishop's celebrated sermons, wrote: "Where he was excellent was in his speeches at luncheon afterwards – gay, easy, cordial, and wonderfully happy."

I think that one gathers from all dispassionate observers of the Bishop that what struck them most in him was the blending of boisterous fun and animal spirits with a deep and abiding sense of the seriousnessof religion. In the philanthropist-father the religions seriousness rather preponderated over the fun ; in the Bishop - son (by a curious inversion of parts) the fun sometimes concealed the religiousness. To those who speculate in race and pedigree and transmitted qualities it is interesting to watch the two elements contending in the character of Canon Basil Wilberforce, the Bishop's youngest and best-beloved son. When you see his graceful figure and clean-shaved ecclesiastical face in the pulpit of his strangely old-fashioned church, or catch the vibrating notes of his beautifully modulated voice in

" The hush of the dread high-altar,
Where the Abbey makes us *We,"*

yon feel yourself in the presence of a born ecclesiastic, called from his cradle by an irresistible vocation to a separate and sanctified career.

When you see him on the platform of some great public meeting, pouring forth argument, appeal, sarcasm, anecdote, fun, and pathos in a never-ceasing flood of admirably chosen English, you feel that you are under the spell of a born orator, who

"Now stirs the uproar, now the murmur stills,
While sobs and laughter answer as he wills."

And yet again, when you see the priest of Sunday, the orator of Monday, presiding on Tuesday with easy yet finished courtesy at the hospitable table of the most beautiful dining - room in London, or welcomed with equal warmth for his racy humor and his unfailing sympathy in the homes of his countless friends, you feel that here is a man naturally framed for society, in whom his father and grandfather live again. Truly a combination of hereditary gifts is displayed in Canon Wilberforce; and the social agreeableness of London received a notable addition when Mr. Gladstone transferred him from Southampton to Dean's Yard.

Of agreeable Canons there is no end, and the Chapter of Westminster is peculiarly rich in them. Mr. Gore's ascetic saintliness of life conceals from the general world, but not from the privileged circle of his intimate friends, the high breeding of a great Whig family and the philosophy of Balliol. Archdeacon Furse has the refined scholarship and delicate literary sense which characterized Eton in its days of glory. Dr. Duckworth's handsome presence has long been welcomed in the very highest of all social circles. Mr. Eyton's massive bulk and warm heart, and rugged humor and sturdy common-sense, produce the effect of a clerical Dr. Johnson. But perhaps we must turn our backs on the Abbey and pursue our walk along the Thames Embankment as far as St. Paul's if we want to discover the very finest flower of canonical culture and charm, for it blushes unseen in the shady recesses of Amen Court. Henry Scott Holland, Canon of St. Paul's, is beyond all question one of the most agreeable men of his time. In fun and geniality and warmhearted hospitality he is a worthy successor of Sydney Smith, whose official house he inhabits; and to those elements of agreeableness he adds certain others which his admirable predecessor could scarcely have claimed. He has all the sensitiveness of genius, with its sympathy, its versatility, its unexpected turns, its rapid transitions from grave to gay, its vivid appreciation of all that is beautiful in art and nature, literature and life. His temperament is essentially musical, and indeed it was from him that I borrowed, in a former paragraph, my description of Jenny Lind and her effect on her hearers. No man in London, I should think, has so many and such devoted friends in every class and stratum; andthose friends acknowledge in him not only the most vivacious and exhilarating of social companions, but one of the moral forces which have done most to quicken their consciences and lift their lives.

Before I have done with the agreeableness of clergymen I must say a word about two academical personages, of whom it was not always easy to remember that they were clergymen, and whose agreeableness struck one in different lights, according as one happened to be the victim or the witness of their jocosity. If any one wishes to know what the late Master of Balliol was really like in his social aspect, I should refer him, not to the two volumes of the conscientious Biography which we have just been reading, nor even to the amusing chit-chat of Mr. Lionel Tolle- mache's I'ecollections, but to the cleverest work of a very clever Balliol man – Mr. W. H. Mallock's *New Republic.* The description of Mr. Jowett's appearance, conversation, and social bearing is photographic, and the sermon which Mr. Mallock puts into his mouth is not a parody, but an absolutely faultless reproduction both of substance and of style. That it excessively irritated the subject of the sketch is the best proof of its accuracy. For my own part, I must freely admit that I do not write as an admirer of Mr. Jowett; but one saying of his, which I had the advantage of hearing, does much to atone, in my judgment, for the snappish impertinences on which his reputation for wit has been generally based. The scene was the Master's own dining-room, and the moment that the ladies had left the room one of the guests began a most outrageous conversation. Every one sat flabbergasted. The Master winced with annoyance; and then, bending down the table towards the offender, said in his shrillest tone : "Shall we continue this conversation in the drawing- room ?" and rose from his chair. It was really a stroke of genius thus both to terminate and to rebuke the impropriety without violating the decorum due from host to guest.

Of the late Master of Trinity – Dr. Thompson – it was said: " He casteth forth his ice like morsels. Who is able to abide his frost ?" The stories of his mordant wit are endless, but an Oxford man can scarcely hope to narrate them with proper accuracy. He was nothing if not critical. At Seeley's Inaugural Lecture as Professor of History his only remark was : " Well, well. I did not think we could so soon have had occasion to regret poor Kings- ley." To a gushing admirer who said that a certain popular preacher had so much taste : " Oh, yes; so very much, and all so very bad." Of a certain Dr. Woods, who wrote elementary mathematical books for schoolboys, and whose statue occupies the most conspicuous position in the ante-chapel of St. John's College: " The Johnian Newton." His hit at the present Chief Secretary for Ireland, when he was a junior Fellow of Trinity, is classical: " We are none of us infallible – not even the youngest of us." But it requires an eye-witness of the scene to do justice to the exordium of the Master's sermon on the Parable of the Talents, addressed in Trinity Chapel to what considers itself, and not without justice, the cleverest congregation in the world : " It would be obviously superfluous in a congregation such as that which I now address to expatiate on the responsibilities of those who have five, or even two, talents. I shall, therefore, confine my observations to the more ordinary case of those of us who have *one talent."* XIX

BEPARTEE

Loed Beacon'sfield, describing Monsignore Berwick in *Lothair,* says that he " could always, when necessary, sparkle with anecdote or blaze with repartee." The former performance is considerably easier than the latter. Indeed, when a man has a varied experience, a retentive memory, and a sufficient copiousness of speech, the facility of story-telling may attain the character of a disease. The "sparkle" evaporates, but the "anecdote" is left; and we feel inclined to agree with another Beaconsfield- ian creation – Mr. Pinto – who remarked that "when a man fell into his anecdotage it was a sign for him to retire from the world." But though anecdotes may become tedious, a repartee is always delightful; and, while by no means inclined to admit the general inferiority of contemporary conversation to that of the last generation, I am disposed to think that in the art of repartee our predecessors excelled us.

If this is true, it may be partly due to the greater freedom of an age when well-bred men and refined women spoke their minds with an uncompromising plainness which would now be voted intolerable. I have said that the old Royal Dukes were distinguished by the racy vigor of their conversation ; and the Duke of Cumberland, afterwards King Ernest of Hanover, was held to excel all his brothers in this respect. I was told by the late Sir Charles Wyke that he was once walking with the Dukeof Cumberland along Piccadilly when the Duke of Gloucester (first cousin to Cumberland, and familiarly known as "Silly Billy") came out of Gloucester House. " Duke of Gloucester, Duke of Gloucester, stop a minute. I want to speak to you," roared the Duke of Cumberland. Poor Silly Billy, whom nobody ever noticed, was delighted to find himself thus accosted, and ambled up smiling. " Who's your tailor ?" shouted Cumberland. " Stultz," replied Gloucester. "Thank you. I only wanted to know, because, whoever he is, he ought to be avoided like the pestilence." Exit Silly Billy.

Of this inoffensive but not brilliant prince (who, by the way, was Chancellor of the University of Cambridge) it is related that once at a levee he noticed a naval friend with a much-tanned face. " How do, admiral ? Glad to see you again. It's a long time since you have been at a levee." "Yes, sir. Since I last saw your Royal Highness I have been nearly to the North Pole." " By God, you look more as if you had been to the South Pole." It is but bare justice to his depreciated memory to observe that the Duke of Gloiicester scored a point against his kingly cousin when, on hearing that William IV. had consented to the Reform Bill, he ejaculated, " Who's Silly Billy now ?" But this is a digression.

Early in this century a famous lady, whose name, for obvious reasons, I forbear to indicate even by an initial, had inherited great wealth under a will which, to put it mildly, occasioned much surprise. She shared an opera- box with a certain Lady D , who loved the flowing

wine-cup not wisely but too well. One night Lady D

was visibly intoxicated at the opera, and her friend told her that the partnership in the box must cease, as she could not appear again in company so disgraceful. "As

you please," said Lady D . " I may have had a glass
of wine too much; but at any rate I never forged myfather's signature, and then murdered the butler to prevent his telling."

Beau Brummell, the Prince of Dandies and the most insolent of men, was once asked by a lady if he would " take a cup of tea." " Thank you, ma'arn," he replied, " I never *take* anything but physic." " I beg your pardon," replied the hostess, "you also take liberties."

The Duchess of Somerset, born Sheridan, and famous as the Queen of Beauty at the Eglinton Tournament of 1839, was pre-eminent in this agreeable art of swift response. One day she called at a shop to inquire for some article which she had purchased the day before, and which had not been sent home. The order could not be traced. The proprietor of the establishment inquired, with great concern : " May I ask who took your Grace's order ? Was it a young gentleman with fair hair ?" "No ; it was an elderly nobleman with a bald head."

Lady W R , an Englishwoman who had spent
her life in diplomatic society abroad and in old age held a "salon" in London, was talking during the Franco- German War of 1870 to the French Ambassador, who complained bitterly that England had not intervened on behalf of France. "But, after all," he said, "it was only what we might have expected. We always believed that you were a nation of shopkeepers, and now we know you
are." "And we," replied Lady W R , "always
believed that you were a nation of soldiers, and now we know you are not" – a repartee worthy to rank with Queen Mary's reply to Lady Lochleven about the sacramental character of marriage, in the third volume of *The Abbot.*

A young lady, who had just been appointed a Maid of Honor, was telling some friends with whom she was dining that one of the conditions of the office was that she should not keep a diary of what went on at Court. Acynical man of the world who was present said : " What a tiresome rule ! I think I should keep my diary all the same." " Then," replied the young lady. " I am afraid you would not be a Maid of *Honor."*

In the famous society of old Holland House a conspicuous and interesting figure was Henry Luttrell. It was known that he must be getting on in life, for he had sat in the Irish Parliament, but his precise age no one knew. At length Lady Holland, whose curiosity was restrained by no considerations of courtesy, asked him point-blank : " Now, Luttrell, we're all dying to know how old you are. Just tell me." Eyeing his questioner gravely, Luttrell made answer: " It is an odd question ; but as you, Lady Holland, ask it, I don't mind telling you. If I lire till next year, I shall be – devilish old."

For the mutual amenities of Melbourne and Alvanley and Rogers and Allen, for Lord Holland's genial humor, and for Lady Holland's indiscriminate insolence, we can refer to Lord Macanlay's Life and Charles Greville's Journals, and the enormous mass of contemporary memoirs. Most of these verbal encounters were fought, with all imaginable good humor, over some social or literary topic; but now and then, when political passion was really roused, they took a fiercely personal tone.

Let one instance of elaborate invective suffice. Sir James Mackintosh, who, as the writer of the *Vindiciae Gal- licae,* had been the foremost apologist for the French Revolution, fell later under the influence of Burke, and proclaimed the most unmeasured hostility to the Revolution and its authors, their works and ways. Having thus become a vehement champion of law and order, he exclaimed one day that O'Coighley, the priest who negotiated between the Revolutionary parties in Ireland and France, was the basest of mankind. "No, Mackintosh," replied that sound though pedantic old Whig, Dr. Parr ; " hemight have been much worse. He was an Irishman; he might have been a Scotsman. He was a priest; he might have been a lawyer. He was a rebel; he might have been a renegade."

These severe forms of elaborate sarcasm belong, I think, to a past age. Lord Beaconsfield was the last man who indulged in them. When the Greville Memoirs – that mine of social information in which I have so often quarried – came out, some one asked Mr. Disraeli, as he then was, if he had read them. He replied : " *No, I* do not feel attracted to them. I knew the author, and he was the most conceited person with whom I have ever been brought in contact, although I have read Cicero and known Bulwer Lytton." This three-edged compliment has seldom been excelled. In a lighter style, and more accordant with feminine grace, was Lady Morley's comment on the decaying charms of her famous rival, Lady Jersey – the Zenobia of *Endymion* – of whom some gushing admirer had said that she looked so splendid going to Court in her mourning array of black and diamonds – "it was like night." "Yes, my dear, but*minuitpasse."* A masculine analogue to this amiable compliment may be cited from the table-talk of Lord Granville – certainly not an unkindly man – to whom the late Mr. Delane had been complaining of the difficulty of finding a suitable wedding-present for a young lady of the house of Roths- child. " It would be absurd to give a Rothschild a costly gift. I should like to find something not intrinsically valuable, but interesting because it is rare." "Nothing easier, my dear fellow ; send her a lock of your hair."

When the *New Review* was started, its accomplished editor designed it to be an inexpensive copy of the *Nineteenth Century.* It was to cost only sixpence, and was to be written by bearers of famous names – those of the British aristocracy for choice. He was complaining in society of the difficulty of finding a suitable title, when a vivacious lady said: " We have got *Cornhill,* and *Ludgate,* and *Strand* – why not call yours *Cheap-side ?"*

Oxford has always been a nursing-mother of polished satirists. Of a small sprig of aristocracy, who was an undergraduate in my time, it was said by a friend that he was like Euclid's definition of a point: he had no parts and no magnitude, but had position. In previous papers I have quoted the late Master of Balliol and Lord Sherbrooke. Professor Thorold Rogers excelled in a Shandean vein. Lord Bowen is immortalized by his emendation to the Judges' address to the Queen, which had contained the Heep-like sentence : " Conscious as we are of our own unworthiness for the great office to which we have been called." " Wouldn't it be better to say, 'Conscious as we are of one another's unworthiness'?" Henry Smith, Professor of Geometry, the wittiest, most learned, and most genial of Irishmen, said of a well-known man of science : "His only fault is that he sometimes mistakes the Editor of Nature for the Author of Nature." A great lawyer who is now a great judge, and has, with good reason, the very highest opinion of himself, stood as a Liberal at the General Election of 1880. His Tory opponents set on foot a rumor that he was an Atheist, and when Henry Smith heard it he said : "Now that's really too bad, for is a man who reluctantly acknowledges the existence of *a Superior Seine/."*

At dinner at Balliol the Master's guests were discussing the careers of two Balliol men, one of whom had just been made a judge and the other a bishop. "Oh," said Henry Smith, "I think the bishop is the greater man. A judge, at the most, can only say ' You be hanged,' but a bishop can say 'You be damned.'" "Yes," characteristically twittered the Master; "but if the judge says 'You be hanged,' you *are* hanged."

Henry Smith, though a delightful companion, was a very unsatisfactory politician – nominally, indeed, a Liberal, but full of qualifications and exceptions. When Mr. Gathorne Hardy was raised to the peerage at the crisis of the Eastern Question in 1878, and thereby vacated his seat for the University of Oxford, Henry Smith came forward as a candidate in the Liberal interest; but his language about the great controversy of the moment was so lukewarm that Professor Freeman said that, instead of sitting for Oxford in the House of Commons, he ought to represent Laodicea in the Parliament of Asia Minor.

Of Dr. Haig-Brown it is reported that, being at a public dinner at Godalming, he was toasted by the Mayor as a man who knew how to combine the *fortlter in re* with the *suavlter in modo.* In replying to the toast he said : "I am really overwhelmed, not only by the quality, but by the *quantity* of the Mayor's eulogium."

It has been a matter of frequent remark that, considering what an immense proportion of parliamentary time has been engrossed during the last seventeen years by Irish speeches, we have heard so little Irish humor, whether conscious or unconscious – whether jokes or "bulls." An admirably vigorous simile was used by the late Mr. O'Sullivan, when he complained that the whiskey supplied at the bar was like "a torch-light procession marching down your throat"; but of Irish bulls in Parliament I have only heard one – proceeding, if my memory serves me, from Mr. T. Healy: " As long as the voice of Irish suffering is dumb, the ear of English compassion is deaf to it." One I read in the columns of the 7mA *Times: "* The key of the Irish difficulty is not to be found in the *empty* pocket of the landlord." The best I ever heard was not an Irish but a Welsh bull. It was uttered by one of the members for the Principalityin the debate on the Welsh Church Bill, in indignant protest against the allegation that the majority of Welshmen now belonged to the Established Church. He said, "It is a lie, sir; and it is high time that we nailed this lie to the mast."

Among tellers of Irish stories, Lord Morris is supreme; one of his best depicts two Irish officials of the good old times discussing, in all the confidence of their after-dinner claret, the principles on which they bestowed their patronage. Said the first, " Well, I don't mind admitting that, *cceterisparibus,* I prefer my own relations." "My dear boy," replied his boon companion, " *cceteris paribus* be damned." The cleverest thing that I have lately heard was from a young lady, who is an Irishwoman, and I hope that its excellence will excuse the personality. It must be premised that Lord Erne is a gentleman who abounds in anecdote, and that Lady Erne is an extremely handsome woman. Their irreverent compatriot has nicknamed them

"The storied Erne and animated bust."

Frances Countess Waldegrave, who had previously been married three times, took as her fourth husband an Irishman, Mr. Chichester Fortescue, who was shortly afterwards made Chief Secretary. The first night that Lady Waldegrave and Mr. Fortescue appeared at the theatre in Dublin, an irreverent wag in the gallery called out, " Which of the four do yon like best, my lady ?" Instantaneous from the Chief Secretary's box came the adroit reply: " Why, the Irishman, of course !"

The late Lord Coleridge was once speaking in the House of Commons in support of Women's Rights. One of his main arguments was that there was no essential difference between the masculine and the feminine intellect. For example, he said, some of the most valuablequalities of what is called the judicial genius – sensibility, quickness, delicacy – are peculiarly feminine. In reply, Sergeant Dowse said: " The argument of the hon. and learned Member, compendiously stated, amounts to this: because some judges are old women, therefore all old women are fit to be judges."

To my friend Mr. Julian Sturgis, himself one of the happiest of phrase-makers, I am indebted for the following gems from America:

Mr. Evarts, formerly Secretary of State, showed an English friend the place where Washington was said to have thrown a dollar across the Potomac. The English friend expressed surprise; "but," said Mr. Evarts, "you must remember that a dollar went farther in those days." A Senator met Mr. Evarts next day, and said that he had been amused by his jest. "But," said Mr. Evarts, "I met a mere journalist just afterwards who said, 'Oh, Mr. Evarts, you should have said that it was a small matter to throw a dollar across the Potomac for a man who had chucked a Sovereign across the Atlantic.3" Mr. Evarts, weary of making many jokes, would invent a journalist or other man and tell a story as his. It was he who, on a kindly busybody expressing surprise at his daring to drink so many different wines at dinner, said that it was only the indifferent wines of which he was afraid.

It was Mr. Motley who said in Boston: " Give me the luxuries of life, and I care not who has the necessaries."

Mr. Tom Appleton, famous for many witty sayings (among them the well-known " Good Americans, when they die, go to Paris "), heard some grave city fathers debating what could be done to mitigate the cruel east wind at an exposed corner of a certain street in Boston. He suggested that they should tether a shorn lamb there.

A witty Bostonian going to dine with a neighbor was met by her with a face of apology. *"1* could not get another man," she said ; " and we are four women, and you will have to take us all into dinner." " Fore-warned is four-armed," said he with a bow.

This gentleman was in a hotel in Boston when the law forbidding the sale of liquor was in force. "What would you say," said an angry Bostonian, " if a man from St. Louis, where they have freedom, were to come in and ask you where he could get a drink ?" Now it was known that spirits could be clandestinely bought in a room under the roof, and the wit, pointing upwards, replied, "I should say, 'Fils de St. Louis, montez au ciel.'"

Madame Apponyi was in London during the debates on the Reform Bill of 1867, and, like all foreigners and not a few Englishmen, was much perplexed by the "Compound Householder," who figured so largely in the discussion. Hayward explained that he was the Masculine of the Femme Incomprise.

One of the best repartees ever made, because the briefest and the justest, was made by "the gorgeous Lady Blessington" to Napoleon III. When Prince Louis Napoleon was living in impecunious exile in London he had been a constant guest at Lady Blessingtou's hospitable and brilliant but Bohemian house. And she, when visiting Paris after the *coup d'etat,* naturally expected to receive at the Tuileries some return for the unbounded hospitalities of Gore House. Weeks passed, no invitation arrived, and the Imperial Court took no notice of Lady Blessington's presence. At length she encountered the Emperor at a great reception. As he passed through the bowing and curtseying crowd, the Emperor caught sight of his former hostess. "Ah, Miladi Blessington ! Restez-vous longtemps a Paris ?" " Et vous, Sire ?" History does not record the usurper's reply.

Henry Philpotts, Bishop of Exeter from 1830 to 1869, lived at a beautiful villa near Torquay, and an enthusiastic lady who visited him there burst into dithyrambics, and cried, " What a lovely spot this is, Bishop ! It is so Swiss." " Yes, ma'am," blandly replied old Harry of Exeter, " it is very Swiss ; only there is no sea in Switzerland, and there are no mountains here." One day one of his clergy desiring to renew a lease of some episcopal property, the Bishop named a preposterous sum as the fine on renewal. The poor parson, consenting with reluctance, said, " Well, I suppose it is better than endangering the lease, but certainly your lordship has got the lion's share." "But, my dear sir, I am sure you would not wish me to have that of the other creature."

Still, after all, for a bishop to score off a clergyman is an inglorious victory ; it is like the triumph of a magistrate over a prisoner or of a don over an undergraduate. Bishop Wilberforce, whose powers of repartee were among his most conspicuous gifts, was always ready to use them where retaliation was possible – not in the safe enclosure of the episcopal study, but on the open battlefield of the platform and the House of Lords. At the great meeting in St. James's Hall in the summer of 1868 to protest against the Disestablishment of the Irish Church some Orange enthusiast, in the hope of disturbing the Bishop, kept interrupting his honeyed eloquence with inopportune shouts of " Speak up, my lord !" " I am already speaking up," replied the Bishop, in his most dulcet tone; " I always speak up ; and I decline to speak down to the level of the ill-mannered person in the gallery." Every one whose memory runs back thirty years will recall the Homeric encounters between the Bishop and Lord Chancellor Westbury in the House of Lords, and will remember the melancholy circumstances under which Lord Westbury had to resign his office."When he was leaving the Royal Closet after surrendering the Great Seal into the Queen's hands, Lord Westbury met the Bishop, who was going in to the Queen. It was a painful encounter, and in reminding the Bishop of the occurrence when next they met, Westbury said, " I felt inclined to say, ' Hast thou found me, 0 mine enemy *?'"* The Bishop in relating this used to say: "I never in my life was so tempted as to finish the quotation, and say, ' Yea, I have found thee, because thou hast sold thyself to work iniquity.' But by a great effort I kept it down, and said, 'Does your lordship remember the end of the quotation ?'" The Bishop, who enjoyed a laugh against himself, used to say that he had once been effectually scored off by a young clergyman whom he had rebuked for his addiction to fox-hunting. The Bishop urged that it had a worldly appearance. The curate replied that it was not a bit more worldly than a ball at Blenheim Palace at which the Bishop had been present. The Bishop explained that he was staying in the house, but was never within three rooms of the dancing. " Oh, if it comes to that," replied the curate, " I never am within three fields of the hounds."

One of the best replies – it is scarcely a repartee – traditionally reported at Oxford was made by the great Saint of the Tractarian Movement, the Rev. Charles Marriott. A brother-Fellow of Oriel had behaved rather outrageously at dinner over night, and, coming out of chapel next morning, essayed to apologize to Marriott: " My friend, I'm afraid I made rather a fool of myself last night." " My dear fellow, I assure you I observed nothing unusual."

In a former paper about the Art of Conversation I referred to the singular readiness which characterized Lord Sherbrooke's talk. A good instance of it was his reply to the strenuous advocate of modern studies, who, presnming on Sherbrooke's sympathy, said, "I have the greatest contempt for Aristotle." "But not that contempt which familiarity breeds, I should imagine," was Sherbrooke's mild rejoinder. " I have got a box at the Lyceum to-night," I once heard a lady say, "and a place to spare. Lord Sherbrooke, will you come ? If you are engaged, I must take the Bishop of Gibraltar." " Oh, that's no good. Gibraltar can never be taken."

In 1872, when University College, Oxford, celebrated the thousandth anniversary of its foundation, Lord Sherbrooke, as an old University College man, made the speech of the evening. His theme was a complaint of the iconoclastic tendency of the New Historians. Nothing was safe from their sacrilegious research. Every tradition, however venerable, however precious, was resolved into a myth or a fable. " For example," he said, " we have always believed that certain lands which this college owns in Berkshire were given to us by King Alfred. Now the Now Historians come and tell us that this could not have been the case, because they can prove that the lands in question never belonged to the King. It seems to me that the New Historians prove too much – indeed, they prove the very point which they contest. If the lands had belonged to the King, he would probably have kept them to himself; but as they belonged to some one else, he made a handsome present of them to the College."

Lord Beaconsfield's excellence in conversation lay rather in studied epigrams than in impromptu repartees. But in his old electioneering contests he used sometimes to make very happy hits. When he came forward, a young, penniless, unknown coxcomb, to contest High Wycombe against the dominating Whiggery of the Greys and the Carringtons, some one in the crowd shouted, "We know all about Colonel Grey; but pray what doyou stand on ?" "I stand on my head," was the prompt reply, to which Mr. Gladstone always renders unstinted admiration. At Aylesbury the Rcidical leader had been a man of notoriously profligate life, and when Mr. Disraeli came to seek re-election as Tory Chancellor of the Exchequer this tribune of the people produced at the hustings the Radical manifesto which Mr. Disraeli had issued twenty years before. " What do you say to that, sir ?" " I say that we all sow our wild oats, and no one knows the meaning of that phrase better than you, Mr. ."

A friend of mine in the diplomatic service, visiting Rome in the old days of the Temporal Power, had the honor of an interview with Pio Nono. The Pope graciously offered him a cigar – "I am told you will find this very fine." The Englishman made that stupidest of all answers, " Thank your Holiness, but I have no vices." " This isn't a vice ; if it was, you would have it." Another repartee from the Vatican reached me a few years ago, when the German Emperor paid his visit to Leo XIII. Count Herbert Bismarck was in attendance on his Imperial master, and when they reached the door of the Pope's audience - chamber the Emperor passed in, and the Count tried to follow. A gentleman of the Papal Court motioned him to stand back, as there must be no third person at the interview between the Pope and the Emperor. "I am Count Herbert Bismarck," shouted the German, as he struggled to follow his master. "That," replied the Roman, with calm dignity, "may account for, but it does not excuse, your conduct."

But, after all these " fashnable fax and polite anny- goats," as Thackeray would have called them, after all these engaging courtesies of kings and prelates and great ladies, I think that the honors in the way of repartee rest with the little Harrow boy who was shouting himself hoarse in the jubilation of victory after an Eton andHarrow match at Lord's, in which Harrow had it hollow. To him an Eton boy, of corresponding years, severely observed: " Well, you Harrow fellows needn't be so beastly cocky. When you wanted a Head Master you had to come to Eton to get one." The small Harrovian was dumbfounded for a moment, and then, pulling himself together for a final effort of deadly sarcasm, exclaimed : " Well, at any rate, no one can say that we ever produced a Mr. Gladstone." XX

TITLES

The List of Honors, usually published on Her Majesty's Birthday, is this year reserved till the Jubilee Day, and to sanguine aspirants I would say, in Mrs. Gamp's immortal words, "Seek not to proticipate." Such a list always contains food for the reflective mind, and some of the thoughts which it suggests may even lie too deep for tears. Why is my namesake picked out for knighthood, while I remain hidden in my native obscurity ? Why is my rival made a C. B., while I "go forth Companionless" to meet the chances and the vexations of another year ? But there is balm in Gilead. If I have fared badly, my friends have done little better. Like Mr. Squeers, when Bolder's father was two-pound- ten short, they have had their disappointments to contend against. A, who was so confident of a peerage, is fobbed off with a baronetcy; and B, whose labors for the Primrose League entitled him to expect the Bath, finds himself grouped with the Queen's footmen in the Royal Victorian Order. As when Sir Robert Peel declined to forma Government in 1839 " twenty gentlemen who had not been appointed Under Secretaries of State moaned over the martyrdom of young ambition," so during the first fortnight of 1897 at least that number of middle-aged self-seekers came to the regretful conelusion that Lord Salisbury was not sufficiently a man of the world for his present position, and inwardly asked why a judge or a surgeon should be preferred before a company-promoter or a party hack. And while feeling is thus fermenting at the base of the social edifice, things are not really tranquil at the summit.

1897.

It is not long since the chief of the princely House of Duff was raised to the first order of the peerage, and one or two opulent earls, encouraged by his example, are understood to be looking upward. Every constitutional Briton, whatever his political creed, has in his heart of hearts a wholesome reverence for a dukedom. Lord Beaconsfield, who understood these little traits of our national character even more perfectly than Thackeray, says of his favorite St. Aldegonde (who was heir to the richest dukedom in the kingdom) that " he held extreme opinions, especially on political affairs, being a Republican of the reddest dye. He was opposed to all privilege, and indeed to all orders of men except dukes, who were a necessity." That is a delicious touch. St. Aldegonde, whatever his political aberrations, voiced the universal sentiment of his less fortunate fellow- citizens ; nor can the most soaring ambition of the British Matron desire a nobler epitaph than that of the lady immortalized by Thomas Ingoldsby :

"She drank prussic acid without any water,
And died like a Duke-and-a-Duchess's daughter."

As, according to Dr. Johnson, all claret would be port if it could, so, presumably, every marquis would like to be a duke; and yet, as a matter of fact, that Elysian translation is seldom made. A marquis, properly regarded, is not so much a nascent duke as an amplified earl. A shrewd observer of the world once said to me : " When an earl gets a marqnisate, it is worth a hundredthousand pounds in hard money to his family." The explanation of this cryptic utterance is that, whereas an earl's younger sons are "misters," a marquis's younger sons are "lords." Each "my lord" can make a "my lady," and therefore commands a distinctly higher price in the marriage market of a wholesomely minded community. Miss Higgs, with her fifty thousand pounds, might scorn the notion of becoming the Honorable Mrs. Percy Popjoy ; but as Lady Magnus Charters she would feel a laudable ambition gratified.

An earldom is, in its combination of euphony, antiquity, and association, perhaps the most impressive of all the titles in the peerage. Most rightly did the fourteenth Earl of Derby decline to be degraded into a brand- new duke. An earldom has always been the right of a Prime Minister who wishes to leave the Commons. In 1880 a member of the House of Russell (in which there are certain Whiggish traditions of jobbery) was fighting a hotly contested election, and his ardent supporters brought out a sarcastic placard – " Benjamin Earl of Beaconsfield! He made himself an earl and the people poor " ; to which a rejoinder was instantly forthcoming – " John Earl Russell! He made himself an earl and his relations rich." The amount of truth in the two statements was about equal. In 1885 this order of the peerage missed the greatest distinction which fate is likely ever to offer it, when Mr. Gladstone declined the earldom proffered by her Majesty on his retirement from office. Had he accepted it, it was understood that the representatives of the last Earl of Liverpool would have waived their claims to the extinct title, and the greatest of the Queen's Prime Ministers would have borne the name of the city which gave him birth.

But, magnificent and euphonious as an earldom is, the children of an earl are the half-castes of the peerage. The eldest son is " my lord," and his sisters are " my lady"; and ever since the days of Mr. Foker, Senior, it has been *de rigueur* for an opulent brewer to marry an earl's daughter; but the younger sons are not distinguishable from the ignominious progeny of viscounts and barons. Two little boys, respectively the eldest and the second son of an earl, were playing on the front staircase of their home, when the eldest fell over into the hall below. The younger called to the footman who picked his brother up, " Is he hurt ?" " Killed, *my lord,"* was the instantaneous reply of a servant who knew the devolution of a courtesy title.

As the marquesses people the debatable land between the dukes and the earls, so do the viscounts between the earls and the barons. A child whom Matthew Arnold was examining in grammar once wrote of certain words which he found it hard to classify under their proper parts of speech that they were " thrown into the common sink, which is adverbs." I hope I shall not be considered guilty of any disrespect if I say that ex-Speakers, ex-Secretaries of State, successful generals, and ambitious barons who are not quite good enough for earldoms, are " thrown into the common sink, which is viscounts." Not only heralds and genealogists, but every one who has the historic sense, must have felt an emotion of regret when the splendid title of twenty-third Baron Dacre was merged by Mr. Speaker Brand in the pinchbeck dignity of first Viscount Hampden.

After viscounts, barons. The baronage of England is headed by the bishops; but we have so recently discoursed of those right reverend peers that, Dante-like, we will not reason of them, but pass on – only remarking, as we pass, that it is held on good authority that no human being ever experiences a rapture so intense as an American bishop from a Western State when he firsthears himself called " My lord" at a London dinnerparty. After the spiritual barons come the secular barons – the " common or garden " peers of the United Kingdom. Of these there are considerably more than three hundred; and of all, except some thirty or forty at the most, it may be said without offence that they are products of the opulent middle - class. Pitt destroyed deliberately and forever the exclusive character of the British peerage when, as Lord Beaconsfield said, he " created a plebeian aristocracy and blended it with the patrician oligarchy." And in order to gain admission to this "plebeian aristocracy," men otherwise reasonable and honest will spend incredible sums, undergo prodigious exertions, associate themselves with the basest intrigues, and perform the most unblushing tergiversations. Lord Hough- ton told me that he said to a well-known politician who boasted that he had refused a peerage: " Then you made a great mistake. A peerage would have secured you three things that you are much in need of – social consideration, longer credit with your tradesmen, and better marriages for your younger children."

It is unlucky that comparatively recent legislation has put it out of the power of a Prime Minister to create fresh Irish peers, for an Irish peerage was a cheap and convenient method of rewarding political service. Lord Palmerston held that, combining social rank with eligibility to the House of Commons, it was the most desirable distinction for a politician. Pitt, when his banker, Mr. Smith (who lived in Whitehall), desired the right of driving through the Horse Guards, said : " No, I can't give you that; but I will make you an Irish peer" ; and the banker became the first Lord Carrington.

What is a baronet ? ask some. Sir Wilfrid Lawson (who ought to know) replies that he is a man " who has ceased to be a gentleman and has not become a nobleman." But this is too severe a judgment. It breathes a spirit of contempt bred of familiarity, which may, without irreverence, be assumed by a member of an exalted Order, but which a humble outsider would do well to avoid. As Major Pendenuis said of a similar manifestation, " It sits prettily enough on a young patrician in early life, though nothing is so loathsome among persons of our rank." I turn, therefore, for an answer to Sir Bernard Burke, who says: " The hereditary Order of Baronets was created by patent in England by King James I. in 1611. At the institution many of the chief estated gentlemen of the kingdom were selected for the dignity. The first batch of baronets comprised some of the principal landed proprietors among the best-descended gentlemen of the kingdom, and the list was headed by a name illustrious more than any other for the intellectual pre-eminence with which it is associated – the name of Bacon. *The Order of Baronets is scarcely estimated at its proper value."*

I cannot help feeling that this account of the baronetage, though admirable in tone and spirit, and actually pathetic in its closing touch of regretful melancholy, is a little wanting in what the French would call "actuality." It leaves out of sight the most endearing, because the most human, trait of the baronetage – its pecuniary origin. On this point let us hear the historian David Hume: " The title of Baronet was sold, and two hundred patents of that species of knighthood were disposed of for so many thousand pounds." This was truly epoch-making. It was one of those " actions of the just" which "smell sweet and blossom in the dust." King James's baronets were the models and precursors of all who to the end of time should traffic in the purchase of honors. Their example has justified posterity, and the precedent which they set is to-day the principal method by which the war - chests of our political parties are replenished.

Another authority, handling the same high theme, tells us that the rebellion in Ulster gave rise to this Order, and " it was required of each baronet on his creation to pay into the Exchequer as much as would maintain thirty soldiers three years at eight-pence a day in the province of Ulster/' and as a historical memorial of their original service the baronets bear as an augmentation to their coats of arms the royal badge of Ulster – a Bloody Hand on a white field. It was in apt reference to this that a famous Whip, on learning that a baronet of his party was extremely anxious to be promoted to the peerage, said, "You can tell Sir Peter Proudflesh, with my compliments, that if he wants a peerage he will have to put his Bloody Hand into his pocket. *We* don't do these things for nothing."

For the female mind the baronetage has a peculiar fascination. As there was once a female Freemason, so there was once a female baronet – Dame Maria Bolles, of Osberton, in the County of Nottingham. The rank of a baronet's wife is not unfrequently conferred on the widow of a man to whom a baronetcy had been promised and who died too soon to receive it. " Call me a vulgar woman!" screamed a lady once prominent in society when some "damned good-natured friend" repeated a critical comment. " Call me a vulgar woman ! me, who was Miss Blank, of Blank Hall, and if I had been a boy should have been a baronet I"

The baronets of fiction are like their congeners in real life – a numerous and a motley band. Lord Beaconsfield described, with a brilliancy of touch which was all his own, the labors and the sacrifices of Sir Vavasour Fire- brace on behalf of the Order of Baronets and the privileges wrongfully withheld from them. " They are evidently the body destined to save this country ; blending all sympathies – the Crown, of which they are the peculiar champions ; the nobles, of whom they are the popular branch ; the people, who recognize in them their natural leaders. . . . Had the poor King lived, we should at least have had the Badge," added Sir Vavasour, mournfully.

"The Badge?"

" It would have satisfied Sir Grosvenor le Draughte ; he was for compromise. But, confound him, his father was only an accoucheur."

A great merit of the baronets, from the novelist's point of view, is that they and their belongings are so uncommonly easy to draw. With the baronet and his family all is plain sailing. He is Sir Grosvenor, his wife is Lady le Draughte, his sons, elder and younger, are Mr. le Draughte, and his daughters Miss le Draughte. The wayfaring man, though a fool, cannot err where the rule is so simple, and accordingly the baronets enjoy a deserved popularity with those novelists who look up to the titled classes of society as men look at the stars, but are a little puzzled about their proper designations. Miss Braddon alone has drawn more baronets, virtuous and vicious, handsome and hideous, than would have colonized Ulster ten times over and left a residue for Nova Scotia. Sir Pitt Crawley and Sir Barnes Newcome will live as long as English novels are read, and I hope that dull forgetfulness will never seize as its prey Sir Alnred Mogyns Smyth de Mogyns, who was born Alfred Smith Muggins, but traced a descent from Hogyn Mogyn of the Hundred Beeves, and took for his motto " Ung Roy ung Mogyns." His pedigree is drawn by the hand of a master in the seventh chapter of the *Book of Snobs,* and is imitated with great fidelity on more than one page oi Burke's Peerage.

An eye closely intent upon the lesser beauties of the natural world will find a very engaging specimen of the genus Baronet in Sir Barnet Skettles, who was so kind to Paul Dombey and so angry with poor Mr. Baps. Sir Leicester Dedlock is on a larger scale – in fact, almost too "fine and large" for life. But I recall a fleeting vision of perfect loveliness among Miss Monflathers's pupils – "a baronet's daughter who by some extraordinary reversal of the laws of nature was not only plain in feature but dull in intellect."

So far we have spoken only of hereditary honors; but our review would be singularly incomplete if it excluded those which are purely personal. Of these, of course, incomparably the highest is the Order of the Garter, and its most characteristic glory is that, in Lord Melbourne's phrase, "there is no damned nonsense of merit about it." The Emperor of Lilliput rewarded his courtiers with three fine silken threads, one of which was blue, one green, and one red. The Emperor held a stick horizontally, and the candidates crept under it, backwards and forwards, several times. Whoever showed the most agility in creeping was rewarded with the blue thread.

Let us hope that the methods of chivalry have undergone some modification since the days of Queen Anne, and that the Blue Ribbon of the Garter, which ranks with the Golden Fleece and makes its wearer a comrade of all the crowned heads of Europe, is attained by acts more dignified than those which awoke the picturesque satire of Dean Swift. But I do not feel sure about it.

Great is the charm of a personal decoration. Byron wrote:

"Ye stars, that are the poetry of heaven."

"A stupid line," says Mr. St. Barbe, in *Endymion; "* lie should have written, 'Ye stars, which are the poetryof dress.'" North of the Tweed the green thread of Swift's imagination – " the most ancient and most noble Order of the Thistle" – is scarcely less coveted than the supreme honor of the Garter; but wild horses should not tear from me the name of the Scottish peer of whom

his political leader said, ' If I gave the Thistle, ho

would eat it."

The Bath tries to make up by the lurid splendor of its ribbon and the brilliancy of its star for its comparatively humble and homely associations. It is the peculiar prize of Generals and Home Secretaries, and is displayed with manly openness on the bosom of the statesman once characteristically described by Lord Beaconsfield as " Mr. Secretary Cross, whom I can never remember to call Sir Richard." But, after all said and done, the institution of knighthood is older than any particular order of knights; and lovers of the old world must observe with regret the discredit into which it has fallen since it became the guerdon of the successful grocer.

When Lord Beaconsfield left office in 1880 he conferred a knighthood – the first of a long series similarly bestowed – on an eminent journalist. The friends of the new knight were inclined to banter him, and proposed his health at dinner in facetious terms. Lord Beacons- field, who was of the company, looked preternaturally grave, and filling his glass, gazed steadily at the flattered editor and said in his deepest tone : " Yes, Sir A. B., I drink to your good health, and I congratulate you. on having attained a rank which was deemed sufficient honor for Sir Philip Sidney and Sir Walter Raleigh, Sir Isaac Newton and Sir Christopher Wren."

But a truce to this idle jesting on exalted themes – too palpably the utterance of social envy and mortified ambition. " They *are* our superiors, and that's the fact/' as the modest author of the *Book of Snobs* exclaims inhis chapter on the Whigs. " I am not a Whig myself ; but, oh, how I should like to be one 1" In a similar spirit of compunctious self-abasement, the present writer may exclaim, "I have not myself been, included in the list of Birthday Honors – but, oh, how I should like to be there *I"* XXI

The Queen's Accession

The writer of these papers would not willingly fall behind his countrymen in the loyal sentiments and picturesque memories proper to the " high midsummer pomps "which begin to-morrow. But there is an almost insuperable difficulty in finding anything to write which shall be at once new and true; and this paper must therefore consist largely of extracts. As the sun of June brings out wasps, so the genial influence of the Jubilee has produced an incredible abundance of fibs, myths, and fables. They have for their subject the early days of our Gracious Sovereign, and round that central theme they play with every variety of picturesque inventiveness. Nor has invention alone been at work. Research has been equally busy. Miss Wynn's description, admirable in its simplicity, of the manner in which the girl-queen received the news of her accession was given to the world by Abraham Hayward in *Diaries of a Lady of Quality* a generation ago. Within the last month it must have done duty a hundred times.

Scarcely less familiar is the more elaborate but still impressive passage from *Sybil,* in which Lord Beacons- field described the same event. And yet, as far as my observation has gone, the citations from this fine description have always stopped short just at the opening of the

Sunday, June 20, 1897. most appropriate passage ; my readers, at any rate, shall see it and judge it for themselves. If there is one feature in the national life of the last sixty years on which Englishmen may justly pride themselves it is the amelioration of the social condition of the workers. Putting aside all ecclesiastical revivals, all purely political changes, and all appeals, however successful, to the horrible arbitrament of the sword, it is Social Reform which has made the Queen's reign memorable and glorious. The first incident of that reign was described in *Sybil* not only with vivid observation of the present, but with something of prophetic insight into the future.

"In a sweet and thrilling voice, and with a composed mien which indicates rather the absorbing sense of august duty than an absence of emotion, The Queen" announces her accession to the throne of her ancestors, and her humble hope that Divine Providence will guard over the fulfilment of her lofty trust. The prelates and captains and chief men of her realm then advance to the throne, and, kneeling before her, pledge their troth and take the sacred oaths of allegiance and supremacy – allegiance to one who rules over the land that the great Macedonian could not conquer, and over a continent of which Columbus never dreamed : to the Queen of every sea, and of nations in every zone.

" It is not of these that I would speak, but of a nation nearer her footstool, and which at this moment looks to her with anxiety, with affection, perhaps with hope. Fair and serene, she has the blood and beauty of the Saxon. Will it be her proud destiny at length to bear relief to suffering millions, and, with that soft hand which might inspire troubadours and guerdon knights, break the last links in the chain of Saxon thraldom ?"

To-day, with pride and thankfulness, chastened though it be by our sense of national shortcomings, we can auswer *Yes* to this wistful question of genius and humanity. We have seen the regulation of dangerous labor, the protection of women and children from excessive toil, the removal of the tax on bread, the establishment of a system of national education; and, in Macaulay's phrase, a point which yesterday was invisible is our goal to-day, and will be our starting-post to-morrow.

Her Majesty ascended the throne on June 20, 1837, and on the 29th the *Times* published a delightfully characteristic article against the Liberal Ministers, " into whose hands the all but infant and helpless Queen has been compelled by her unhappy condition to deliver up herself and her indignant people." Bating one word, this might be an extract from an article on the formation of Mr. Gladstone's Home Rule Government. Surely the consistency of the *Times* in evil-speaking is one of the most precious of our national possessions. On June 30 the Royal Assent was given by commission to forty Bills – the first Bills which became law in the Queen's reign ; and, the clerks in the House of Lords having been accustomed ever since the days of Queen Anne to say "His Majesty" and "Le Roy le veult," there was hopeless bungling over the feminine appellations, now after 130 years revived. However, the Bills scrambled through somehow, and among them was the Act which abolished the pillory – an auspicious commencement of a humane and reforming reign. On July 8 came the rather belated burial of William IV. at Windsor, and on the llth the newly completed Buckingham Palace was occupied for the first time, the Queen and the Duchess of Kent moving thither from Kensington.

On July 17 Parliament was prorogued by the Queen in person. Her Majesty's first speech from the Throne referred to friendly relations with Foreign Powers, the diminution of capital punishment, and " discreet improvements in ecclesiastical institutions." It was read in a clear and musical voice, with a fascinating grace of accent and elocution which never faded from the memory of those who heard it. As long as Her Majesty continued to open and prorogue Parliament in person the same perfection of delivery was always noticed. An old M. P., by no means inclined to be a courtier, told me that when Her Majesty approached the part of her speech relating to the estimates, her way of uttering the words "Gentlemen of the House of Commons " was the most winning address he had ever heard : it gave to an official demand the character of a personal request. After the Prince Consort's death in 1861 the Queen did not again appear at Westminster till the opening of the new Parliament in 1866. On that occasion the speech was read by the Lord Chancellor, and the same usage has prevailed whenever Her Majesty has opened Parliament since that time. But on several occasions of late years she has read her reply to addresses presented by public bodies, and I well recollect that at the opening of the Imperial Institute in 1893, though the *timbre* of her voice was deeper than in early years, the same admirable elocution made every syllable audible.

In June, 1837, the most lively emotion in the masses of the people was the joy of a great escape. I have said before that grave men, not the least given to exaggeration, told me their profound conviction that had Princess Victoria died in youth, and her uncle, Ernest Duke of Cumberland, succeeded to the throne on the death of William IV., no earthly power could have averted a revolution. Into the causes of that intense unpopularity this is not the occasion to enter ; but let me just describe a curious print of the year 1837 which lies before me as I write. It is headed " The Contrast," and is divided into See frontispiece.

two panels. On your left hand is a young girl, simply dressed in mourning, with a pearl necklace and a gauzy shawl, and her hair coiled in plaits, something after the fashion of a crown. Under this portrait is " *Victoria.* " On the other side of the picture is a hideous old man, with shaggy eyebrows and scowling gaze, wrapped in a military cloak with fur collar and black stock. Under this portrait is *"Ernest,"* and running the whole length of the picture is the legend :

"Look here upon *this* picture – and on *this* –

The counterfeit presentment of two Sovereigns."

This print was given to me by a veteran Ref ormer, who told me that it expressed in visible form the universal sentiment of England. That sentiment was daily and hourly confirmed by all that was heard and seen of the girl-queen. We read of her walking with a gallant suite upon the terrace at Windsor, dressed in scarlet uniform and mounted on her roan charger, to receive with uplifted hand the salute of her troops ; or seated on the throne of the Plantagenets at the opening of her Parliament, and invoking the divine benediction on the labors which should conduce to " the welfare and contentment of My people." We see her yielding her bright intelligence to the constitutional guidance, wise though worldly, of her first Prime Minister, the sagacious Melbourne. And then, when the exigencies of parliamentary government forced her to exchange her Whig advisers for the Tories, we see her carrying out with exact propriety the constitutional lessons taught by " the friend of her youth," and extending to each premier in turn, whether personally agreeable to her or not, the same absolute confidence and loyalty.

As regards domestic life, we have been told by Mr. Gladstone that "even among happy marriages her marriage was exceptional, so nearly did the union of thought, heart, and action both fulfil the ideal and bring duality near to the borders of identity."

And so twenty years went on, full of an evergrowing popularity, and a purifying influence on the tone of society never fully realized till the personal presence was withdrawn. And then came the blow which crushed her life – "the sun going down at noon" – and total disappearance from all festivity and parade and social splendor, but never from political duty. In later years we have seen the gradual resumption of more public offices; the occasional reappearances, so earnestly anticipated by her subjects, and hedged with something of a divinity more than regal; the incomparable majesty of personal bearing which has taught so many an onlooker that dignity has nothing to do with height, or beauty, or splendor of raiment; and, mingled with that majesty and unspeakably enhancing it, the human sympathy with suffering and sorrow, which has made Queen Victoria, as none of her predecessors ever was or could be, the Mother of her People.

And the response of the English people to that sympathy – the recognition of that motherhood – is written, not only in the printed records of the reign, but on the "fleshly tables" of English hearts. Let one homely citation suffice as an illustration. It is taken from a letter of condolence addressed to the Queen on the death of Prince "Eddie," Duke of Clarence, in 1892:

" *To our beloved Queen, Victoria.*

"Dear Lady, – "We, the surviving widows and mothers of some of the men and boys who lost their lives by the explosion which occurred in the Oaks Colliery, near Barnsley, in December, 1866, desire to tell your Majesty how stunned we all feel by the cruel and unexpectedblow which has taken Prince Eddie from his dear Grandmother, his loving parents, his beloved intended, and an admiring nation. The sad news affected us deeply, we , ill believing that his youthful strength would carry him through the danger. Dear Lady, we feel more than we can express. To tell you that we sincerely condole with your Majesty and the Prince of Wales in your and their sad bereavement and great distress is not to tell you all we feel; but the widow of Albert the Good and the parents of Prince Eddie will understand what we feel when we say that we feel all that widows and mothers feel who have lost those who were dear as life to them. Dear Lady, we remember with gratitude all that you did for us Oaks widows in the time of our great trouble, and we cannot forget you in yours. We have not forgotten that it was you, dear Queen, who set the example, so promptly followed by all feeling people, of forming a fund for the relief of our distress – a fund which kept us out of the workhouse at the time and has kept us out ever since. . . . We wish it were in our power, dear Lady, to dry up your tears and comfort you, but that we cannot do. But what we can do, and will do, is to pray God, in His mercy and goodness, to comfort and strengthen you in this your time of great trouble. – Wishing your Majesty, the Prince and Princess of Wales, and the Princess May all the strength, consolation, and comfort which God alone can give, and which He never fails to give to all who seek Him in truth and sincerity, we remain, beloved Queen, your loving and grateful though sorrowing subjects,

" The Oaks Widows.

"(Signed on behalf of the widows by Sarah BradLey, one of them.)

" Poor Eddie! to die so young, and so much happiness in prospect. Oh ! 'tis hard."

The historic associations, half gay, half sad, of the week on which we are just entering tempt me to linger on this fascinating theme, and I cannot illustrate it better than by quoting the concluding paragraphs from a sermon, which now has something of the dignity of fulfilled prophecy, and which was preached by Sydney Smith in St. Paul's Cathedral on the Sunday after the Queen's accession.

The sermon is throughout a noble composition, grandly conceived and admirably expressed. It begins with some grave reflections on the " folly and nothingness of all things human " as exemplified by the death of a king. It goes on to enforce on the young Queen the paramount duties of educating her people, avoiding war, and cultivating personal religion. It concludes with the following passage, which in its letter, or at least in its spirit, might well find a place in some of to-morrow's sermons: "The Patriot Queen, whom I am painting, reverences the National Church, frequents its worship, and regulates her faith by its precepts; but she withstands the encroachments and keeps down the ambition natural to Establishments, and by rendering the privileges of the Church compatible with the civil freedom of all sects, confers strength upon and adds duration to that wise and magnificent institution. And then this youthful Monarch, profoundly but wisely religions, disdaining hypocrisy, and far above the childish follies of false piety, casts herself upon God, and seeks from the Gospel of His Blessed Son a path for her steps and a comfort for her soul. Here is a picture which warms every English heart, and would bring all this congregation upon their bended knees to pray it may be realized. What limits to the glory and happiness of the native land if the Creator should in His mercy have placed in the heart of this royal woman the rudiments of wisdomand mercy ? And if, giving them time to expand, and to bless our children's children with her goodness, He should grant to her a long sojourning upon earth, and leave her to reign over us till she is well stricken in years, what glory! what happiness! what joy! what bounty of God ! I of course can only expect to see the beginning of such a splendid period; but when I do see it I shall exclaim: ' Lord, now lettest Thou Thy servant depart in peace, for mine eyes have seen Thy salvation.'"

As respects the avoidance of war, the event has hardly accorded with the aspiration. It is melancholy to recall the idealist enthusiasms which preceded the Exhibition of 1851, and to contrast them with the realities of the present hour. Then the arts of industry and the competitions of peace were to supplant for ever the science of bloodshed. Nations were to beat their swords into ploughshares and their spears into pruuing-hooks, and men were not to learn war any more. And this was on the eve of the Crimea – the most ruinous, the most cruel, and the least justifiable of all campaigns. In one corner of the world or another, the war-drum has throbbed almost without intermission from that day to this.

But when we turn to other aspirations the retrospect is more cheerful. Slavery has been entirely abolished, and, with all due respect to Mr. George Curzon, is not going to be re-established under the British flag. The punishment of death, rendered infinitely more impressive, and therefore more deterrent, by its withdrawal from the public gaze, is reserved for offences which even Romilly would not have condoned. The diminution of crime is an acknowledged fact. Better laws and improved institutions – judicial, political, social, sanitary – we flatter ourselves that we may claim. National Education dates from 1870, and its operation during a quarter of a century has changed the face of the industrial world. Queen Victoria in her later years reigns over an educated people.

Of the most important theme of all – our national advance in religion, morality, and the principles of humane living – I have spoken in previous papers, and this is not the occasion for anything but the briefest recapitulation. " Where is boasting ? It is excluded." There is much to be thankful for, much to encourage, something to cause anxiety, and nothing to justify bombast. No one believes more profoundly than I do in the providential mission of the English race, and the very intensity of my faith in that mission makes me even painfully anxious that we should interpret it aright. Men who were undergraduates at Oxford in the seventies learned the interpretation, in words of unsurpassable beauty, from John Buskin:

"There is a destiny now possible to us – the highest ever set before a nation, to be accepted or refused. We are still nndegenerate in race; a race mingled of the best northern blood. We are not yet dissolute in temper, but still have the firmness to govern and the grace to obey. We have been taught a religion of pure mercy, which we must either now finally betray or learn to defend by fulfilling. And we are rich in an inheritance of honor, bequeathed to us through a thousand years of noble history, which it should be our daily thirst to increase with splendid avarice, so that Englishmen, if it be as in to covet honor, should be the most offending souls alive.

"Within the last few years we have had the laws of natural science opened to us with a rapidity which has been blinded by its brightness, and means of transit and communication given to us which have made but one kingdom of the habitable globe. One kingdom – butwho is to be its King ? Is there to be no King in it, think you, and every man to do that which is right in his own eyes ? Or only kings of terror, and the obscene Empires of Mammon and Belial ? Or will yon, youths of England, make your country again a royal throne of Kings, a sceptred isle, for all the world a source of light, a centre of peace; mistress of learning and of the arts; faithful guardian of great memories in the midst of irreverent and ephemeral visions; faithful servant of time- tried principles, under temptation from fond experiments and licentious desires; and, amid the cruel and clamorous jealousies of the nations, worshipped in her strange valor of good-will towards men ?

" *Vexilla Regis prodeunt.* Yes, but of which King ? There are the two oriflammes ; which shall we plant on the furthest islands – the one that floats in heavenly fire, or that which hangs heavy with foul tissue of terrestrial gold ?" XXII

"PRINCEDOMS, VIRTUES, POWEBS "

The celebrations of the past week have set us all upon a royal tack. Diary-keepers have turned back to their earliest volumes for stories of the girl-queen ; there has been an unprecedented run on the *Annual Register* for 1837; and every rusty old print of Princess Victoria in the costume of Kate Mckleby has been paraded as a pearl of price.

As I always pride myself on following what Mr. Matthew Arnold used to call "the great mundane movement/' I have been careful to obey the impulse of the hour. I have cudgelled my memory for Collections and Recollections suitable to this season of retrospective enthusiasm. Last week I endeavored to touch some of the more serious aspects of the Jubilee, but now that the great day has come and gone – "Bedtime, Hal, and all well" – a lighter handling of the majestic theme may not be esteemed unpardonable.

Those of my fellow-chroniclers who have blacked themselves all over for the part have acted on the principle that no human life can be properly understood without an exhaustive knowledge of its grandfathers and grandmothers. They have resuscitated George III. and called Queen Charlotte from her long home. With a less heroic insistence on the historic method, I leave grandparents out of sight, and begin my gossip with the Queen'suncles. Of George IV. it is less necessary that I should speak, for has not his character been faithfully drawn in Thackeray's *Lectures on the Four Georges ?*

June 20-7, 1897.

" The dandy of sixty, who bows with a grace,
And has taste in wigs, collars, cuirasses, and lace,
Who to tricksters aud fools leaves the State and its treasure.
And, while Britain's in tears, sails about at his pleasure,"

was styled, as we all know, " the First Gentleman in Europe." I forget if I have previously narrated the following instance of gentlemanlike conduct. If I have, it will bear repetition. The late Lord Charles Russell (1807-1894), when a youth of eighteen, had just received a commission in the Blues, and was commanded, with the rest of his regiment, to a full-dress ball at Carlton House, where the King then held his Court. Unluckily for his peace of mind, the young subaltern dressed at his father's house, and, not being used to the splendid paraphernalia of the Blues' full dress, he omitted to put on his aiguillette. Arrived at Carlton House, the company, before they could enter the ball-room, had to advance in single file along a corridor in which the old King, bewigged and bestarred, was seated on a sofa. When the hapless youth who lacked the aignillette approached the presence, he heard a very high voice exclaim, " Who is this damned fellow ?" Retreat was impossible, and there was nothing for it but to shuffle on and try to pass the King without further rebuke. Not a bit of it. As he neared the sofa the King exclaimed, " Good-evening, sir. I suppose you are the regimental doctor ?" and the imperfectly accoutred youth, covered with confusion as with a cloak, fled blushing into the ball-room, and hid himself from further observation. And yet the narrator of this painful story always declared that George IV. could be very gracious when the fancy took him ; thathe was uniformly kind to children ; and that on public occasions his manner was the perfection of kingly courtesy. His gorgeous habits and profuse expenditure made him strangely popular. The people, though they detested his conduct, thought him " every inch a King." Lord Shaftesbury, noting in his diary for May 19, 1849, the attempt of Hamilton upon the Queen's life, writes: " The profligate George IV. passed through a life of selfishness and sin without a single proved attempt to take it. This mild and virtuous young woman has four times already been exposed to imminent peril."

The careers of the King's younger brothers and sisters would fill a volume of "queer stories." Of the Duke of York, Mr. Gold win Smith genially remarks, that '-'the only meritorious action of his life was that he once risked it in a duel." The Duke of Clarence – Burns's "Royal young tarry-breeks" – lived in disreputable seclusion till he ascended the throne, and then was so excited by his elevation that people thought he was going mad. The Duke of Cumberland was the object of a popular detestation, of which the grounds can be discovered in the *Annual Register* for 1810. The Duke of Sussex made two marriages in defiance of the Royal Marriage Act, and took a political part as active on the Liberal side as that of the Duke of Cumberland among the Tories. The Duke of Cambridge is chiefly remembered by his grotesque habit (recorded, by the way, in *Happy Thoughts)* of making loud responses of his own invention to the service in church. "Let us pray," said the clergyman. " By all means," said the Duke. The clergyman begins the prayer for rain. The Duke exclaims : " No good as long as the wind is in the east."

Clergyman: " ' Zacchseus stood forth and said, Behold, Lord, the half of my goods I give to the poor.'"

Duke : "Too much, too much ; don't mind tithes, butcan't stand that." To two of the Commandments, which I decline to discriminate, the Duke's responses were: " Quite right, quite right, but very difficult sometimes "; and " No, no ! It was my brother Ernest did that."

Those who care to pursue these curious byways of not very ancient history are referred to the unfailing Gre- ville; to Lady Anne Hamilton's *Secret History of the Court of England;* and to the *Recollections of a Lady of Quality,* commonly ascribed to the late Lady Charlotte Bury. The closer our acquaintance with the manners and habits of the last age, even in what are called " the highest circles," the more wonderful will appear the social transformation which dates from Her Majesty's accession. Thackeray spoke the words of truth and soberness when, after describing the virtues and the limitations of George III., he said : "I think we acknowledge in the inheritrix of his sceptre a wiser rule and a life as honorable and pure; and I am sure that the future painter of our manners will pay a willing allegiance to that good life, and be loyal to the memory of that unsullied virtue."

For the earlier years of the Queen's reign Greville continues to be a fairly safe guide, though his footing at the palace was by no means so intimate as it had been in the roystering days of George IV. and William IV. Of course, Her Majesty's own volumes and Sir Theodore Martin's *Life of the Prince Consort* are of primary authority. Interesting glimpses are to be caught in the first volume of Bishop Wilberforce's Life, ere yet his tergiversation in the matter of Bishop Hampden had forfeited the Royal favor; and the historian of the future will probably make great use of the Letters of Sarah Lady Lyttelton – Governess to the Queen's children – which, being printed for private circulation, are unluckily withheld from the present generation.

A rather pleasing instance of the ultra-German etiquette fomented by Prince Albert was told me by an eyewitness of the scene. The Prime Minister and his wife were dining at Buckingham Palace very shortly after they had received an addition to their family. When the ladies retired to the drawing-room after dinner, the Queen said most kindly to the Premier's wife., " I know

you are not very strong yet, Lady ; so I beg you will
sit down. And, when the Prince comes in, Lady D
shall stand in front of you." This device of screening a breach of etiquette by hiding it behind the portly figure of a British Matron always struck me as extremely droll.

Courtly etiquette, with the conditions out of which it springs and its effect upon the character of those who are subjected to it, has, of course, been a favorite theme of satirists time out of mind, and there can scarcely be a more fruitful one. There are no heights to which it does not rise, nor depths to which it does not sink. In the service for the Queen's Accession the Christological Psalms are boldly transferred to the Sovereign by the calm substitution of "her" for "Him." A few years back – I do not know if it is so now – I noticed that in the prayer-books in St. George's Chapel at Windsor all the pronouns which referred to the Holy Trinity were spelled with small letters, and those which referred to the Queen with capitals. So much for the heights of etiquette, and for its depths we will go to Thackeray's account of an incident stated to have occurred on the birth of the Duke of Connaught:

" Lord John he next alights,
And who comes here in haste ?
The Hero of a Hundred Fights,
The caudle for to taste.
" Then Mrs. Lily the nuss,
Towards them steps with joy ;
Says the brave old Duke, ' Come tell to us,
Is it a gal or boy ?'
" Saya Mrs. L. to the Duke,
'Your Grace, it is a *Prince.*'
And at that nurse's bold rebuke
He did both laugh and wince."

Such was the etiquette of the Royal nursery in 1850; but little Princes, even though ushered into the world under such very impressive circumstances, grow up into something not very unlike other little boys when once they go to school. Of course, in former days young Princes were educated at home by private tutors. This was the education of the Queen's uncles and of her sons. A very different experience has been permitted to her grandsons. The Prince of Wales's boys, as we all remember, were middies; Princess Christian's sons were at Wellington; Prince Arthur of Connaught is at Eton. There he is to be joined next year by the little Duke of Albany, who is now at a private school in the New Forest. He has among his school-fellows his cousin Prince Alexander of Battenberg, of whom a delightful story is current just now. Like many other little boys, he ran short of pocket-money, and wrote an ingenious letter to his august Grandmother asking for some slight pecuniary assistance. He received in return a just rebuke, telling him that little boys should keep within their limits, and that he must wait till his allowance next became due. Shortly afterwards the undefeated little Prince resumed the correspondence in something like the following form: "My dear Grandmamma, – I am sure you will be glad to know that I need not trouble yon for any money just now, for I sold your last letter to another boy here for 30s."

As Royalty emerges from infancy and boyhood intothe vulgar and artificial atmosphere of the grown -np world, it is daily and hourly exposed to such sycophancy that Royal persons acquire, quite unconsciously, a habit of regarding every subject in heaven and earth in its relation to themselves. An amusing instance of this occurred a few years ago on an occasion when one of our most popular Princesses expressed a gracious wish to present a very smart young gentleman to the Queen. This young man had a remarkably good opinion of himself ; was the eldest son of a peer, and a Member of Parliament ; and it happened that he was also related to a lady who belonged to one of the Royal Households. So the Princess led the young exquisite to the august presence, and then sweetly said, "I present Mr. , who

is" – not Lord A.'s eldest son or Member for Loamshire, but – " nephew to dear Aunt Cambridge's lady." My young friend told me that he had never till that moment realized how completely he lacked a position of his own in the universe of created being.

SECTION 12

XXIII

LORD BEACONSFIELD

Archbishop Tait wrote on February 11, 1877 : " Attended this week the opening of Parliament, the Queen being present, and wearing for the first time, some one says, her crown as Empress of India. Lord Beaconsfield was on her left side, holding aloft the Sword of State. At five the House again was crammed to see him take his seat; and Slingsby Bethell, equal to the occasion, read aloud the writ in very distinct tones. All seemed to be founded on the model, ' What shall be done to the man whom the king delighteth to honor ?' "

Je ne suis pas la rose, mais j'ai vecu pr&s d'elle. For the last month onr thoughts have been fixed upon the Queen to the exclusion of all else. But now the regal splendors of the Jubilee have faded. The majestic theme is, in fact, exhausted; and we turn, by a natural transition, from the Royal Rose to its subservient primrose; from the wisest of Sovereigns to the wiliest of Premiers ; from the character, habits, and life of the Queen to the personality of that extraordinary child of Israel who, though he was not the Rose, lived uncommonly near it; and who, more than any other Minister before or since his day, contrived to identify himself in the public view with the Crown itself. There is nothing invidious in this use of a racial term. It was one of Lord Beaconsfield's finest qualities that he labored all through his life to make his race glorious and admired. To a Jewish boy – a friend of my own – who was presented to him in his old age he said: " You and I belong to a race which can do everything but fail."

June, 1897.

Is Lord Beaconsfield's biography ever to be given to the world ? Not in our time, at any rate, if we may judge by the signs. Perhaps Lord Rowton finds it more convenient to live on the vague but splendid anticipations of future success than on the admitted and definite failure of a too cautious book. Perhaps he finds his personal dignity enhanced by those mysterious Sittings to Windsor and Osborne, where he is understood to be comparing manuscripts and revising proofs with an Illustrious Personage. But there is the less occasion to lament Lord Rowton's tardiness, because we already possess Mr. Froude's admirable monograph on Lord Beacons- field in the series of *The Queen's Prime Ministers,* and an extremely clear-sighted account of his relations with the Crown in Mr. Reginald Brett's *Yoke of Empire.*

My present purpose is not controversial. I do not intend to estimate the soundness of Lord Beaconsfield's opinions or the permanent value of his political work. It is enough to recall what the late German Ambassador – Count Miinstcr – related to me after the Congress of Berlin, and what, in a curtailed form, has been so often quoted. Prince Bismarck said: "I think nothing of their Lord Salisbury. He is only a lath painted to look like iron. But that old Jew means business." This is merely a parenthesis. I am at present concerned only with Lord Beaconsfield's personal traits. When I first encountered him he was already an old man. He had left far behind those wonderful days of the black velvet dress-coat lined with white satin, the "gorgeous gold flowers on a splendidly embroidered waistcoat," the jewelled rings worn outside the white gloves, the evening cane of ivory inlaid with gold and adorned with a tassel of black silk. " We were none of us fools," said one of his most brilliant contemporaries, " and each man talked his best; but we all agreed that the cleverest fellow in the party was the young Jew in the green velvet trousers." Considerably in the background, too, were the grotesque performances of his middle life, when, makiiig up for the character of a country gentleman, he "rode an Arabian mare for thirty miles across country without stopping," attended Quarter Sessions in drab breeches and gaiters, and wandered about the lanes round Hugh- enden pecking up primroses with a spud.

When I first saw Mr. Disraeli, as he then was, all these follies were matters of ancient history. They had played their part and were discarded. He was dressed much like other gentlemen of the Sixties – in a black frock coat, gray or drab trousers, a waistcoat cut rather low, and a black cravat which went once round the neck and was tied in a loose bow. In the country his costume was a little more adventurous. A black velveteen jacket, a colored waistcoat, a Tyrolese hat, lent picturesque incident and variety to his appearance. But the brilliant colors were reserved for public occasions. I never saw him look better than in his peer's robes of scarlet and ermine when he took his seat in the House of Lords, or more amazing than when, tightly buttoned up in the Privy Councillor's uniform of blue and gold, he stood in the "general circle" at the Drawing-room or Levee. In his second Administration he looked extraordinarily old. His form was shrunk, and his face of a death-like pallor. Ever since an illness in early manhood he had always dyed his hair, and the contrast between the artificial blackness and the natural paleness was extremely startling. The one sign of vitality which his appearance presented was the brilliancy of his dark eyes, which still flashed with penetrating lustre.

The immense powers of conversation of which we read so much in his early days, when he " talked like a racehorse approaching the winning-post," and held the whole company spellbound by his tropical eloquence, had utterly vanished. He seemed, as he was, habitually oppressed by illness or discomfort. He sat for hours together in moody silence. When he opened his lips it was to pay an elaborate (and sometimes misplaced) compliment to a lady, or to utter an epigrammatic judgment on men or books, which recalled the conversational triumphs of his prime. Skill in phrasemaking was perhaps the literary gift which he most admired. In a conversation with Mr. Matthew Arnold shortly before his death he said, with a touch of pathos: " You are a fortunate man. The young men read you ; they no longer read me. And you have invented phrases which every one quotes – such as ' Philistinism' and ' Sweetness and light.'" It was a characteristic compliment, for he dearly loved a good phrase. From the necessities of his position as a fighting politician, his own best performances in that line were sarcasms; and indeed sarcasm was the gift in which, from first to last, in public and in private, in writing and in speaking, he peculiarly excelled. To recall the instances would be to rewrite his political novels and to transcribe those attacks on Sir Robert Peel which made his fame and fortune.

It was my good fortune when quite a boy to be present at the debates in the House of Commons on the Tory Reform Bill of 1867. Never were Mr. Disraeli's gifts of sarcasm, satire, and ridicule so freely displayed, and never did they find so responsive a subject as Mr. Gladstone. As school-boys say, " he rose freely." The Bill was read a second time without a division, but in Committee the fun waxed fast and furious, and was marked by the liveliest encounters between the Leader of the House and the Leader of the Opposition. At the conclusion of one of these passages of arms Mr. Disraeli gravely congratulated himself on having such a substantial piece of furniture as the table of the House between himself and his energetic opponent. In May, 1867, Lord Houghton writes thus: "I met Gladstone at breakfast. He seems quite awed with the diabolical cleverness of Dizzy, who, he says, is gradually driving all ideas of political honor out of the House, and accustoming it to the most revolting cynicism." Was it cynicism, or some related but more agreeable quality, which suggested Mr. Disraeli's reply to the wealthy manufacturer, newly arrived in the House of Commons, who complimented him on his novels ? "I can't say I've read them myself. Novels are not in my line. But my daughters tell me they are uncommonly good." " Ah," said the Leader of the House, in his deepest note, " this, indeed, is fame." The mention of novels reminds me of a story which I heard twenty years ago, when Mr. Mallock produced his first book – the admirable *Neio Republic.* A lady who was his constant friend and benefactress begged Lord Beacons- field to read the book and say something civil about it. The Prime Minister replied with a groan: "Ask me anything, dear lady, except this. I am an old man. Do not make me read your young friends' romances." "Oh, but he would be a great accession to the Tory party, and a civil word from you would secure him forever." " Oh – well, then, give me a pen and a sheet of paper," and, sitting down in the lady's drawing - room, he wrote :

" Dear Mrs. , – I am sorry that I cannot dine with

yon, but I am going down to Hughenden for a week. Would that my solitude could be peopled by the bright creations of Mr. Mallock's fancy." " Will that do foryour young friend ?" Surely, as an appreciation of a book which one has not read, this is absolutely perfect.

When Lord Beaconsfield was driven from office by the General Election of 1880, one of his supporters in the House of Commons begged a great favor – " May I bring my boy to see you, and will you give him some word of counsel which he may treasure all his life as the utterance of the greatest Englishman who ever lived ?" Lord Beaconsfield groaned, but consented. On the appointed day the proud father presented himself with his young hopeful in Lord Beaconsfield's presence. " My dear young friend," said the statesman, "your good papa has asked me to give you a word of counsel which may serve you all your life. Never ask who wrote the Letters of Junius, or on which side of Whitehall Charles I. was beheaded ; for if you do you will be considered a bore – and that is something too dreadful for you at your tender age to understand." For these last two stories I by no means vouch. They belong to the flotsam and jetsam of ephemeral gossip. But the following, which I regard as eminently characteristic, I had from Lord Randolph Churchill.

Towards the end of Lord Beaconsfield's second Premiership a younger politician asked the Premier to dinner. It was a domestic event of the first importance, and no pains were spared to make the entertainment a success. When the ladies retired, the host came and sat where the hostess had been, next to his distinguished guest. "Will you have some more claret, Lord Beacons- field ?" " No, thank you, my dear fellow. It is admirable wine – true Falernian – but I have already exceeded my prescribed quantity, and the gout holds me in its horrid clutch." When the party had broken up, the host and hostess were talking it over. "I think the chief enjoyed himself," said the host, "and I know heliked his claret." "Claret!" exclaimed the hostess; " why, he drank brandy-and-water all dinner-time."

I said in an earlier paragraph that Lord Beaconsfield's flattery was sometimes misplaced. An instance recurs to my recollection. He was staying in a country house where the whole party was Conservative with the exception of one rather plain, elderly lady, who belonged to a great Whig family. The Tory leader was holding forth on politics to an admiring circle when the Whig lady came into the room. Pausing in his conversation, Lord Beaconsfield exclaimed, in his most histrionic manner, "But, hush ! We must not continue these Tory heresies until those pretty little ears have been covered up with those pretty little hands" – a strange remark under any circumstances, and stranger still if, as his friends believed, it was honestly intended as an acceptable compliment.

Mr. Brett, who shows a curious sympathy with the personal character of Lord Beaconsfield, acquits him of the charge of flattery, and quotes his own description of his method : " I never contradict; I never deny ; but I sometimes forget," On the other hand, it has always been asserted by those who had the best opportunities of personal observation that Lord Beaconsfield succeeded in converting the dislike with which he had once been regarded in the highest quarters into admiration and even affection, by his elaborate and studied acquiescence in every claim, social or political, of Royalty, and by his unflagging perseverance in the art of flattery. He was a courtier, not by birth or breeding, but by genius. What could bo more skilful than the inclusion of *Leaves from the Journal of our Life in the Highlands* with *Coningsby* and *Sybil* in the phrase " We authors" ? – than his grave declaration, "Your Majesty is the head of the literary profession " – than his announcement at the dinner-tableat Windsor, with reference to some disputed point of regal genealogy, " We are in the presence of probably the only Person in Europe who could tell us" ? In the last year of his life he said to Mr. Matthew Arnold, in a strange burst of confidence which showed how completely he realized that his fall from power was final: " You have heard me accused of being a flatterer. It is true. I am a flatterer. I have found it useful. Every one likes flattery; and when you come to Royalty you should lay it on with a trowel." As a courtier Lord Bcaconsfield excelled. Once, sitting at dinner by the Princess of Wales, he was trying to cut a hard dinner - roll. The knife slipped and cut his finger, which the Princess, with her natural grace, instantly wrapped up in her handkerchief. The old gentleman gave a dramatic groan, and exclaimed, " I asked for bread and they gave me a stone; but I had a Princess to bind my wounds."

The atmosphere of a Court naturally suited him, and he had a quaint trick of transferring the grandiose nomenclature of palaces to his own very modest domain of Hnghenden. He called his simple drawing-room the saloon ; he styled his pond the lake ; he expatiated on the beauties of the terrace - walks, the " Golden Gate," and the "German Forest." His style of entertaining was more showy than comfortable. Nothing could excel the grandeur of his state coach and powdered footmen; but when the ice at dessert came up melting, one of his friends exclaimed, "At last, my dear Dizzy, we have got something hot" ; and in the days when he was Chancellor of the Exchequer some critical guest remarked of the soup that it was apparently made with Deferred Stock. When Lady Beaconsfield died he sent for his agent and said: "I desire that Her Ladyship's remains should be borne to the grave by the tenants of the estate." Presently the agent came back with a troubled countenance and said," I regret to say there are not tenants enough to carry a coffin."

Lord Beaconsfield's last years were tormented by a bronchial asthma of gouty origin, against which he fought with tenacious and uncomplaining courage. The last six weeks of his life, described all too graphically by Dr. Kidd in an article in the *Nineteenth Century,* were a hand-to-hand struggle with death. Every day the end was expected, and his early compatriot, companion, and so-called friend, Bernal Osborne, found it in his heart to remark, "Ah, overdoing it – as he always overdid everything."

For my own part, I never was numbered among Lord Beaconsfield's friends, and I regarded the Imperialistic and pro-Turkish policy of his latter days with an equal measure of indignation and contempt. But I place his political novels among the masterpieces of Victorian literature, and I have a sneaking affection for the man who wrote the following passage : " We live in an age when to be young and to be indifferent can be no longer synonymous. We must prepare for the coming hour. The claims of the Future are represented by suffering millions, and the Youth of a Nation are the Trustees of Posterity." XXIV

FLATTERERS AND BORES

Can a flatterer be flattered ? Does he instinctively recognize the commodity in which he deals ? And, if he does so recognize it, does he enjoy or dislike the application of it to his own case ? These questions are suggested to my mind by the ungrudging tribute paid in my last chapter to Lord Beaconsfield's pre-eminence in the art of flattery.

" Supreme of heroes, bravest, noblest, best I"

No one else ever flattered so long and so much, so boldly and so persistently, so skilfully and with such success. And it so happened that at the very crisis of his romantic career he became the subject of an act of flattery quite as daring as any of his own performances in the same line, and one which was attended with diplomatic consequences of infinite pith and moment.

It fell out on this wise. When the Congress of the Powers assembled at Berlin in the summer of 1878, our Ambassador in that city of stucco palaces was the loved and lamented Lord Odo Russell, afterwards Lord Ampt- hill, a born diplomatist if ever there was one, with a suavity and affectionateness of manner and a charm of voice which would have enabled him, in homely phrase, to whistle the bird off the bough. On the evening before the formal opening of the Congress Lord Beacons- field arrived in all his plenipotentiary glory, and was re-

ceived with high honors at the British Embassy. In the course of the evening one of his private secretaries came to Lord Odo Rnssell and said: "Lord Odo, we are in a frightful mess, and we can only turn to you to help us out of it. The old chief has determined to open the proceedings of the Congress in French. He has written out the devil's own long speech in French and learned it by heart, and is going to fire it off at the Congress tomorrow. We shall be the laughing-stock of Europe. He pronounces *epicier* as if it rhymed with *overseer,* and all his pronunciation is to match. It is as much as our places are worth to tell him so : can yon help us ?" Lord Odo listened with amused good humor to this tale of woe, and then replied: " It is a very delicate mission that you ask me to undertake, but then I am fond of delicate missions. I will see what I can do." And so he repaired to the state bedroom, where our venerable Plenipotentiary was beginning those very elaborate processes of the toilette with which he prepared for the couch. " My dear lord," began Lord Odo, " a dreadful rumor has reached us." " Indeed! Pray what is it?" "We have heard that you intend to open the proceedings to-morrow in French." "Well, Lord Odo, what of that ?" " Why, of course, we all know that there is no one in Europe more competent to do so than yourself. But then, after all, to make a French speech is a commonplace accomplishment. There will be at least half a dozen men at the Congress who could do it almost, if not quite, as well as yourself. But, on the other hand, who but you can make an English speech ? All these Plenipotentiaries have come from the various Courts of Europe expecting the greatest intellectual treat of their lives in hearing English spoken by its greatest living master. The question for you, my dear lord, is – Will you disappoint them ?" Lord Beaconsfield puthis glass in his eye, fixed his gaze on Lord Odo, and then said: " There is much force in what you say. I will consider the point." And next day he opened the proceedings in English. Now the psychological conundrum is this – Did he swallow the flattery, and honestly believe that the object of Lord Odo's appeal was to have the pleasure of hearing him speak English ? Or did he see through the manoeuvre, and recognize a polite intimation that a French speech from him would throw an air of comedy over all the proceedings of the Congress, and perhaps kill it with ridicule ? The problem is well fitted to be made the subject of a Prize Essay; but personally I incline to believe that he saw through the manoeuvre and acted on the hint. If this be the true reading of the case, the answer to my opening question is that the flatterer cannot be flattered.

We saw in my last paper how careful Lord Beaconsfield was, in the great days of his political struggles, to flatter every one who came within his reach. To the same effect is the story that when he was accosted by any one who claimed acquaintance but whose face he had forgotten he always used to inquire, in a tone of affectionate solicitude, "And how is the old complaint?" But when he grew older, and had attained the highest objects of his political ambition, these libtle arts, having served their purpose, were discarded, like the green velvet trousers and tasselled canes of his aspiring youth. There was no more use for them, and they were dropped. He manifested less and less of the apostolic virtue of suffering bores gladly ; and, though always delightful to his intimate friends, he was less and less inclined to curry favor with mere acquaintances. A characteristic instance of this later manner has been given to the world in a book of chit-chat by a prosy gentleman whose name it would be unkind to recall.

This worthy soul narrates with artless candor that towards the end of Lord Beaconsfield's second Administration he had the honor of dining with the great man, whose political follower he was, at his official residence in Downing Street. When he arrived he found his host looking ghastly ill, and apparently incapable of speech. He made some commonplace remark about the weather or the House, and the only reply was a dismal groan. A second remark was similarly received, and the visitor then abandoned the attempt in despair. " I felt he would not survive the night. Within a quarter of an hour, all being seated at dinner, I observed him talking to the Austrian Ambassador with extreme vivacity. During the whole of dinner their conversation was kept up; I saw no sign of nagging. *This is difficult to account for."* And the worthy man goes on to theorize about the cause, and suggests that Lord Beaconsfield was in the habit of taking doses of opium which were so timed that their effect passed off at a certain moment!

This freedom from self-knowledge which bores enjoy is one of their most striking characteristics. One of the principal clubs in Pall Mall has the misfortune to be frequented by a gentleman who is by common consent the greatest bore and button-holer in London. He always reminds me of the philosopher described by Sir George Trevelyan, who used to wander about asking " Why are we created ? Whither do we tend ? Have we an inner consciousness ?" till all his friends, when they saw him from afar, used to exclaim : " Why was Tompkins created ? Is he tending this way ? Has he an inner consciousness that he is a bore ?"

Well, a few years ago this good man, on his return from his autumn holiday, was telling all his acquaintances at the club that he had been occupying a house at the Lakes not far from Mr. Kuskin, who, he added, wasin a very melancholy state. "I am truly sorry for that," said one of his hearers. " What is the matter with him ?" "Well," replied the button-holer, "I was walking one day in the lane which separated Buskin's house from mine, and I saw him coming down the lane towards me. The moment he caught sight of me he darted into a wood which was close by, and hid behind a tree till I had passed. Oh, very sad indeed." But the truly pathetic part of it was one's consciousness that what Mr. Ruskin did we should all have done, and that not all the trees in Birnam Wood and the Forest of Arden combined would have hidden the multitude of brother - clubmen who sought to avoid the narrator.

The faculty of boring belongs, unhappily, to no one period of life. Age cannot wither it, nor custom stale its infinite variety. Middle life is its heyday. Perhaps infancy is free from it, but I strongly suspect that it is a form of original sin, and shows itself very early. Boys are notoriously rich in it; with them it takes two forms, the loquacious and the awkward ; and in some exceptionally favored cases the two forms are combined. I once was talking with an eminent educationist about the characteristic qualities produced by various Public Schools, and when I asked him what Harrow produced he replied: *"A* certain shy bumptiousness." It was a judgment which wrung my Harrovian withers, but of which I could not dispute the truth.

One of the forms which shyness takes in boyhood is a7i inability to get up and go. When Dr. Vaughan was Head Master of Harrow, and had to entertain his boys at breakfast, this inability was frequently manifested, and was met by the Doctor in a most characteristic fashion. When the muffins and sausages had been devoured, the perfunctory inquiries about the health of "your people" made and answered, and all permissible schooltopics discussed, there used to ensue a horrid silence, while " Dr. Blimber's young friends " sat tightly glued to their chairs. Then the Doctor would approach with cat-like softness, and, extending his hand to the shyest and most loutish boy, would say, " Must yon go ? Can't you stay ?" and the party broke up with magical celerity. Such at least was our Harrovian tradition.

Nothing is so refreshing to a jaded sense of humor as to be the recipient of one of your own stories retold you with appreciative fervor but with all the point left out. This was my experience not long ago with reference to the story of Dr. Vaughan and his boy-bores which I have just related. A Dissenting minister was telling me, with extreme satisfaction, that he had a son at Trinity College, Cambridge. He went on to praise the Master, Dr. Butler, whom he extolled to the skies, winding up his eulogy with, "He has such wonderful tact in dealing with shy undergraduates." I began to scent my old story from afar, but held my peace and awaited results. " Yon know," he continued, " that young men are sometimes a little awkward about making a move and going away when a party is over. Well, when Dr. Butler has undergraduates to breakfast, if they linger inconveniently long when he wants to be busy, he has such a happy knack of getting rid of them. It is so tactful, so like him. He goes up to one of them and says, ' *Can't you go ? Must you stay 9'* and they are off immediately." So, as Macau- lay says of Montgomery's literary thefts, may such ill-got gains ever prosper.

My Dissenting minister had a congener in the late

Lord P , who was a rollicking man about town

thirty years ago, and was famous, among other accomplishments, for this peculiar art of so telling a story as to destroy the point. When the two large houses at Albert Gate, of which one is now the French Embassy andthe other the abode of Mr. Arthur

Sassoon, were built, their size and cost were regarded as prohibitive, and some wag christened them " Malta and Gibraltar, because they can never be taken." Lord P thought

that this must be an excellent joke, because every one laughed at it; and so he ran round the town saying to each man he met: " I say, do you know what they call those houses at Albert Gate ? They call them Malta and Gibraltar, because they can never be let. Isn't it awfully good ?" We all remember an innocent riddle of our childhood – " Why was the elephant the last animal to get into the Ark ?" – to which the answer was, " Because he had to pack his trunk." Lord P asked the

riddle, and gave as the answer, " Because he had to pack his portmanteau," and was beyond measure astonished when his hearers did not join in his uproarious laughter.

Poor Lord P ! he was a fellow of infinite jest,

though not always exactly in the sense that he intended. If he had only known of it, he might with advantage have resorted to the conversational device of old Samuel Rogers, who, when he told a story which failed to produce a laugh, used to observe in a reflective tone, " The curious part of that story is that stupid people never see the point of it"; and then loud, though belated, guffaws resounded round the table.

13

SECTION 13

XXV

EPITAPHS

word more, and I hare done." This immemorial sentence, the unfailing refuge of the parliamentary orator who feels that he is boring the House, I now apply to my dissertations on Lord Beaconsfield. "One word more" about him, "and I have done." Suitably enough, that one word relates to his epitaph; or, to speak more strictly, to the inscription on his monument in Hughenden Church. It was penned, I believe, by an illustrious hand:

TO THE DEAU AND HONORED MEMORY
Op BENJAMIN, EARL Of BEACONSFIELD,
THIS M RMOIU. U, IS PLACED BY
HIS GRATEFUL AND AFFECTIONATE
SOVEREIGN AND FRIEND,
VICTORIA, B. I.

Kings love him that speaketh right. – Prov. xvi. 13

When this tablet was erected, the memories of Lord Beaconsfield's Eastern policy were still rankling in the minds of at least half England, and there were critics who observed that it would have been better to avoid the too obvious inference that Queens love him that speaketh wrong. Others remarked that language so eulogistic had never before been inscribed by a Sovereign's hand upon a Minister's tomb, although the Crown of England had been served by a long succession of men at least as eminent, as conscientious. and as loyal as Benjamin Disraeli.

Of course the Disraelitish faction in the press and the whole Conservative party revelled in the unprecedented character of the inscription, and said triumphantly, though perhaps indecorously, that it showed the absolute concord which had existed between the Sovereign and the late Premier. They pointed out that no such language of confidence and affection was likely to be used towards Lord Beaconsfield's successor; and they seemed even to feel a kind of second-hand glory reflected on themselves, as the disciples and inheritors of a tradition which had been so signally honored. But the Dis- raelites boasted all too soon. Two years later the following inscription appeared in the church-yard of Crathie, N. B.:

THIS STONE
IS ERECTED IN AFFECTIONATE REMEMBRANCE OP
JOHN BROWN,

the devoted and faithful personal attendant and beloved friend of Queen Victoria. ..." That friend on whose fidelity you count, that friend given you by circumstances over which you have no control, was God's own gift."

Profound was the mortification which the appearance of this epitaph produced among the Disraelites. It was at least as cordial, as appreciative, and as honorific as the inscription at Hughenden; and all the elaborate edifice of partisan swagger and unconstitutional suggestion which had been so carefully reared was seen to be utterly baseless. Alike in the inscription at Hughenden and in the epitaph at Crathie there was the frank expression of a warm-hearted and grateful nature towards a departed friend on whom it had leaned for succor and assistance; and although Tory paragraphists might snarl and sneer, the ordinary Englishman, and especially the ordinary Radical, saw with pleasure thatat least as high a tribute was paid to the gillie as to the Minister.

From the epitaph in particular to epitaphs in general the transition is natural and easy. Mr. Gladstone, whose knowledge of such matters is extensive and peculiar, once told me the precise number – I have forgotten what it is – of books in the English language about epitaphs. Any one who is curious about such matters can find them all in St. Deiniol's Library at Hawarden. But although I am not versed in the literature of epitaphs, epitaphs themselves have always been a favorite study of mine. The late Dean Burgon once gave a lecture on epitaphs, and appealed for striking instances to all his friends, among others to dear old " Bodley Coxe " – the Bodleian Librarian at Oxford. Coxe took a pencil and instantly wrote an epitaph which he had read on au infant's grave in Eglingham church-yard, Northumberland:

"When the Archangel's trump shall blow
And souls to bodies join,
Thousands will wish their life below
Had been as brief as mine."

Putting aside the hideousness of the rhyme "join" and "mine" (whichever way you take the sound), the quatrain must be admitted to contain a thrilling thought in an effective phrase.

It is now a quarter of a century since I read in the Cathedral church-yard at Ripon the following inscription:

"Bold Infidelity, turn pale and die,
Beneath this stone three infants' ashes lie :
Say – Are they lost or saved ?
If Death's by sin, they sinned, because they're here :
If Heaven's by works, in Heaven they can't appear.
Reason – Ah! how depraved!
Revere the Bible's page – the knot's untied :
They died, for Adam sinned; they live, for Christ has died."

All Evangelical theology is contained in this strange ditty.

The following I found only last year at the west end of Lincoln Minster:

HERE IS ENTOMBED
DAME HARRIOT, Daughter Op Lieu.-general Churchill,
WIFE IN HER FIRST MARRIAGE TO 6R. EVERARD FAWKENER, KT. IN HER SECOND TO GOVEUNOUR POWNALL.
SHE DYED FEB. *G,* 177T, AGED 51.
HER PERSON WAS THAT OF ANIMATED, ANIMATING BEAUTY, WITH A COMPLEXION OF THE MOST EXQUISITE BRILLIANCY,
UNFADED WHEN SHE FELL.
HER UNDERSTANDING WAS OF SUCH QUICKNESS AND REACH OF THOUGHT THAT HER KNOWLEDGE, ALTHOUGH SHE HAD
LEARNING, WAS INSTANT AND ORIGINAL.
HER HEART WARMED WITH UNIVERSAL BENEVOLENCE
TO THE HIGHEST DEGREE OF SENSIBILITY,
HAD A READY TEAR FOR PITY,
GLOWED WITH FRIENDSHIP AS WITH A SACRED AND INVIOLATE FIRE. HER LOVE TO THOSE WHO WERE BLEST WITH IT
WAS HAPPINESS.
HER SENTIMENTS WERE CORRECT, REFINED, ELEVATED,
HER MANNER SO CHEARFUL, ELEGANT, WINNING, AND AIMIABLE
THAT, WHILE SHE WAS ADMIRED, SHE WAS BELOVED,
AND, WHILE SHE ENLIGHTENED, SHE ENLIVENED.
SHE WAS THE DELIGHT OF THE WORLD IN WHICH SHE LIVED,
SHE WAS FORMED FOR LIFE,
SHE WAS PREPARED FOR DEATH,
WHICH BEING
A GENTLE WAFTING TO IMMORTALITY,
SHE LIVES
WHERE LIFE IS REAL.

The style feels the century; but, though the rhetorical elaboration may raise a smile, this is excellent English of its time and class. And what a delightful woman must Lady Fawkener have been! To have kept her complexion to the last, and to have so combined amnsingness with information that "while she enlightened, she enlivened," was a twofold triumph not often achieved. One cannot help pausing on the last line of the epitaph, with its curious touch of rebuke to, or at least dissent from, the prevailing materialism of the time. That the invisible life is the real life, and that all earthly existence is but " a figure of the true," is a thought which seems to belong rather to antiquity, or to the religious sentiment of the present hour, than to the deadest period of the most unspiritnal century.

For the epitaph which appears on the following page, in an altogether different style of excellence, I am not personally responsible. It is stated in the *Annual Register* to exist in a church-yard in Northumberland.

If the epitaph is not a genuine transcript, it does infinite credit to the wag who invented it. A more perfect study in character I have never read. "Temperate, chaste, and charitable, but proud, peevish, and passionate," is as good as the " bland, passionate, and deeply religious " of the best-known of all epitaphs ; and the type of economy which, while liberal in larger matters, " would sacrifice one's eyes to a farthing candle," is drawn by the hand of a master. " She was a professed enemy to flattery" is an excellent *litotes* (as the grammarians would say) for the plainer statement that she was contradictory and censorious. It reminds me of the Rev. C. P. Golightly – the "old Golly" of my Oxford days – whose excess of charity made it impossible for him to express even the mildest censure on his friends. Some of the Fellows of Oriel, who had long groaned under the dry temper and mordant tongue of their old Provost, Dr. Hawkins, were joining in an outcry against his intolerable coldness and severity. Truth would not allow Go- lightly to dissent, and charity forbade him to agree, so he liberated his soul by gently remarking: "If I were

HERE LIK THE BODIES

Op THOMAS BOND And MARY His Wife.

SHE WAS TEMPERATE, CHASTE, AND CHARITABLE ;

BUT

SHE WAS PROUD, PEEVISH, AND PASSIONATE.

SHE WAS AN AFFECTIONATE WIFE AND A TENDER MOTHER ;

BUT

HER HUSBAND AND CHILD, WHOM SHE LOVED,

SELDOM SAW HER COUNTENANCE WITHOUT A DISGUSTING FROWN, WHILST SHE RECEIVED VISITORS WHOM SHE DESPISED WITH AN ENDEARING SMILE.

HER BEHAVIOR WAS DISCREET TOWARDS STRANGERS ;

BUT

IMPRUDENT IN HER FAMILY. ABROAD, HER CONDUCT WAS INFLUENCED BY GOOD BREEDING;

BUT

AT HOME, BY ILL-TEMPER.

SHE WAS A PROFESSED ENEMY TO FLATTERY,

AND WAS SELDOM KNOWN TO PRAISE OR COMMEND,

BUT

THE TALENTS IN WHICH SHE PRINCIPALLY EXCELLED WERE DIFFERENCE OF OPINION, AND DISCOVERING FLAWS AND IMPERFECTIONS.

SHE WAS AN ADMIRABLE ECONOMIST,
AND, WITHOUT PRODIGALITY,
DISPENSED PLENTY TO EVERY PERSON IN HER FAMILY;
BUT
WOULD SACRIFICE THEIR EYES TO A FARTHING CANDLE.
SHE SOMETIMES MADE HER HUSBAND HAPPY WITH HER GOOD QUALITIES;
BUT
MUCH MORE FREQUENTLY MISERABLE WITH HER MANY FAILINGS. INSOMUCH THAT IN THIRTY YEARS' COHABITATION HE OFTEN
LAMENTED THAT, MAUGRE ALL HER VIRTUES, HE HAD NOT, IN THE WHOLE, ENJOYED TWO YEARS OF MATRIMONIAL
COMFORT.
AT LENGTH,
FINDING THAT SHE HAD LOST THE AFFECTIONS OF HER HUSBAND,
AS WELL AS THE REGARD OF HER NEIGHBOURS,
FAMILY DISPUTES HAVING BEEN DIVULGED BY SERVANTS,
SHE DIED OF VEXATION, JULY 20, 1708,
AGED 48 YEARS.
HER WORN-OUT HUSBAND SURVIVED HER FOUR MONTHS AND TWO DAYS, AND DEPARTED THIS LIFE NOV. 28, 1768,
IN THE 54TH YEAR OF HIS AGE.
WILLIAM BOND, BROTHER TO THE DECEASED, ERECTED THIS STONE, AS A *WEEKLY MOXITOR* TO THE SURVIVING WIVES OF THIS PARISH
THAT THEY MAY AVOID THE INFAMY
OF HAVING THEIR MEMORIES HANDED TO POSTERITY
WITH A *PATCH-WORK* CHARACTER.

forced to choose an epithet to describe the dear Provost, I think the last I should choose would be 'gushing.'" But this is a digression to the *litotes* of the common-room from the *litotes* of the tombstone.

In the church-yard of Harrow-on-the-Hill is an epitaph remarkable for its happy combination of verse and prose:

TO THE MEMORY OF
THOMAS PORT,
BON OP JOHN POBT, OP BURTON-UPON-TRENT,
IN THE COUNTY OP STAFFORD, HAT MANUFACTURER,
"WHO NEAR THIS TOWN HAD BOTH HIS LEGS
SEVERED FROM HIS BODY BY THE *RAILWAY TRAIN.*
WITH THE GREATEST FORTITUDE HE BOBE A
SECOND AMPUTATION BY THE SURGEONS, AND
DIED FROM LOSS OF BLOOD.
AUGUST T", 1838. AGED 33 YEARS.

" Bright rose the morn and vigrous rose poor *Port,*
Gay on the *Train* he used his wonted sport.
Ere noon arrived, his mangled form they bore,

With pain distorted and o'erwhelmed with gore ;
When evening came to close the fatal day,
A mutilated corpse the sufferer lay."

In St. Anne's church-yard, Soho, is read:

NEAR THIS PLACE IS INTERRED
THEODORE, KING Of CORSICA,
WHO DIED IN THIS PARISH, DEC. 11,
1756,
IMMEDIATELY AFTER LEAVING
THE KING'S BENCH PRISON,
BY THE BENEFIT OF THE ACT OF INSOLVENCY,
IN CONSEQUENCE OF WHICH
HE REGISTERED THE KINGDOM OF CORSICA
FOR THE USE OF HIS CREDITORS.
"The grave, great teacher, to a level brings
Heroes and beggars, galley-slaves and kings."

In Winchester Cathedral yard :

IN MEMORY OP
THOMAS THATCHER,
A Grenadier Op The Ninth Regiment
Op Hants Militia, Who Died Op A
Violent Fever, Contracted By Drinking
Small Beer When Hot The 12th Op May,
1769, Aged 26 Years.
In Grateful Remembrance Op
Whose Universal
Goodwill Towards His Comrades
This Stone
Is Placed Here At Their Expense,
As A Small
Testimony Op Their Regard And Concern.
Here Sleeps In Peace A Hampshire Grenadier
Who Caught His Death By Drinking Cold Small Beer.
Soldiers, Be Wise From His Untimely Fall,
And When Ye're Hot, Drink Strong Or None At All.
THIS MEMORIAL BEING DECAYED, WAS RESTORED BY
THE OFFICERS OF THE GARRISON A. D. 1781.
AN HONEST SOLDIER NEVER IS FORGOT,
WHETHER HE DIED BY MUSKET OR BY POT.
THIS STONE WAS PLACED BY THE NORTH HANTS
MILITIA WHEN DISEMBODIED AT WINCHESTER
ON 26TH APRIL, 1802, IN CONSEQUENCE OF
THE ORIGINAL STONE BEING DESTROYED.

With professedly comic epitaphs – the *crambe repetita* of " Cheltenham Waters" and " The Landlord of the Lion " – I do not purpose to insult the intelligence of my readers. But I cannot forbear to quote a sarcastic epitaph suggested by the famous Lord Alvanley for a noble friend of his who had been expelled from society for cheating at whist:

HERE LIES
HENRY WILLIAM, Twenty-Second LORD ,
IN JOYFUL EXPECTATION OP THE LAST TRUMP.

In its point and brevity this is as good as a Greek epigram.

What I am about to quote is indeed not an epitaph, for it is not, so far as I am aware, inscribed on any tomb; but, as an elegiac poem, it is in nature congruous to the epitaph, and alike in metre and in sentiment it is too remarkable to be left in obscurity. I copied it from a Yorkshire newspaper two years ago, and I now give it verbally and literally, only altering the last two lines, so as to avoid mentioning the name of the good man in whose honor it was composed :

A beloved Christian gentleman has yielded his breath
And passed away, but for the truly *good* there is no death.
His work bears fruit which sweet undying fragrance gives,
And in vivid and ineffaceable deeds the good man ever lives.
He was a philanthropist in its true and broadest sense,
Who wrought much good secretly and sought no recompense.
An administrator of justice and advocate of the helpless and
weak,
His life and actions to the world most eloquently speak.
Sympathy true and deep surrounds the lady of noble birth
Who bears his name, and whom *all* revere for sterling worth !
Who takes a noble part in every sweet and gracious deed,
For whom, in her great *sorrow,* every heart must bleed.
To him that's gone many appealed, on whom all could depend,
And in him rich and poor have lost a *mined friend !*
And ever shall be cherished in men's hearts (a deathless roll)
The revered familiar name of John Thomas Peter Pole.

The following performance, in a similar vein, I bought in the streets of London from an itinerant minstrel who vended his own compositions :

A FEW LINES UPON THE LATE EMPEROR FREDERICK

Listen to the church bells tolling,
How they sound so clear in the air,
Telling us of the lost one who in his country was so dear.
He has lingered through his illness,
Although he suffered many a pain ;
Now to think he has been taken,
Just as he succeeded his Father's reign !
He was a noble Emperor, he was good to all mankind.
So gently toll the bell, and quietly draw the blind.
He will be missed by many now that he has left this shore,
Because he was a man for Peace, he was not the one for War.
No one can say that while he lived but what he did his best

To keep the country around him in quietness and rest.
Her dear Empress Victoria will take it much to heart.
For she was a fond and loving wife, and now they have to part.
He was a noble Emperor, so gentle and so kind,
So gently toll the bell, and quietly draw the blind.
It was while driving with the King of Italy in the autumn, 1886,
When the Emperor got wet through, which caused this dreadful
fix;
He tried his best to shake it off, but no, it was to be his fate, All the doctors could not save him, for he was in such a dreadful state ;
Now he has been called away, there is not the slightest doubt,
But what the people in the country will be very much put about.
By what is being said now, and what has been said before,
It seems very plainly there means to be a war.
He was a noble Emperor, a nobleman in miud,
So gently toll the bell, and quietly draw the blind. XXVI

ADVERTISEMENTS

Lately, when hunting in my diary for Epitaphs, I came upon a collection of Advertisements. No branch of literature is more suggestive of philosophical reflections. I take my specimens quite at random, just as they turn up in my diary, and the first which meets my eye is printed on the sad sea-green of the *Westminster Gazette:*

" Guardian, whose late ward merits the highest encomiums, seeks for him the Position of Secretary to a Nobleman or Lady of Position: one with literary tastes preferred : the young gentleman is highly connected, distinguished-looking, a lover of books, remarkably steady, and exceptionally well read, clever and ambitious: has travelled much: good linguist, photographer, musician: a moderate fortune, but debarred by timidity from competitive examination."

I have always longed to know the fate of this lucky youth. Few of us can boast of even " a moderate fortune," and fewer still of such an additional combination of gifts, graces, and accomplishments. On the other hand, most of us, at one time or another in our career, have felt " debarred by timidity from competitive examination." But, unluckily, we have had fathers of our flesh who corrected us, and college dons who forced us to face the agonies of the Schools, instead of an amiable guardian who bestowed on us "the highest encomiums,"
"

and sought to plant us on Ladies of Position, "with literary tastes preferred."

Another case, presenting some points of resemblance to the last, but far less favored by fortune, was notified to the compassionate world by the *Morning Post,* in 1889:

" Will any rich person Take a gentleman and Board him ? Of good family: age 27: good musician: thoroughly conversant with all office-work: *no objection to turn Jew:* lost his money through dishonest trustee: excellent writer."

I earnestly hope that this poor victim of fraud has long since found his desired haven in some comfortable Hebrew home, where he can exercise his skill in writing and office-work during the day and display his musical accomplishments after the family supper. I have known not a few young Gentiles who would be glad to be adopted on similar terms.

The next is extracted from the *Manchester Guardian* of 1894:

"A Child of God, seeking employment, would like to take charge of property and collect rents; has a slight knowledge of architecture and sanitary; can give unexceptionable references; aged 31; married."

What offers ? Very few, I should fear, in a community so shrewdly commercial as Manchester, where, I understand, religious profession is seldom taken as a substitute for technical training. The mention of that famous city reminds me that not long ago I was describing Cheetham College to an ignorant outsider, who, not realizing how the name was spelled, observed that it sounded as if Mr. Squeers had been caught by the Oxford Movement and the Gothic Revival, and had sought to give an ecclesiastical air to his famous seminary of Dotheboys Hall by transforming it into "Cheat'em College."

That immortal pedagogue owed much of his deserved success to his skill in the art of drawing an advertisement:

"At Mr. Wackford Squeers's Academy, Dotheboys Hall, at the delightful village of Dotheboys, in Yorkshire, youth are boarded, clothed, booked, furnished with pocket-money, provided with all necessaries, in-. strncted in all languages, living and dead, mathematics/ orthography, geometry, astronomy, trigonometry, the use of the globes, algebra, singlestick (if required), writing, arithmetic, fortification, and every other branch of classical literature. Terms, twenty guineas per annum. No extras, no vacation, and diet unparalleled."

Now, mark what follows. Wackford Squeers the younger was, as we all know, destined by his parents to follow the school-master's profession, to assist his father as long as assistance was required, and then to take the management of the Hall and its pupils into his own hands. " Am I to take care of the school when I grow up a man, father ?" said Wackford, junior. " You are, my son," replied Mr. Squeers, in a sentimental voice. " Oh, my eye, won't I give it to the boys!" exclaimed the interesting child, grasping his father's cane – " won't I make 'em squeak again!" But we know also that, owing to the pressure of pecuniary and legal difficulties, and the ill-timed interference of Mr. John Browdie, the school at Dotheboys Hall was at any rate temporarily broken up. So far we have authentic records to rely on; the remainder is pure conjecture. But I am persuaded that Wackford Squeers the younger, with all the dogged perseverance of a true Yorkshireman, struggled manfully against misfortune; resolved to make a home for his parents and sister; and, as soon as he could raise the needful capital, opened a private school in the South of England, as far as possible from the scene of earlier misfortune. Making due allowance for change of timeand circumstances, I trace a close similarity of substance and style between the advertisement which I quoted above and that which I give below, and I feel persuaded that young Wackford inherited from his more famous father this peculiar power of attracting parental confidence by means of picturesque statement. We have read the earlier manifesto ; let us now compare the later :

"Vacancies now occur in the establishment of a gentleman who undertakes the care and education of a few backward boys, who are beguiled and trained to study by kind discipline, without the least severity (which too often frustrates the end desired). Situation extremely healthy. Sea and country air; deep gravelly soil. Christian gentility assiduously cultivated on sound Church principles. Diet unsurpassed. Wardrobes carefully preserved. The course of instruction comprises English, classics, mathematics, and science. Inclusive terms, 30 guineas per annum, quarterly in advance. Music, drawing, and modern languages are extras, but moderate. Address , Chichester."

Was it Vivian Grey or Pelham who was educated at a private school where "the only extras were pure milk and the guitar"?

I believe that there is no charitable institution which more thoroughly deserves support than the Metropolitan Association for Befriending Young Servants, affectionately contracted by its supporters into the "Mabys." Here is one of its advertisements, from which, I am bound to say, the alluring skill displayed by Mr. Squeers is curiously absent:

"Will any one undertake as Servant a bright, clean, neat girl, who is deceitful, lazy, and inclined to be dishonest ? Address, Hon. Secretary, M. A. B. Y. S., 21 Charlotte Street, S. E."

I remember some years ago an advertisement whichsought a kind master and a pleasant home for a large, savage dog; and I remember how admirably *Punch* described the kind of life which the "large, savage dog" would lead the "kind master" when he got him. But really the vision of a bright maid-servant who is " deceitful, lazy, and inclined to be dishonest," and the havoc which she might work in a well-ordered household, is scarcely less appalling. A much more deserving case is this which I append :

',' Under-Housekeeper, under - Matron, desired by a Young Woman, age 22. Energetic, domesticated. Great misfortune in losing right arm, but good artificial one. Happy home, with small remuneration. Ap-

ply – "

It is not, I fear, in my power to make a contribution of permanent value to the "Great Servant Question." But, having given instances of insufficient qualification in people seeking to be employed, I now turn to the opposite side of the account, and, after perusing what follows, would respectfully ask, Who is sufficient for these things ?

" Can any lady or gentleman recommend a Man and Wife (Church of England)? Man useful indoors and out. Principal duties large flower-garden, small conservatory, draw bath-chair, must wait at table, understand lamps, non-smoker, wear dress suit except in garden. Clothes and beer not found. Family, lady and child, lady-help. House-parlor-maid kept. Must not object to small bedroom. Wife plain cook (good), to undertake kitchen offices, dining-room, and hall (ish clothes). Joint wages *501.,* all found. ." *9*

Now there is really a study in exacting eccentricity which Thackeray might have made the subject of a "Roundabout Paper." In the first place, the two servants must be man and wife. Unmarried people neednot apply, and yet they must be contented with a small bedroom. The family consists of a lady (apparently an invalid), a child, a lady-help, and a house-parlor-maid. For these the wife must cook, and cook well, besides cleaning the dining-room, hall, and offices, and washing the clothes. Her husband, yet more accommodating, must attend to a large flower-garden and a small conservatory, must draw a bath-chair, wait at table, and clean lamps. After all these varied and arduous labors, he is denied the refreshment of a pipe ; but, as a kind of compensation, he is not obliged to wear his dress suit when he is gardening! The joint wages are 50?., with all found except clothes and beer ; and the lucky recipients of this overpowering guerdon must be members of the Church of England.

This last requirement reminds me of a letter from a girl-emigrant written to Lady Laura Ridding, wife of the Bishop of Southwell, who had befriended her at home. " Dear Madam, – I hope this finds you as well as it leaves me. The ship is in the middle of the Red Sea, and it is fearfully hot. I am in a terrible state of melting all day long. But, honored Madam, I know you will be pleased to hear that I am still a member of the Church of England." I hope the good plain cook and her nonsmoking, bath-chair-drawing, large-gardening husband may be able to comfort themselves with the same reflection when the varied toils of the day are ended and they seek their well-earned repose in the " small bedroom."

From these lowly mysteries of domestic service I pass at a bound to the exalted atmosphere of courtly life :

"The Great-niece of a Lord Chamberlain to King George III. Requires a Situation as Companion to a lady, or Cicerone to young ladies. Her mind is highly cultivated. *English habits and Parisian accent.* Apply,

by letter, Caesar, ."

"Vieille ecole, bonne ecole, begad *I"* cried Major Pen- dennis, and here would have been a companion for Mrs. Pendennis or a cicerone for Laura after his own heart. The austere traditions of the Court of George III. and Queen Charlotte might be expected to survive in the grand-niece of their Lord Chamberlain; and what a tactful concession to the prejudices of Mrs. Grundy in the statement that, though the accent may be Parisian, the habits are English ! This excellent lady – evidently a near relation to Mrs. General, in *Little Dorrit* – reintro- dnces us to the genteel society in which we are most at home ; and here I may remark that the love of aristocracy which is so marked and so amiable a feature of our national character finds its expression not only in the advertisement columns, but in the daily notices of deaths and marriages. For example : " On the 22d inst., at Lisbon, William Thorold Wood, cousin to the Bishop of Rochester, to Sir John Thorold, of Syston Park, and brother to the Rector of Widmerpool. He was a man of great mental endowments and exemplary conduct." I dare say he was, but I fear they would have gone unrecorded had it not been for the more impressive fact that he was kinsman to a Bishop and a Baronet.

Here is a gem of purest ray serene, extracted by me from the *Morning Post* of 1893 :

" Copper Wedding.

"DE Courcelles – St. AuBYNT. – On the 7th November, 1883, at St. Marylebone Church, W., by the Rev. Grant E. Thomas, B. C. L., and privately, owing to family bereavements, the Rev. J. Hector de Courcelles, M. A., Worcester College, Oxford, and some time incumbent of St. Andrew's, Ardrossan, to Matilda Chrysogoria, daughter of the late Rev. William John St. Aubyn, M. A., rector of Stoke Damerel, Devonport, and granddaughter of Sir John St. Aubyn, F. R. S., fifth Baronet of Clowance and St. Michael's Mount, in the county of Cornwall, and also icranddaughter of the late

Sir Thomas Barrett Lennard, Bart., of Belhus, Essex, and his wife Dorothy, Lady Lennard, sister and co-heir of the above- named Sir John St. Aubyn, Bart., F. R. S."

Was the following skit, which appeared in the same paper directly afterwards, undeserved ?

"brazen Wedding.

" Poyntz-d'argent – Champignon. – On November 9, 1888, at St. Wombat's, Stony Stratford, by the Bev. Peter Broke Poyntz-d'Argent, father of the bridegroom, and privately, owing to affliction in bride's family, the Rev. Maximus Cadwallader Poyntz - d'Argent, B. A., Brasenose, and some time curate-in-charge of Cabbidge, Beds, to Rosy Gillian, only surviving child of Vane Champignon, Esq., of Champignon, Beds, and granddaughter of the late Sir De Horsey Champignon, Kt., of Muckross, and maternal great - grandniece of the late Honorable Carolina A. W. Skeggs."

The closing allusion to the *Vicar of Wdkefield* redeems the ribaldry with a touch of literary grace.

I cannot quit the subject of Advertisements without saying a word about the Medical branch of this fine art; and, knowing the enormous fortunes which have often been made out of a casual prescription for *acne* or *alopecia,* I freely place at the disposal of any aspiring young chemist who reads this paper the following tale of enterprise and success. A few years ago, according to the information before me, a London doctor had a lady patient who complained of an incessant neuralgia in her face and jaw. The doctor could detect nothing amiss, but exhausted his skill, his patience, and his remedies in trying to comfort the complainant, who, however, refused to be comforted. At length, being convinced that the case was one of pure hypochondria, he wrote to the afflicted lady, saying that he did not feel justified in any longer taking her money for a case which was evidently beyond his powers, but recommended her to try change of air, to live in the country, and to trust for her cure to the *edax rerum* which sooner or later cures all human ills.

The lady departed in sorrow, but in faith ; obeyed her doctor's intructions to the letter, and established herself not a hundred miles from the good city of Newcastle. Once established there, her first care was to seek the local chemist and to place her doctor's letter in his hands. A smart young assistant was presiding at the counter; he read the doctor's letter, and promptly made up a bottle, which he labelled " *Edax Rerum.* To be taken twice a day before meals," and for which he demanded 7s. *GcL* The lady rejoicingly paid, and requested that a similar bottle might be sent to her every week till further notice. She continued to use and to pay for this specific for a year and a half, and then, finding her neuralgia considerably abated, she came np to London for a week's amusement. Full of gratitude, she called on her former doctor, and said that though she had felt a little hurt at the abrupt manner in which he had dismissed so old a patient, still she could not forbear to tell him that his last prescription had done her far more good than any of its predecessors, and that, indeed, she now regarded herself as practically cured. Explanations followed ; inquires were set on foot; the chemist's assistant sailed for South Africa; and " *Edax Rerum "* is now largely in demand among the unlettered heroes who bear the banner of the Chartered Company.

14

SECTION 14

XXVII

PARODIES IN PROSE

"Parody," wrote Mr. Matthew Arnold in 1882, "is a vile art, but I must say I read *Poor Matthias,* in the *World,* with an amused pleasure." It was a generous appreciation, for the original *Poor Matthias* – an elegy on a canary – is an exquisite little poem, and the *World's* parody of it is a rather dull imitation. On the whole, I agree with Mr. Arnold that parody is a vile art; but the dictum is a little too sweeping. A parody of anything really good, whether in prose or verse, is as odious as a burlesque of Hamlet; but, on the other hand, parody is the appropriate punishment for certain kinds of literary affectation. There are, and always have been, some styles of poetry and of prose which no one endowed with an ear for rhythm and a sense of humor could forbear to parody. Such, to a generation brought up on Milton and Pope, were the styles of the various poetasters satirized in *Rejected Addresses ;* but excellent as are the metrical parodies in that famous book, the prose is even better. Modern parodists, of whom I will speak more particularly in a future paper, have, I think, surpassed such poems as *The Baby's Debut* and *A Tale of Drury Lane,* but in the far more difficult art of imitating a prose style none that I know of has even approached the author of the *Hampshire Farmer's Address* and *Johnson's Ghost.* Does any one read William

Cobbett nowadays ? If so, let him compare what follows with the recorded specimens of Cobbett's public speaking:

"Most thinking People, – When persons address an audience from the stage, it is usual, either in words or gesture, to say 'Ladies and gentlemen, your servant.' If I were base enough, mean enough, paltry enough, and *brute beast* enough to follow that fashion, I should tell two lies in a breath. In the first place, you are not ladies and gentlemen, but, I hope, something better – that is to say, honest men and women ; and, in the next place, if you were ever so much ladies, and ever so much gentlemen, I am not, *nor ever will be,* your humble servant."

With Dr. Johnson's style – supposing we had ever forgotten its masculine force and its balanced antitheses – we have been made again familiar by the erudite labors of Dr. Birkbeck Hill and Mr. Augustine Birrell. But even those learned critics might, I think, have mistaken a copy for an original if in some collection of old speeches they had lighted on the ensuing address :

" That which was organized by the moral ability of one has been executed by the physical efforts of many, and Drttry Laxe Theatre is now complete. Of that part behind the curtain, which has not yet been destined to glow beneath the brush of the varnisher or vibrate to the hammer of the carpenter, little is thought by the public, and little need be said by the Committee. Truth, however, is not to be sacrificed to the accommodation of either, and he who should pronounce that our edifice has received its final embellishment would be disseminating falsehood without incurring favor, and risking the disgrace of detection without participating in the advantage of success."

An excellent morsel of Johnsonese prose belongs to a more recent date. It became current about the time when the scheme of Dr. Murray's Dictionary of theEnglish Language was first made public. It took the form of a dialogue between Dr. Johnson and Boswell in the shades: i

"Boswell: Pray, sir, what would you say if you were told that the next dictionary of the English language would be written by a Scotchman and a Presbyterian domiciled at Oxford ?

"Dr. J.: Sir, in order to be facetious, it is not necessary to be indecent."

When Bulwer-Lytton brought out his play *Not so Bad as we Seem,* his friends good-naturedly altered its title to *Not so Good as we Expected.* And when a lady's newspaper advertised a work called " How to dress on fifteen pounds a year, as a Lady. By a Lady," *Punch* was ready with the characteristic parody: "How to dress on nothiug a year, as a Kaffir. By a Kaffir."

Mr. Gladstone's authority compels me to submit the ensuing imitation of Macaulay – the most easily parodied of all prose writers – to the judgment of my readers. It was written by the late Abraham Hayward. Macaulay is contrasting, in his customary vein of over-wrought and over-colored detail, the evils of arbitrary government with those of a debased currency :

" The misgovernment of Charles and James, gross as it had been, had not prevented the common business of life from going steadily and prosperously on. While the honor and independence of the State were sold to a foreign Power, while chartered rights were invaded, while fundamental laws were violated, hundreds of thousands of quiet, honest, and industrious families labored and traded, ate their meals, and lay down to rest in comfort and security. Whether Whigs or Tories, Protestants or Jesuits were uppermost, the grazier drove his beasts to market; the grocer weighed out his currants; the draper measured out his broadcloth; the hum of buyersand sellers was as loud as ever in the towns; the harvest-home was celebrated as joyously as ever in the hamlets ; the cream overflowed the pails of Cheshire; the apple juice foamed in the presses of Herefordshire ; the piles of crockery glowed in the furnaces of the Trent; and the barrows of coal rolled fast along the timber railways of the Tyne."

This reads like a parody, but is a literal transcript of the original; and Hayward justly observes that there is no reason why this rigmarole should ever stop, as long as there is a trade, calling, or occupation to be particularized. The pith of the proposition (which needed no proof) is contained in the first sentence. Why not continue thus ?

" The apothecary vended his drugs as usual the poulterer crammed his turkeys ; the fishmonger skinned his eels; the wine-merchant adulterated his port; as many hot-cross buns as ever were eaten on Good Friday, as many pancakes on Shrove Tuesday, as many Christmas pies on Christmas Day; on area steps the domestic drudge took in her daily pennyworth of the chalky mixture which Londoners call milk ; through area bars the feline tribe, vigilant as ever, watched the arrival of the cat's- meat man; the courtesan flaunted in the Haymarket; the cab rattled through the Strand; and, from the suburban regions of Fulham and Putney, the cart of the market-gardener wended its slow and midnight way along Piccadilly to deposit its load of cabbages and turnips in Covent Garden."

Twice has Mr. Gladstone publicly called attention to the merits of this "effective morsel of parody," as he styles it; and he judiciously adds that what follows (by the late Dean Hook) is "a like attempt, but less happy." Most people remember the attack on the constitution of the Court of Chancery in the preface to *Bleak House.*Dean Hook, in a laudable attempt to soothe the ruffled feelings of his old friend Vice-Chancellor Page Wood, of whom Dickens in that preface had made fun, thus endeavors to translate the accusation into Macanlayese :

"REIGN OF VICTORIA – 1856.

" The Courts Of Justice.

" The Court of Chancery was corrupt. The guardian of lunatics was the cause of insanity to the suitors in his court. An attempt at reform was made when Wood was Solicitor-General. It consisted chiefly in increasing the number of judges in the Equity Court. Government was pleased by an increase of patronage; the lawyers approved of the new professional prizes. The Government papers applauded. Wood became Vice-Chancellor. At the close of 1855 the Equity Courts were without business. People had become weary of seeking justice where justice was not to be found. The state of the Bench was unsatisfactory. Cranworth was feeble; Knight Bruce, though powerful, sacrificed justice to a joke ; Turner was heavy; Romilly was scientific; Kin- dersley was slow; Stuart was pompous; Wood was at Bealings."

If I were to indulge in quotations from, well-known parodies of prose, this chapter would soon overflow all proper dimensions. I forbear, therefore, to do more than remind my readers of Thackeray's *Novels by Eminent Hands* and Bret Harte's *Sensation Novels,* only remarking, with reference to the latter book, that " Miss Mix" is in places really indistinguishable from *Jane Eyre.* The sermon by Mr. Jowett in Mr.

Mallock's *New Republic* is so perfect an imitation, both in substance and in style, that it suggested to some readers the idea that it had been reproduced from notes of an actual discourse. On spoken, as distinguished from written, eloquence there are some capital skits in the *Anti-Jacobin,* where (under the name of Macfungus) excellent fun is made of the too mellifluous eloquence of Sir James Mackintosh.

The differentiating absurdities of after-dinner oratory are photographed in Thackeray's *Dinner in the City,* where the speech of the American Minister seems to have formed a model for a long series of similar performances. Dickens's experience as a reporter in the gallery of the House of Commons had given him a perfect command of that peculiar style of speaking which is called Parliamentary, and he used it with great efEect in his accounts of the inaugural meeting of the " United Metropolitan Improved Hot Muffin and Crumpet Baking and Punctual Delivery Company" in *Nicholas Nickleby* (where he introduces a capital sketch of Tom Duncombe, Radical Member for Finsbury); and in the interview between Mr. Gregsbury, M. P., and his constituents in a later chapter of the same immortal book.

The parliamentary eloquence of a later day was admirably reproduced in Mr. Edward Jenkins's prophetic squib (published in 1872), *Barney Geoghegan, M. P., and Home Rule at St. Stephen's.* As this clever little book has, I fear, lapsed into complete oblivion, I venture to cite a passage. It will vividly recall to the memory of middle-aged politicians the style and tone of the verbal duels which, towards the end of Mr. Gladstone's first Administration, took place so frequently between the Leader of the House and the Leader of the Opposition. Mr. Geoghegan has been returned, a very early Home Ruler, for the Borough of Rashkillen, and for some violent breaches of order is committed to the custody of the Sergeant - at - Arms. On this the Leader of the House rises and addresses the Speaker:

"Sir, – The House cannot but sympathize with you in the eloquent and indignant denunciation you have uttered against the painful invasion of the decorum of the House which we have just witnessed. There can be no doubt in any mind, even in the minds of those with whom the hon. member now at the bar usually acts, that of all methods of argument which could be employed in this House, he has selected the least politic. Sir, may I be permitted, with great deference, to say a word upon a remark that fell from the Chair, and which might be misunderstood ? Solitary and anomalous instances of this kind could never be legitimately used as arguments against general systems of representation or the course of a recent policy. I do not, at this moment, venture to pronounce an opinion upon the degree of criminality that attaches to the hon. member now unhappily in the custody of the officer of the House. It is possible – I do not say it is probable, I do not now say whether I shall be prepared to commit myself to that hypothesis or not – but it is not impossible that the hon. member or some of his friends may be able to urge some extenuating circumstances – (Oh ! oh !) – I mean circumstances that, when duly weighed, may have a tendency in a greater or less degree to modify the judgment of the House upon the extraordinary event that has occurred. Sir, it becomes a great people and a great assembly like this to be patient, dignified, and generous. The honorable member, whom we regret to see in his present position, no doubt represents a phase of Irish opinion unfamiliar to this House. (Cheers and laughter.) . . . The House is naturally in a rather excited state after an event so unusual, and I venture to urge that it should not hastily proceed to action. AVe must be careful of the feelings of the Irish people. (Oh! oh!) If we are to govern Ireland according to Irish ideas we must make allowance for personal, local, and

transitory ebullitions of Irish feeling, having no general or universal consequence or bearing. . . . The course, therefore, which I propose to take is this – to move that the lion, member shall remain in the custody of the Ser- geant-at-Arms, that a Committee be appointed to take evidence, and that their report be discussed this day month."

To this replies the Leader of the Opposition : " The right hon. gentleman is to be congratulated on the results of his Irish policy. (Cheers and laughter.) . . . Sir, this, I presume, is one of the right hon. gentleman's contented and pacified people ! I deeply sympathize with the right hon. gentleman. His policy produces strange and portentous results. A policy of concession, of confiscation, of truckling to ecclesiastical arrogance, to popular passions and ignorant prejudices, of lenity to Fenian revolutionists, has at length brought us to this, that the outrages of Galway and Tipperary, no longer restricted to those charming counties, no longer restrained to even Her Majesty's judges, are to reach the interior of this House and the august person of its Speaker. (Cheers.) Sir, I wash my hands of all responsibility for this absurd and anomalous state of things. Whenever it has fallen to the Tory party to conduct the affairs of Ireland, they have consistently pursued a policy of mingled firmness and conciliation with the most distinguished success. All the great measures of reform in Ireland may be said to have had their root in the action of the Tory party, though, as usual, the praise has been appropriated by the right hon. gentleman and his allies. We have preferred, instead of truckling to prejudice or passion, to appeal, and we still appeal, to the sublime instincts of an ancient people !"

I hope that an unknown author, whose skill in reproducing an archaic style I heartily admire, will forgive mefor quoting the following narrative of certain doings decreed by the General Post Office on the occasion of the Jubilee of the Penny Post. Like all that is truly good in literature, it will be seen that this narrative was not for its own time alone, but for the future, and has its relevancy to events of the present day :

"1. Now it came to pass in the month June of the Post-office Jubilee, that Raikes, the Postmaster-General, said to himself, Lo ! an opening whereby I may find grace in the sight of the Queen!

"2. And Raikes appointed an Executive Committee; and Baines, the Inspector - General of Mails, made he Chairman.

" 3. He called also Cardin, the Receiver and Account- ant-General; Preece, Lord of the Lightning ; Thompson, the Secretarial Officer; and Tombs, the Controller.

"4. Then did these four send to the Heads of Departments, the Postmasters and Sub-Postmasters, the Letter Receivers, the Clerks-in-Charge, the Postal Officers, the Telegraphists, the Sorters, the Postmen; yea, from the lowest even unto the highest sent they out.

"5. And the word of Baines and of them that were with him went forth that the Jubilee should be kept by a conversazione at the South Kensington Museum on Wednesday the second day of the month July in the year 1890.

" 6. And Victoria the Queen became a patron of the Jubilee celebration; and her heart was stirred within her; for she said, For three whole years have I not had a Jubilee.

" 7. And the word of Baines and of them that were with him went forth again to the Heads of Departments, the Postmasters and Sub-Postmasters, the Letter Receivers, the Clerks-in-Charge, the Postal Officers and Telegraphists, the Sorters and the Postmen.

" 8. Saying unto them, Lo ! the Queen is become Patron of the Rowland Hill Memorial and Benevolent Fund, and of the conversazione in the Museum; and we the Executive Committee bid you, from the lowest even to, the highest, to join with us at the tenth hour of the conversazione in a great shouting to praise the name of the Queen our patron.

"9. Each man in his Post Office at the tenth hour shall shout upon her name; and a record thereof shall be sent to us that we may cause its memory to endure forever.

" 10. Then a great fear came upon the Postmasters, the Sub-Postmasters, and the Letter Receivers, which were bidden to make thejecord.

" 11. For they said, If those over whom we are set in authority shout not at the tenth hour, and we send an evil report, we shall surely perish.

" 12. And they besought their men to shoot aloud at the tenth hour, lest a worse thing should befall.

" 13. And they that were of the tribes of Nob and of Snob rejoiced with an exceeding great joy, and did shout with their whole might; so that their voices became as the voices of them that sell tidings in the street at nightfall.

" 14. But the Telegraphists and the Sorters and the Postmen, and them that were of the tribes of Rag and of Tag, hardened their hearts, and were silent at the tenth hour; for they said among themselves, ' Shall the poor man shout in his poverty, and the hungry celebrate his lack of bread ?'

"15. Now Preece, Lord of Lightning, had wrought with a cord of metal that they who were at the conversazione might hear the shouting from the. Post Offices.

"16. And the tenth hour came ; and lo ! there was no great shout; and the tribes of Nob and Snob were as the voice of men calling in the wilderness.

"17. Then was the wrath of Baines kindled against the tribes of Rag and Tag for that they had not shouted according to his word; and he commanded that their chief men and counsellors should be cast out of the Queen's Post Office.

"18. And Raikes, the Postmaster-General, told the Queen all the travail of Baines, the Inspector-General, and of them that were with him, and how they had wrought all for the greater glory of the Queen's name.

" 19. And the Queen hearkened to the word of Raikes, and lifted up Baines to be a Centurion of the Bath ; also she placed honors upon Cardin, the Receiver-General and Accountant-General; upon Preece, Lord of Lightning; upon Thompson, the Secretarial Officer; and upon Tombs, the Controller, so that they dazzled the eyes of the tribe of Snob, and were favorably entreated of the sons of Nob.

" 20. And they lived long in the land; and all men said pleasant things unto them.

"21. But they of Tag and of Rag that had been cast out were utterly forgotten ; so that they were fain to cry aloud, saying, 'How long, 0 ye honest and upright in heart, shall Snobs and Nobs be rulers over us, seeing that they are but men like unto us, though they imagine us in their hearts to be otherwise ?'

"22. And the answer is not yet." XXVIII

PARODIE8 IN VERSE

To-day I embark on the shoreless sea of metrical parody, and I begin my cruise by reaffirming that in this department *Rejected Addresses,* though distinctly good for their time, have been left far behind by modern achievements. The sense of style seems to have grown acuter, and the art of reproducing it has been brought to absolute perfection. The theory of development is instructively illustrated in the history of metrical parody.

Of the same date as *Rejected Addresses,* and of about equal merit, is the *Poetry of the Anti-Jacobin,* which our grandfathers, if they combined literary taste with Conservative opinions, were never tired of repeating. The extraordinary brilliancy of the group of men who contributed to it guaranteed the general character of the book. Its merely satiric verse is a little beside my present mark; but as a parody the ballad of *Duke Smithson of Northumberland,* founded on *Chevy Chase,* ranks high, and the inscription for the cell in Newgate, where Mrs. Brownrigg, who murdered her apprentices, was imprisoned, is even better. Southey, in his Radical youth, had written some lines on the cell in Chepstow Castle where Henry Marten the Regicide was confined :

" For thirty years secluded from mankind
Here Marten lingered . . .
Dost thou ask his crime ?
He had rebell'd against the King, and sate
In judgment on him."

Here is Canning's parody :

"For one long term, or e'er her trial came,
Here Brownrigg lingered . . .
Dost tbou ask her crime ?
She whipped two female 'prentices to death,
And hid them in a coal-hole."

The time of *Rejected Addresses* and the *Anti-Jacobin* was also the heyday of parliamentary quotation, and old parliamentary hands used to cite a happy instance of instantaneous parody by Daniel O'Connell, who, having noticed that the speaker to whom he was replying had his speech written out in his hat, immediately likened him to Goldsmith's village schoolmaster, saying :

" And still they gazed, and still the wonder grew
That one small *hat* could carry all he knew."

Another instance of the same kind was O'Connell's extemporized description of three ultra - Protestant members, Colonel Verner, Colonel Vandeleur, and Colonel Sibthorpe, the third of whom was conspicuous in a closely shaven age for his profusion of facial hair :

" Three Colonels, in three different counties born,
Armagh and Clare and Lincoln did adorn.
The first in direst bigotry surpassed :

The next in impudence : in both the last.
The force of nature could no further go –
To beard the third, she shaved the former two. "

A similarly happy turn to an old quotation was given by Baron Parke, afterwards Lord Wensleydale. His old friend and comrade at the Bar, Sir David Duudas, had just been appointed Solicitor-General, and, in reply to Baron Parke's invitation to dinner, he wrote that he could not accept it, as he had been already invited byseven peers for the same evening. He promptly received the following couplets:

" Seven thriving cities fight for Homer dead
Through which the living Homer begged his bread."
" Seven noble Lords ask Davie to break bread
Who wouldn't care a d were Davie dead."

The *Ingoldsby Legends* – long since, I believe, deposed from their position in public favor – were published in 1840. Their principal merits are a vein of humor, rollicking and often coarse, but genuine and infectious; great command over unusual metres ; and an unequalled ingenuity in making double and treble rhymes – *e. g. :*

" The poor little page, too, himself got no quarter, but Was found the next day with his head in the water-butt."

There is a general flavor of parody about most of the ballads. It does not as a rule amount to more than a rather clumsy mockery of medisevalism, but the verses prefixed to the *Lay of St. Gengulphus* are really rather like a fragment of a black-letter ballad. The book contains only one parody, borrowed from Samuel Lover's *Lyrics of Ireland,* and then the result is truly offensive, for the poem which he chooses for his experiment is one of the most beautiful in the language – the *Burial of Sir John Moore,* which is transmuted into a stupid story of vulgar debauch. Of much the same date as the *Ingolds- by Legends* was the *Old Curiosity Shop,* and no one who has a really scholarly acquaintance with Dickens will forget the delightful scraps of Tom Moore's amatory ditties with which, slightly adapted to current circumstances, Dick Swiveller used to console himself when Destiny seemed too strong for him. And it will be remembered that Mr. Slum composed some very telling parodies ofthe same popular author as advertisements for Mrs. Jar- ley's Waxworks; but I forbear to quote here what is so easily accessible.

By way of tracing the development of the Art of Parody, I am taking my samples in chronological order. In 1845 the Newdigate Prize for an English poem at Oxford was won by J. W. Burgon, afterwards Dean of Chichester. The subject was Petra. The successful poem was, on the whole, not much better and not much worse than the general run of such compositions ; but it contained one couplet which Dean Stanley regarded as an absolute gem – a volume of description condensed into two lines :

" Match me such marvel, save in Eastern clime –
A rose-red city, half as old as time."

The couplet was universally praised and quoted, and, as a natural consequence, parodied. There resided then (and long after) at Trinity College, Oxford, an extraordinarily old don called Short. When I was an undergraduate he was still tottering about, and there was a tradition – based on what authority I know not – that the great

Sir Robert Peel had " coached " with him for his degree. To his case the University parodists instantly adapted Burgon's beautiful couplet, saying thus :

" Match me such marvel, save in college port –
That rose-red liquor, half as old as Short."

In 1845 the poet of Young England was the, present Duke of Rutland, who, as Lord John Manners, produced in *England's Trust* some chivalric songs which, in their own way, have never been surpassed. I suppose there has seldom been a couplet so often or so deservedly quoted as :

" Let wealth and commerce, laws and learning die,
But leave us still our old nobility."

Far better than any parody is this chivalric aspiration from the same poem :

" Oh ! would some noble dare again to raise
The feudal banner of forgotten days,
And live, despising slander's harmless hate,
The potent ruler of his petty state !
Then would the different classes once again
Feel the kind pressure of the social chain."

All this mediaeval mummery was peculiarly distasteful to
the mordant mind of Thackeray, and he made fun of
Lord John's chivalric aspirations in Lord Southdown's
Lines upon my Sister's Portrait:

" The castle towers of Bareacres are fair upon the lea, Where the cliffs of bonny Diddlesex rise up from out the
sea:
I stood upon the donjon-keep – it is a sacred place,
Where floated for eight hundred years the banner of my
race.
Argent, a dexter sinople, and *gules* an azure field –
There ne'er was nobler cognizance on knightly warrior's
shield."

The *Ballads of Bon Gaultier,* published anonymously in 1855, had a success which would only have been possible at a time when really artistic parodies were unknown. Bon Gaultier's verses are not as a rule much more than rough - and - ready imitations ; and, like so much of the humor of their day, and of Scotch humor in particular, they generally depend for their point upon drinking and drunkenness. Some of the different forms of the Puff Poetical are amusing, especially the advertisement of Doudney Brothers' waistcoats, and the Puff Direct in which Parr's Life-pills are glorified after the manner of a German ballad. *The Laureate* is a fair hit at some of Tennyson's earlier mannerisms :

" Who -would not be
The Laureate bold,
With his butt of sherry
To keep him merry,
And nothing to do but pocket his gold ?"

But *The Lay of the Lovelorn* is a clumsy and rather vulgar skit on *Locksley Hall* – a poem on which two such writers as Sir Theodore Martin and Professor Aytoun would have done well not to lay their sacrilegious hands. We have now passed through the middle stage of the development which I am trying to trace ; we are leaving clumsiness and vulgarity behind ns, and are approaching the age of perfection. Sir George Trevelyan's parodies are transitional. He was born in 1838, three times won the prize poem at Harrow, and brought out his Cambridge squibs in and soon after the year 1858. *Horace at the University of Athens,* originally written for acting at the famous " A. D. C.," still holds its own as one of the wittiest of extravaganzas. It contains a really pretty imitation of the 10th Eclogue, and it is studded with imitations of Horace adapted to the events of undergraduate life, of which the only possible fault is that, for the general reader, they are too topical. Here is a sample :

" *'Donee grains eram tibi.'*
" *Hor.* While still you loved your Horace best
Of all my peers who round you pressed
(Though not in expurgated versions),
More proud I lived than King of Persians.
" *Lyd.* And while as yet no other dame
Had kindled in your breast a flame
(Though Niebuhr her existence doubt),
I cut historic Ilia out.
" *Hor.* Dark Chloe now my homage owns,
Skilled on the banjo and the bones;
For whom I would not fear to die,
If death would pass my charmer by.
" *Lyd.* I now am lodging at the *rus-*
In-urbe of young Decius Mus.
Twice over would I gladly die
To see him hit in either eye.
"*Hor.* But should the old love come again,
And Lydia her sway retain,
If to my heart once more I take her,
And bid black CUIoe wed the baker ?
"*Lyd.* Though you be treacherous as audit
When at the fire you've lately thawed it,
For Decius Mus no more I'd care
Than for their plate the Dons of Clare."

Really this is a much better rendering of the famous ode than nine-tenths of its more pompous competitors ; and the allusions to the perfidious qualities of Trinity Audit Ale and the mercenary conduct of the Fellows of Clare need no explanation for Cambridge readers, and little for others. But it may be fairly objected that this is not, in strictness, a parody. That is true, and indeed as a parodist Sir George Trevelyan belongs to the metrical miocene. His Horace, when serving as a volunteer in the Republican Army, bursts into a pretty snatch of song which has a flavor of Moore :

" The minstrel boy from the wars is gone,

All out of breath you'll find him ;
He has run some five miles, off and on.
And his shield has flung behind him."

And the Bedmaker's Song in one of the Cambridge scenes is sweetly reminiscent of a delightful and forgotten bard :

" I make the butter fly, all in an hour;
I put aside the preserves and cold meats,
Telling my master the cream has turned sour,
Hiding the pickles, purloining the sweets.
"I never languish for husband or dower ;
I never sigh to see ' gyps' at my feet;
I make the butter fly, all in an hour,
Taking it home for my Saturday treat."

This, unless I greatly err, is a very good parody of Thomas Haynes Bayly, author of some of the most popular songs of a sentimental cast which were chanted in our youth and before it. But this is ground on which I must not trench, for Mr. Andrew Lang has made it his own. The most delightful essay in one of his books of Reprints deals with this amazing bard, and contains some parodies so perfect that Mr. Haynes Bayly would have rejoicingly claimed them as his own.

Charles Stuart Calverley is by common consent the king of metrical parodists. All who went before merely adumbrated him and led up to him ; all who have come since are descended from him and reflect him. Of course he was infinitely more than a mere imitator of rhymes and rhythms. He was a true poet; he was one of the most graceful scholars that Cambridge ever produced; and all his exuberent fun was based on a broad and strong foundation of Greek, Latin, and English literature. *Verses and Translations, "by C. S. C.,* which appeared in 1862, was a young man's book, although its author had already established his reputation as a humorist by the inimitable Examination-Paper on *Pickwick;* and, being a young man's book, it was a book of unequal merit. The translations I leave on one side, as lying outside my present purview, only remarking as I pass that if there is a finer rendering than that of Ajax – 645- 692 – I do not know where it is to be found. My business is with the parodies. It was not till ten years later that in *Fly Leaves* Calverley asserted his supremacy in the art, but even in *Verses and Translations* he gave good promise of what was to be.

Of all poems in the world, I suppose *Horatius* has been most frequently and most justly parodied. Every Public School magazine contains at least one parody of it every year. In my Oxford days there was current an admirable version of it (attributed to the Rev. W. W. Merry, now Rector of Lincoln College), which began –

" Augustus Smalls, of Boniface,
By all the powers he swore
That, though he had been ploughed three times,
He would be ploughed no more,"

and traced with curious fidelity the successive steps in the process of preparation till the dreadful day of examination arrived :

"They said he made strange quantities,
Which none might make but he ;

And that strange things were in his Prose,
Canine to a degree;
But they called his *Viva Voce* fair,
They said his ' Books' would do;
And native cheek, where facts were weak,
Brought him triumphant through.
And in each Oxford college
In the dim November days,
When undergraduates fresh from hall
Are gathering round the blaze;
When the 'crusted port' is circling,
And the Moderator's lit,
And the weed glows in the Freshman's mouth,
And makes him turn to spit;
With laughing and with chaffing
The story they renew,
How Smalls of Boniface went in,
And actually got through."

So much for the Oxford rendering of Macaulay's famous lay. " C. S. C." thus adapted it to Cambridge, and to a different aspect of undergraduate life :

" On pinnacled St. Mary's
Lingers the setting sun ;
Into the street the blackguards
Are skulking one by one ;
Butcher and Boots and Bargeman
Lay pipe and pewter down,
And with wild shout come tumbling out
To join the Town and Gown.
" 'Twere long to tell how Boxer
Was countered on the cheek,
And knocked into the middle
Of the ensuing week ;
How Barnacles the Freshman
Was asked his name and college,
And how he did the fatal facts
Reluctantly acknowledge."

Quite different, but better because more difficult, is this essay in *Proverbial Philosophy:*

I heard the wild notes of the lark floating far over the blue sky. And my foolish heart went after him, and, lo ! I blessed him as he
rose ;
Foolish ! for far better is the trained boudoir bullfinch,
Which pipeth the semblance of a tune and mechanically draweth
up water.

For verily, O my daughter, the world is a masquerade, And God made thee one thing that thou mightest make thyself another.

A maiden's heart is as champagne, ever aspiring and struggling, And it needed that its motions be checked by the silvered cork of

Propriety.

He that can afford the price, his be the precious treasure, Let him drink deeply of its sweetness, nor grumble if it tasteth of the cork.

Enoch Arden was published in 1864, and was not enthusiastically received by true lovers of Tennyson, though people who had never read him before thought it wonderfully fine. A cousin of mine always contended that the story ended wrongly, and that the truly human, and therefore dramatic, conclusion would have been as follows :

" For Philip's dwelling fronted on the street,
And Enoch, coming, saw the house a blaze
Of light, and Annie drinking from a mug –
A funuy mug, all blue, with strange device
Of birds and waters and a little man.
And Philip held a bottle; and a smell
Of strong tobacco, with a fainter smell –
But still a smell, and quite distinct – of gin,
Was there. He raised the latch, and, stealing by
The cupboard, where a row of teacups stood,
Hard by the genial hearth, he paused behind
The luckless pair; then drawing back his foot –
His manly foot, all clad in sailors' hose-
He swung it forth with such a grievous kick
That Philip, in a moment, was propelled
Against his wife, though not his wife ; and she
Fell forwards, smashing saucers, cups, and jug ;
Fell in a heap. All shapeless on the floor
Philip and Annie and the crockery lay.
Then Enoch's voice accompanied his foot,
For both were raised, with horrid oath and kick,
Till constables came in with Miriam Lane
And bare them all to prison, railing loud.
Then Philip was discharged and ran away,
And Enoch paid a fine for the assault ;
And Annie went to Philip, telling him
That she would see old Enoch further first
Before she would acknowledge him to be
Himself, if Philip only would return.
But Philip said that he would rather not.
Then Annie plucked such handfuls of his hair
Out of his head that ho was nearly bald.
But Enoch laughed and said, 'Well done, my girl.'

And so the two shook hands and made it up."

In 1869 Lewis Carroll published a little book of rhymes called *Phantasmagoria.* It chiefly related to Oxford. Partly because it was anonymous, partly because it was mainly topical, the book had no success. But it contained two or three parodies which deserve to rank with the best in the language. Unluckily I have not the book at hand, and if I give samples it must be from memory, and therefore with some risk of slips. One that I remember is an imitation of a ballad in black- letter. It runs something like this :

"I have a horse, a right good horse ;
Ne do I envy those
Who onward urge their heady course
Till sodayne on their nose
They light with unexpected force –
It is a Horse of Clothes."

Then, again, there is excellent metaphysical fooling in *The Three Voices.* But far the best parody in the book – and the most richly deserved by the absurdity of its original – is *Hiaivatha's Photographing.* It has the double merit of absolute similarity in cadence and lifelike realism. Here again I rely on memory, and the limits of space forbid complete citation :

"From his shoulders Hiawatha
Took the camera of rosewood,
Made of folding, sliding rosewood.
In its case it lay compacted,
Folded into next to nothing.
But he pulled the joints and hinges,
Pulled and pushed the joints and hinges,
Till it looked all squares and oblongs,
Like a complicated figure
In the Second Book of Euclid.
This he perched upon a tripod,
And the family in order
Sate before it for their portraits.
Mystic, awful was the process.
Every one as he was taken
Volunteered his own suggestions,
His invaluable suggestions.
First the Governor, the Father.
He suggested velvet curtains,
And the corner of a table,
Of a rosewood dining-table.
He would hold a scroll of something;
Hold it firmly in his left hand ;
He would have his right hand buried
(Like Napoleon) in his waistcoat;
He would contemplate the distance.

With a look of pensive meaning,
As of ducks that die in thunder.
Grand, heoric, was the notion,
Yet the picture failed completely,
Failed, because he moved a little;
Moved, because he could not help it."

Who does not know that Father in the flesh ? *and* who has not seen him – velvet curtains, dining-table, scroll, and all – on the most conspicuous "wall of the Royal Academy ? The Father being disposed of,

"Next his better half took courage,
She would have her portrait taken."

But her restlessness and questionings proved fatal to the result.

"Next the son, the Stunning Cantab.
He suggested curves of beauty,
Curves pervading all the figure,
Which the eye might follow onward,
Till they centred in the breastpin,
Centred in the golden breastpin.
He had learnt it all from Ruskin,
Author of the *Stones of Venice."*

But, in spite of such culture, the portrait was a failure, and the elder sister fared no better. Then the younger brother followed, and his portrait was so awful that –

"By comparison, the others
Might be thought to have succeeded –
To have partially succeeded."

Undaunted by these repeated failures, Hiawatha, by a great final effort, "tumbled all the tribe together "in the manner of a family group, and –

"Did at last obtain a picture
Where the faces all succeeded,
Each came out a perfect likeness.
Then they joined and all abused it.
Unrestrainedly abused it,
As the worst and ugliest picture
They could possibly have dreamed of;
Giving one such strange expressions,
Sulkiness, conceit, and meanness.
Really any one would take us
(Any one who didn't know us)
For the most unpleasant people.
Hiawatha seemed to think so,
Seemed to think it not unlikely."

How true to life is this final touch of indignation at the unflattering truth ! But time and space forbid me further to pursue the photographic song of Hiawatha.

Phantasmagoria filled an aching void during the ten years which elapsed between the appearance of *Verses and Translations* and that of *Fly Leaves.* The latter book is small, only 124 pages in all, including the Pic- wick Examination-Paper, but what marvels of mirth and poetry and satire it contains ! How secure its place in the affections of all who love the gentle art of parody ! My rule is not to quote extensively from books which are widely known ; but I must give myself the pleasureof quoting just six lines which even appreciative critics generally overlook. They relate to the conversation of the travelling tinker:

" Thus on he prattled like a babbling brook.
Then I: ' The sun hath slipt behind the hill,
And my Aunt Vivian dines at half-past six.'
So in all love we parted ; I to the Hall,
He to the village. It was noised next noon
That chickens had been miss'd at Syllabub Farm."

Will any one stake his literary reputation on the assertion that these lines are not really Tennyson's ?

SECTION 15

XXIX

PARODIES *IN* VERSE

I embarked upon the subject of metrical parody I said that it was a shoreless sea. For my own part, I enjoy sailing through these rippling waters, and cannot be induced to hurry the pace. Let us put in for a moment at Belfast. There in 1874 the British Association held its annual meeting, and Professor Tyndall delivered an inaugural address in which he revived and glorified the Atomic Theory of the Universe. His glowing peroration ran as follows : " Here I must quit a theme too great for me to handle, but which will be handled by the loftiest minds ages after you and I, like streaks of morning cloud, shall have melted into the infinite azure of the past." Shortly afterwards *Blackivood's Magazine,* always famous for its humorous and satiric verse, published a rhymed abstract of Tyndall's address, of which I quote (from memory) the concluding lines :

" Let us greatly honor the Atom, so lively, so wise, and so small;
The Atomists, too, let us honor – Epicurus, Lucretius, and all.
Let us damn with faint praise Bishop Butler, in whom many atoms combined
To form that remarkable structure which it pleased him to call his mind.
Next praise we the noble body to which, for the time, we belong

(Ere yet the swift course of the Atom hath hurried us breathless along) –
The British Association – like Leviathan worshipped by Hobbes,
The incarnation of wisdom built up of our witless nobs ;
Which will carry on endless discussion till I, and probably you,
Have *melted in infinite azure – and,* in short, till all is blue."

Surely this translation of the Professor's misplaced dithyrambics into the homeliest of colloquialisms is both good parody and just criticism.

In 1876 there appeared a clever little book (attributed to Sir Frederick Pollock) which was styled *Leading Cases done into English, by an Apprentice of Lincoln's Inn.* It appealed only to a limited public, for it is actually a collection of sixteen important law cases set forth, with explanatory notes, in excellent verse, imitated from poets great and small. Chaucer, Browning, Tennyson, Swinburne, Clough, Rossetti, and James Rhoades supply the models, and I have been credibly informed that the law is as good as the versification. Mr. Swinburne was in those days the favorite butt of young parodists, and the gem of the book is the dedication to " J. S.," or " John Styles," a mythical person, nearly related to John Doe and Richard Roe, with whom all budding jurists had in old days to make acquaintance. The disappearance of the venerated initials from modern law- books inspired the following:

" When waters are rent with commotion
Of storms, or with sunlight made whole,
The river still pours to the ocean
The stream of its effluent soul;
You, too, from all lips of all living,
Of worship disthroned and discrowned,
Shall know by these gifts of my giving
That faith is yet found ;
" By the sight of my song-flight of cases
That bears, on wings woven of rhyme,
Names set for a sign in high places
By sentence of men of old time;
From all counties they meet and they mingle,
Dead suitors whom Westminster saw ;
They are many, but your name is single,
Pure flower of pure law.
" So I pour you this drink of my verses,
Of learning made lovely with lays,
Song hitter and sweet that rehearses
The deeds of your eminent days;
Yea, in these evil days from their reading
Some profit a student shall draw,
Though some points are of obsolete pleading,
And some are not law.
" Though the Courts, that were manifold, dwindle
To divers Divisions of One,
And on fire from your face may rekindle

The light of old learning undone ;
We have suitors and briefs for our payment,
While, so long as a Court shall hold pleas,
We talk moonshine with wigs for our raiment,
Not sinking the fees."

Some five - and - twenty years ago there appeared the first number of a magazine called *The Dark Blue.* It was published in London, but was understood to represent in some occult way the thought and life of Young Oxford, and its contributors were mainly Oxford men. The first number contained an amazing ditty called " The Sun of my Songs." It was dark, and mystic, and transcendental, and unintelligible. It dealt extensively in strange words and cryptic phrases. One verse I must transcribe: –

" Yet all your song
Is – 'Ding dong.
Summer is dead,
Spring is dead –
O my heart, and O my head I
Go a-singing a silly song,
All wrong,
For all is dead.
Ding dong,
And I am dead !
Dong!' "

I quote thus fully because Cambridge, never backward in poking fun at her more romantic sister on the Isis, shortly afterwards produced an excellent little magazine named sarcastically *The Light Green,* and devoted to the ridicule of its cerulean rival. The poem from which I have just quoted was thus burlesqued, if indeed burlesque of such a composition were possible :

" Ding dong, ding dong,
There goes the gong;
Dick, come along,
It is time for dinner.
Wash your face,
Take your place.
Where's your grace,
You little sinner ?
Baby cry,
(Wipe his eye.
Baby good,
Give him food.
Baby sleepy,
Go to bed.
Baby naughty,
Smack his head !"

The Light Green, which had only an ephemeral life, was, I have always heard, entirely, or almost entirely, the work of one undergraduate. I believe that his name was Hilton, and that he died young. Beyond that I have never been able to get any account of him; but he certainly had the knack of catching and reproducing style. The " May Exam." is a really good imitation of"The May Queen." The departing undergraduate thus addresses his "gyp":

"When the men come up again, Filcher, and the Term is at its
height,
You'll never see me more in these long gay rooms at night; When the 'old dry wines' are circling, and the claret-cup flows
cool, And the loo is fast and furious, with a fiver in the pool."

In 1872 Lewis Carroll brought out *Through the Looking-glass,* and every one who has ever read that pretty work of poetic fancy, will remember the ballad of the Walrus and the Carpenter. It was parodied in *The Light Green* under the title of the "Vulture and the Husbandman." This poem described the agonies of a *viva-voce* examination, and it derived its title from two facts of evil omen – that the Vulture plucks its victim, and that the Husbandman makes his living by ploughing:

" Two undergraduates came up,
And slowly took a seat,
They kuit their brows, and bit their thumbs,
As if they found them sweet;
And this was odd, because, you know,
Thumbs are not good to eat.
"'The time has come,' the Vulture said,
' To talk of many things –
Of Accidence and Adjectives,
And names of Jewish Kings ;
How many notes a Sackbut has,
And whether Shawms have strings.'
" ' Please, sir,' the Undergraduates said,
Turning a little blue,
'We did not know that was the sort
Of thing we had to do.'
'We thank you much,' the Vulture said;
' Send up another two.'"

The base expedients to which an examination reduces its victims are hit off with much dexterity in "The Heathen Pass-ee " – a parody of an American poem which is too familiar to justify quotation:

" Tom Crib was his name,
And I shall not deny,
In regard to the same.
What that name might imply ;
But his face it was trustful and childlike,
And he had the most innocent eye.
" On the cuffs of his shirt
He had managed to get
What he hoped had been dirt,

But which proved, I regret,
To be notes on the Rise of the Drama –
A question invariably set.
" In the crown of his cap
Were the Furies and Fates,
And a delicate map
Of the Dorian States ;
And we found in his palms, which were hollow,
What are frequent in palms – that is, dates."

Deservedly dear to the heart of English youth are the Nonsense Rhymes of Edward Lear. It will be recollected that the form of the verse as originally constructed reproduced the final word of the first line at the end of the fifth, thus :

"There was an old person of Basing
Whose presence of mind was amazing ;
He purchased a steed
Which he rode at full speed,
And escaped from the people of Basing."

But in the process of development it became unusual to find a new word for the end of the fifth line, thus atonce securing a threefold rhyme and introducing the element of unexpectedness, instead of inevitableness, into the conclusion. Thus *The Light Green* sang of the Colleges in which it circulated :

"There was an old Fellow of Trinity,
A Doctor well versed in divinity;
But he took to free-thinking,
And then to deep drinking,
And so had to leave the vicinity."

And –

"There was a young genius of Queen's
Who was fond of explosive machines;
He blew open a door,
But he'll do so no more ;
For it chanced that that door was the Dean's."

And –

"There was a young gourmand of John's
Who'd a notion of dining off swans ;
To the 'Backs' he took big nets
To capture the cygnets,
But was told they were kept for the Dons."

So far *The Light Green,*

Not at all dissimilar in feeling to these ebullitions of youthful fancy were the parodies of nursery rhymes which the lamented Corney Grain invented for one of his most popular entertainments, and used to accompany on the piano in his own inimitable style. I well remember the opening verse of one, in which an incident in the social career of a Liberal millionaire was understood to be immortalized :

" Old Mr. Parvenu gave a great ball,

And of all his smart guests he knew no one at all;
Old Mr. Parvenu went up to bed,
And his guests said good-night to the butler instead."

Twenty years ago we were in the crisis of the great Jingo fever, and Lord Beaconsfield's antics in the East were frightening all sober citizens out of their senses. It was at that period that the music-halls rang with the "Great MacDermott's" Tyrtaean strain :

" We don't want to fight; but, by Jingo, if we do, We've got the ships, we've got the men, we've got the money too,"

and the word "Jingo" took its place in the language as the recognized symbol of a warlike policy. At Easter, 1878, it was announced that the Government were bringing black troops from India to Malta to aid our English forces in whatever enterprises lay before them. The refrain of the music-hall was instantly adapted with great effect, even the grave *Spectator* giving currency to the parody :

"We don't want to fight; but, by Jingo, if we do,
We won't go to the front ourselves, but we'll send the mild Hindoo."

Two years passed. Lord Beaconsfield was deposed. The tide of popular feeling turned in favor of Liberalism, and " Jingo" became a term of reproach. Mr. Tennyson, as he then was, endeavored to revive the patriotic spirit of his countrymen by publishing "Hands All Round " – a poem which had the distinguished honor of being quoted in the House of Commons by Sir Ellis Ash- mead-Bartlett. Forthwith an irreverent parodist – some say Mr. Andrew Lang – appeared with the following counterblast :

DRINKS ALL ROUND.

(Being an attempt to arrange Mr. Tennyson's noble words for truly patriotic, Protectionist, and Anti-aboriginal circles.)

"A health to Jingo first, and then
A health to shell, a health to shot!
The man who hates not other men
I deem no perfect patriot.
To all who hold all England mad
We drink ; to all who'd tax her food!
We pledge the man who hates the Rad.!
We drink to Bartle Frere and Froude 1
"Drinks all round!
Here's to Jiugo, king and crowned !
To the great cause of Jingo drink, my boys,
And the great name of Jingo, round and round 1
" To all the companies that long
To rob, as folk robbed years ago ;
To all that wield the double thong,
From Queensland round to Borneo 1
To all that, under Indian skies,
Call Aryan man a 'blasted nigger";
To all rapacious enterprise;
To rigor everywhere, and vigor 1

" Drinks all round !
Here's to Jingo, king and crowned !
To the great name of Jingo drink, my boys,
And every filibuster, round and round 1
" To all our Statesmen, while they see
An outlet new for British trade,
Where British fabrics still may be
With British size all overweighed!
Wherever gin and guns are sold
We've scooped the artless nigger in;
Where men give ivory and gold,
We give them measles, tracts, and gin 1
" Drinks all round !
Here's to Jingo, king and crowned !
To the great name of Jingo drink, my boys,
And to Adulteration, round and round I"

The Jingo fever having abated, another malady appeared in the body politic. Trouble broke out in Ireland, and in January, 1881, Parliament was summoned to pass Mr. Forster's Coercion Act. My diary for that date supplies me with the following excellent imitation of a veteran Poet of Freedom rushing with ardent sympathy into the Irish struggle against Gladstonian tyranny :

A L'IRLANDE.
Par Victor Hugo.

O Irlande, grand pays du shillelagh et du bog,
Oft les patriotes vont toujours ce qu'on appelle le whole hog,
Aujourd'hui je prends la plume, moi qui est vieux,
Pour dire au grand patriot Parnell, ' How d'ye do ?'
Erin, aux armes ! le whisky vous donne la force
De se battre l'un pour l'autre comme les fameux FrtSres Corses.
Votre Land League et vos Home Rulers sont des liberateurs.
Payez la valuation de Griffith et n'ayez pas peur.
De la tenure la fixite c'est l'astre de vos rSves,
Que Rory des Collines vit et que les lanclgrabbers crevent;
Moi, je suis vieux, mais dans l'ombre je vois clair,
Bient6t serez-vous maltres de vos bonnes pommes de terre.
C'est le brave Biggar, le T. P. O'Connor, et les autres
Qui sont vos sauveurs, comme Gambetta etait le noire ;
Suivez-les, et la victoire sera tou jours 8, vous,
Si & Milbank ce cher Forster ne vous envoie pas. Hooroo !"

By the time that these lines were written the late Mr. J. K. Stephen – affectionately known by his friends as "Jem Stephen" – was beginning to be recognized as an extraordinarily good writer of humorous verse. His performances in this line were not collected till ten years later ("Lapsus Calami," 1891), and his brilliant career was cut short by the results of an accident in 1892. I reproduce the following sonnet, not only because I think it an excellent criticism aptly expressed, but because I desire to pay my tribute of admiration to the memory of one of whom all men spoke golden words :

" Two voices are there : one is of the deep;
It learns the storm-cloud's thunderous melody,
Now roars, now murmurs with the changing sea,
Now bird-like pipes, now closes soft in sleep;
And one is of an old, half-witted sheep
Which bleats articulate monotony,
And indicates that two and one are three,
That grass is green, lakes damp, aud mountains steep;
And, Wordsworth, both are thine. At certain times
Forth from the heart of thy melodious rhymes
The form and pressure of high thoughts will burst;
At other times – Good Lord I I'd rather be
Quite unacquainted with the A, B, C
Than write such hopeless rubbish as thy worst."

I hope that there are few among my readers who have not in their time known and loved the dear old ditty which tells us how

"There was a youth, and a well-belovSd youth,
And he was a squire's son,
And he loved the Bailiff's daughter dear
Who dwelt at Islington."

Well, to all who have followed that touching story of love and grief I commend the following version of it. French, after all, is the true language of sentiment:

"II y avait un gargon,
Fort aimable et fort bon,
Qui etait le flls du Lord Mayor;
Et il aimait la fille
D'un sergent de ville
Qui dcmeurait 3, Leycesster Sqvare.
"Mais elle etait un peu prude,
Et n'avait pas 1'babitude
De coqueter, comme les autres demoiselles ;
Jusqu'3, ce que Lord Mayor
(Homme brutal, comme tous les pSres)
L'eloigna de sa tourterelle.
"Apres quelques ans d'absence
Au rencontre elle s'elance ;
Elle se fait une toilette de tres bon goflt –
Des pantoufles sur les pieds,
Bes lunettes sur le uez,
Et un collier sur le cou – c'etait tout!
" Mais bientot elle s'assit
Dans la rue Piccadilli,
Car il f aisait extrSmement chaud ;

Et 1& elle vit s'avancer

L'unique objet de ses pensees,

Sur le plus magniflque de chevaux I

" ' Je suis pauvre et sans ressource !

Prfite, pr§te-moi ta bourse,

Ou ta montre, pour me montrer confiance.' ' Jeune femme, je ne vous connais, Ainsi il faut me donner

Une adresse et quelques references.'

" 'Mou adresse – c'est Leycesster Sqvare, Et pour reference j'espere

Que la statue de Shakespeare vous suffira.' ' Ah ! connais tu, ma mie, La die du sergent ?' ' Si; Mais elle est movte comme un rat 1'

" ' Si defunte est ma belle, Prenez, s'il vous plait, ma selle,

Et ma bride, et mon cheval incomparable ; Car il ne faut rien dire, Mais vite, vite m'ensevelir Dans un desert sec et desagreable.'

" 'Ah ! mon brave, arrfite-toi.

Je suis ton unique choix ;

La fille du sergent sans peur!

Pour mon trousseau, c'est modeste,

Vous le voyez ! Pour le reste,

Je t'epouse dans une demi-heure 1"

" Mais le jeune homme epouvant§

Sur son cheval vite remontait,

La liberte lui etait trop chere 1 Et la pauvre fille degofitee N'avait qu'a, reprendre sa route, et Son adresse est encore Leycesster Sqvare."

The chiefs of the Permanent Civil Service are not usually, as Swift said, " Blasted with poetic fire," but this delightful ditty is from the pen of Mr. Henry Graham, the Clerk of the Parliaments.

Of the metrical parodists of the present hour two are extremely good. Mr. Owen Seaman is, beyond and before all his rivals, " up to date," and pokes his lyrical fun at such songsters as Mr. Alfred Austin, Mr. William Watson, Mr. Rudyard Kipling, and Mr. Richard Le Gal- lienne. But " Q " is content to try his hand on poets of more ancient standing; and he is not only of the school but of the lineage of " C. S. C." I have said before that I forbear as a rule to quote from books as easily accessible as *Green Bays*; but is there a branch of the famous " Omar Khayyam Club" in Manchester ? If there be, to it I dedicate the last handful of precious stuff which I have gathered on this long voyage, only apologizing to the uninitiated reader for the pregnant allusiveness, which none but a sworn Khayyamite can perfectly apprehend :

"MEASURE FOR MEASURE.

" Wake ! for the closed Pavilion doors Lave kept

Their silence while the white-eyed Kaffir slept,

And wailed the Nightingale with 'Jug, jug, jug!'

Whereat, for empty cup, the White Rose wept.

" Enter with me where yonder door hangs out

Its Red Triangle to a world of drought,

Inviting to the Palace of the Djinn,

Where death, Aladdin, waits as Chuckerout.
" Melhought, last night, that one in suit of woe
Stood by the Tavern-door and whispered, ' Lo 1
The Pledge departed, what avails the Cup ?
Then take the Pledge and let the Wine-cup go.'
' But I: ' For every thirsty soul that drains
This Anodyne of Thought its rim contains –
Freewill the *can,* Necessity the *must;*
Pour off the *must,* and, see, the *can* remains.
' 'Then, pot or glass, why label it *"With care"1*
Or why your Sheepskin with my Gourd compare ?
Lo! here the Bar and I the only Judge: O, Dog that bit me, I exact a hair!'"

VERBAL INFELICITIES

Se non I vero, said a very great Lord Mayor within the last few weeks, $ *ben traviata.* His lordship's linguistic slip served him right. Latin is fair play, though some of us are in the condition of the auctioneer in *The Mill on the Floss* who had brought away with him from Mud- port Grammar School "a sense of understanding Latin generally, though his comprehension of any particular Latin was not ready." Bnt to qnote from any other language is to commit an outrage on your guests. The late Sir Robert Fowler was, I believe, the only Lord Mayor who ever ventured to quote Greek, but I have heard him do it, and have seen the turtle-fed company smile with alien lips in the painful attempt to look as if they understood it, and in abject terror lest their neighbor should ask them to translate. The late Mr. James Payn used to tell a pleasing tale of a learned clergyman who quoted Greek at dinner. The lady who was sitting by Mr. Payn inquired in a whisper what one of these quotations meant. He gave her to understand, with a well-assumed blush, that it was scarcely fit for a lady's ear. " Good heavens !" she exclaimed ; " you don't mean to say – " " Please don't ask any more," said Payn, pleadingly, " I really could not tell you." Which was true to the ear, if not to the sense.

Municipal eloquence has been time out of mind a storehouse of delight. It was, according to tradition, aprovincial mayor who, blessed with a numerous progeny, publicly expressed the pious hope that his sons might grow up to be better citizens than their father, and his daughters more virtuous women than their mother. There was a worthy alderman at Oxford in my time who was entertained at a public dinner on his retirement from civic office. In replying to the toast of his health, he said it had always been his anxious endeavor to administer justice without swerving to " partiality on the one hand or impartiality on the other." Surely he must have been near kin to the moralist who always tried to tread "the narrow path which lay between right and wrong"; or, perchance, to the newly elected mayor who, in returning thanks for his elevation, said that during his year of office he should lay aside all his political prepossessions and be, " like Caesar's wife, all things to all men." It was said of my old friend the late Dean Burgon that once, in a sermon on the transcendent merits of the Anglican School of Theology, he exclaimed, with a fervor which was all his own, "May I live the life of a Taylor, and die the death of a Bull!"

The admirable Mr. Brooke, when he purposed to contest the Borough of Middlemarch, found Will Ladislaw extremely useful, because he "remembered what the right quotations are – *Omne tulit punctum,* and that sort of thing." And certainly an apt quotation is one of the most effective decorations of a public speech; but the dangers of inappositeness are correspondingly formidable. I have always heard that the most infelicitous quotation on record was made by the fourth Lord Fitz- william at a county meeting held at York to raise a fund for the repair of the Minster after the fire which so nearly destroyed it in 1829. Previous speakers had, naturally, appealed to the pious munificence of Churchmen. Lord Fitzwilliam, as the leading Whig of thecounty, thought that it would be an excellent move to enlist the sympathies of the rich Nonconformists, and that he was the man to do it. So he perorated somewhat after the following fashion : " And if the liberality of Yorkshire Churchmen proves insufficient to restore the chief glory of our native county, then, with all confidence, I turn to our excellent Dissenting brethren, and I exclaim, with the Latin poet,

"Flectere si nequco superos, Acheronta movebo."

Mr. Anstey Guthrie has some pleasant instances of texts misapplied. He was staying once in a Scotch country-house where, over his bed, hung an illuminated scroll with the inscription, "Occupy till I come," which, as Mr. Guthrie justly observes, is an unusually extended invitation, even for Scottish notions of hospitality. According to the same authority, the leading citizen of a seaside town erected some iron benches on the sea front, and, with the view of at once commemorating his own munificence and giving a profitable turn to the thoughts of the sitters, inscribed on the backs –

THESE BEATS

WERE PRESENTED TO THE TOWN OP SHINGLETON

BY

JOSEPH BUGGINS, Esq.,

J. P. FOB THE BOROUGH.

"the Bea is His And He Made It."

Nothing is more deeply rooted in the mind of the average man than that certain well-known aphorisms of piety are to be found in the Bible – possibly in that lost book, the Second Epistle to the Ephesians, which Dickens must have had in his mind when he wrote in *Dombey and Son* of the First Epistle to that Church. "In the midst of life we are in death" is a favoritequotation from this imaginary Scripture. "His end was peace " holds its place on many a tomb in virtue of a similar belief. " He tempers the wind to the shorn lamb" is, I believe commonly attributed to Solomon; and a charming song which was popular in my youth declared that, though the loss of friends was sad, it would have been much sadder

"Had we ne'er heard that Scripture word,

'Not lost, but gone before.'"

Mrs. Gamp, with some hazy recollections of the New Testament floating in her mind, invented the admirable aphorism that "Bich folks may ride on camels, but it ain't so easy for 'em to see out of a needle's eye." And a lady of my acquaintance, soliloquizing on the afflictions of life and the serenity of her own temper, exclaimed, "How true it is what Solomon says, 'A contented spirit is like a perpetual dropping on a rainy day!'"

A Dissenting minister, winding up a week's mission, is reported to have said, "And if any spark of grace has been kindled by these exercises, oh, we pray thee, *water that spark."* An old peasant-woman in Buckinghamshire, extolling the merits of her favorite curate, said to the rector, " I do say that Mr. Woods is quite an angel in sheep's clothing;" and Dr. Liddon told me of a Presbyterian minister who was called on at short notice to officiate at the parish-church of Crathie in the presence of the Queen, and, transported by this tremendous experience, burst forth in rhetorical supplication : " Grant that as she grows to be an old woman she may be made a new man; and that in all righteous causes she may go forth before her people like a he-goat on the mountains."

Undergraduates, whose wretched existence for a week before each examination is spent in the hasty acquisition of much ill-assorted and indigestible knowledge, are not seldom the victims of similar confusions. At Oxford – and, for all I know, at Cambridge too – a hideous custom prevails of placing before the examinee a list of isolated texts, and requiring him to supply the name of the speaker, the occasion, and the context.

Question. "'My punishment is greater than I can bear.' Who said this ? Under what circumstances ?"

Answer. "Agag, when he was hewn in pieces."

One wonders at what stage of the process he began to think it was going a little too far. " What' is faith *?"* inquired an examiner in " Pass-Divinity." "Faith is the faculty by which we are enabled to believe that which we know is not true," replied the undergraduate;. who had learned his definition by heart, but imperfectly, frm a popular cram-book. A superficial knowledge of HteKr ture may sometimes be a snare. " Can you give me any particulars of Oliver Cromwell's death ?" asked an Examiner in History in 1874. " Oh yes, sir," eagerly replied the victim; " he exclaimed, ' Had I but served my God as I have served my King, He would not in mine age have left me naked to mine enemies.'"

" Things one would rather have expressed differently" are, I believe, a discovery of Mr. Punch's. Of course he did not create them. They must be as old as human nature itself. The history of their discovery is not unlike that of another epoch-making achievement of the same great genius, as set forth in the preface to *The Book of Snobs.* First, the world was made ; then, as a matter of course, snobs ; they existed for years arid years, and were no more known than America. But presently – *ingens patebat tellus* – people became darkly aware that there was such a race. Then in time a name arose to designate that race. That name has spread over England like railroads. Snobs are known and recognized throughout an Empire on which the sun never sets. *Punch* appeared at the ripe season to chronicle their history, and the individual came forth to write that history in *Punch.*

Mutatis mutandis, we may apply this historical method to the origin and discovery of " Things one would rather have expressed differently." They must have existed as loug as language; they must have flourished wherever men and women encountered one another in social intercourse. But the glory of having discovered them, recognized them, classified them, and established them among the permanent sources of human enjoyment belongs to Mr. Punch alone.

He was the first that ever burst
Into that silent sea.
Let us humbly follow in his wake.

We shall see later on that no department of human speech is altogether free from " Things one would rather have expressed differently "; but, naturally, the great bulk of them belong to social conversation; and just as the essential quality of a " bull" is that it expresses substantial sense in the guise of verbal nonsense, so the social " Thing one would rather have expressed differently," to be really precious, must show a polite intention struggling with verbal infelicity. Mr. Corney Grain, narrating his early experiences as a social entertainer, used to describe

an evening party given by the Dowager Duchess of S
at which he was engaged to play and sing. Late in the
evening the young Duke of S came in, and Mr. Grain
heard his mother prompting him in an anxious undertone : " Pray go and say something civil to Mr. Grain. You know he's quite a gentleman – not a common professional person." Thus instructed, the young Duke strolled up to the piano and said: " Good evening, Mr. Grain. I'm sorry I am so late, and have missed your performance.

Bnt I was at Lady 's. *We had a dancing-dog there."*

The married daughter of one of the most brilliant men of the Queen's reign has an only child. An amiable matron of her acquaintance, anxious to be thoroughly kind,
said, "Oh, Mrs. W , I hear that you have such a
clever little boy." Mrs. W., beaming with a mother's pride, replied, " Well, yes, I think Roger is rather a sharp little fellow." " Yes," replied her friend. "How often one sees that – the talent skipping a generation !" A stately old rector in Buckinghamshire – a younger son of a great family – whom I knew well in my youth, had, and was justly proud of, a remarkably pretty and well- appointed rectory. To him an acquaintance, coming for the first time to call, genially exclaimed : " What a delightful rectory ! Really a stranger arriving in the village, and not knowing who lived here, would take it for a gentleman's house." One of our best-known novelists, the most sensitively courteous of men, arriving very late at a dinner-party, was overcome with confusion – " I am truly sorry to be so shockingly late." The genial hostess, only meaning to assure him that he was not the last,
emphatically replied: "Oh, Mr. , you can't come too
late." A member of the present Cabinet was engaged with his wife and daughter to dine at a friend's house in the height of the season. The daughter fell ill at the last moment, and her parents first telegraphed her excuses for dislocating the party, and then repeating them earnestly on arriving. The hostess, receiving them with the most cordial sympathy, exclaimed : " Oh, it doesn't matter the least to us, we are only so sorry for your daughter." An eminent authoress who lives not a hundred miles from Richmond Hill was asked, in my hearing, if she had been to "write her name" at White Lodge, in Richmond Park (where the late Duchess of Teck lived), on the occasion of an important event in the Duchess's family. She replied that she had not, because she did not know the Duchess, and saw no use in adding another stranger's signature to

the enormous list. " Oh, that's a pity," was the rejoinder; " the Eoyal Family think more of the quantity of names than the quality."

In all these cases the courtesy of the intention was manifest; but sometimes it is less easy to discover. Not long ago Sir Henry Irving most kindly went down to one of our great Public Schools to give some Shake- sperian recitations. Talking over the arrangements with the Head Master, who is not a man of felicities and facilities, he said: "Each piece will take about an hour; and there must be fifteen minutes' interval between the two." "Oh! certainly," replied the Head Master; "yon couldn't expect the boys to stand two hours of it without a break." The newly appointed rector of one of the chief parishes in London was entertained at dinner by a prominent member of the congregation. Conversation turned on the use of stimulants as an aid to intellectual and physical effort, and Mr. Gladstone's historic egg-flip was cited. " Well, for my own part," said the divine, " I am quite independent of that kind of help. The only occasion in my life when I used anything of the sort was when I was in for my tripos at Cambridge, and then, by the doctor's order, I took a dose of strychnine, in order to clear the brain." The hostess, in a tone of the deepest interest, inquired, " How soon did the effect pass off ?" and the rector, a man of academical distinction, who had done his level best in his inaugural sermons on the previous Sunday, didn't half like the question.

Not long ago I was dining with one of the City Companies. On my right was another guest – a member of the Worshipful Company of Butchers. We had a long and genial conversation on the state of trade and othertopics relevant to Smithfield, when, in the midst of it, I was suddenly called on to return thanks for the visitors. The chairman, in proposing the toast, was good enough to speak of my belongings and myself in far too nattering terms, to which I hope that I suitably responded. When I resumed my seat my butcher-friend exclaimed, with the most obvious sincerity: "I declare, sir, I'm quite ashamed of myself. To think that I have been sitting alongside of a gentleman all the evening, and never found it out!"

The doorkeepers and attendants at the House of Commons are all old servants, who generally have lived in great families, and have obtained their places through influential recommendations. One of these fine old men encountered, on the opening day of a new Parliament, a young sprig of a great family who had just been for the first time elected to the House of Commons, and thus accosted him with tears in his eyes : " I am glad indeed, sir, to see you here; and when I think that I helped to put your noble grandfather and grandmother both into their coffins, it makes me feel quite at home with you." Never, surely, was a political career more impressively auspicated.

These Verbal Infelicities are by no means confined to social intercourse. Lord Cross, when the House laughed at his memorable speech in favor of Spiritual Peers, exclaimed in solemn remonstrance, " I hear a smile." When the Bishop of Southwell, preaching in the London Mission of 1885, began his sermon by saying, " I feel a feeling which I feel you all feel," it is only fair to assume that he said something which he would rather have expressed differently. Quite lately I heard a Radical rhetorician exclaim, " If the Liberal party is to maintain its position, it must move forward." A clerically minded orator, fresh from a signal triumph at a Diocesan Conference, informed me, together with some hundreds of other hearers, that when his Resolution was put " quite a shower of hands went up "; and at a missionary meeting I once heard that impressive personage, " the Deputation from the parent society," involve himself very delightfully in extemporaneous imagery. He had been explaining that here in England we hear so much of the rival systems and operations of the Society for the Propagation of the Gospel and the Church Missionary Society that we are often led to regard them as hostile institutions; whereas if, as he himself had done, his hearers would go out to the mission field and observe the working of the societies at close quarters, they would find them to be in essential unison. " Even so," he exclaimed ; " as I walked in the beautiful park which adjoins your town to-day, I noticed what appeared at a distance to be one gigantic tree. It was only when I got close to it and sat down under its branches that I perceived that what I had thought was one tree was really two trees – as completely distinct in origin, growth, and nature as if they had stood a hundred miles apart." No one in the audience (besides myself) noticed the infelicity of the illustration; nor do I think that the worthy "Deputation," if he had perceived it, would have had the presence of mind to act as a famous preacher did in like circumstances, and, throwing up his hands, exclaim, " Oh, blessed contrast *I"*

But it does not always require verbal infelicity to produce a " Thing one would rather have expressed differently." The mere misplacement of a comma will do it. A highly distinguished graduate of Oxford determined to enter the Nonconformist ministry, and, quite unnecessarily, published a manifesto setting forth his reasons and his intentions. In his enumeration of the various methods by which he was going to mark his aloofness fromthe sacerdotalism of the Established Church, he wrote : – " I shall wear no clothes, to distinguish me from my fellow-Christians." Need I say that all the picture-shops of the University promptly displayed a fancy portrait of the newly fledged minister clad in what Artemus Ward called "the scandalous style of the Greek slave," and bearing the unkind inscription: " The Rev. X. Y. Z. distinguishing himself from his fellow-Christians"?

An imperfect sympathy with the prepossessions of one's environment may often lead the unwary talker to give a totally erroneous impression of his meaning. Thus the Professor of Sanskrit at Oxford once brought an Indian army - chaplain to dine at the high table of Oriel, and in the common-room after dinner the Fellows courteously turned the conversation to the subject of life and work in India, on which the chaplain held forth with fluency and zest. When he had made an end of speaking, the Professor of Anglo - Saxon, who was not only a very learned scholar, but also a very devout clergyman, leaned forward and said, "I am a little hard of hearing, sir, but from what I could gather I rejoice to infer that you consider the position of an army-chaplain in India a hopeful field." "Hopeful field indeed," replied the chaplain ; " I should rather think so ! You begin at $400 a year *I"*

A too transparent honesty which reveals each transient emotion through the medium of suddenly chosen words is not without its perils. None that heard it can ever forget Norman Macleod's story of the Presbyterian minister who, when he noticed champagne - glasses on the dinner - table, began his grace, " Bountiful Jehovah !" but, when he saw only claret-glasses, subsided into, "We are not worthy of the least of Thy mercies." I deny the right of Bishop Wilberforce in narrating this story in his diary to stigmatize this good man as "gluttonous." Hewas simply honest, and his honesty led him into one of those " Things one would rather have expressed differently." But, however expressed, the meaning would have been the same, and equally sound.

Absence of mind, of course, conversationally slays its thousands, though perhaps more by the way of " Things one would rather have left unsaid " than by " Things one would rather have expressed differently." The late Archbishop Trench, a man of singularly vague and dreamy habits, resigned the See of Dublin on account of advancing years, and settled in London. He once went back to pay a visit to his successor, Lord Plunket. Finding himself back again in his old palace, sitting at his old dinner - table, and gazing across it at his old wife, he lapsed in memory to the days when he was master of the house, and gently remarked to Mrs. Trench, " I am afraid, my dear, that we must put this cook down among our failures." Delight of Lord and Lady Plunket!

Medical men are sometimes led by carelessness of phrase into giving their patients shocks. The country doctor who, combining in his morning's round a visit to the Squire and another to the Vicar, said that he was trying to kill two birds with one stone, would probably have expressed himself differently if he had premeditated his remark ; and a London physician who found his patient busy composing a book of Recollections, and asked, " Why have you put it off so long ?" uttered a " Thing one would rather have left unsaid." The "donniest" of Oxford dons in an unexampled fit of good nature once undertook to discharge the duties of the chaplain of Oxford jail during the Long Vacation. Unluckily it so fell out that he had to perform the terrible office of preparing a condemned felon for execution, and it was felt that he said a " Thing one would rather have expressed differently," when, at the close of his final interview, heleft the condemned cell observing, "Well, at eight o'clock to-morrow morning, then."

The path of those who inhabit Courts is thickly beset with pitfalls. There are so many things that must be left unsaid, and so many more that must be expressed differently. Who does not know the " Copper Horse " at Windsor – that equestrian statue at the end of the Long Walk, to which (and back again) the local flyman always offers to drive the tourist ? The Queen was entertaining a great man, who, in the afternoon, walked from the Castle to Cumberland Lodge. At dinner Her Majesty, full, as always, of gracious solicitude for the comfort of her guests, said, " I hope you were not tired by your long walk?" "Oh, not at all, thank yon, ma'am. I got a lift back as far as the Copper Horse." " As far as what ?" inquired Her Majesty, in palpable astonishment. " Oh, the Copper Horse, at the end of the Long Walk !" " That's not a copper horse. That's my grandfather !"

A little learning is proverbially dangerous, and often lures vague people into unsuspected perils. One of the most charming ladies of my acquaintance, remonstrating with her mother for letting the fire go out on a rather chilly day, exclaimed : " Oh ! dear mamma, how could yon be so careless ? If yon had been a Vestal Virgin you would have been bricked up." When the London County Council first came into existence, it used to assemble in the Guildhall, and the following dialogue took place between a highly cultured councillor and one of his commercial colleagues:

Cultured Councillor: " The acoustics of this place seem very bad."

Commercial Councillor (sniffing): " Indeed, sir ? I haven't perceived anything unpleasant."

A well-known lady had lived for some years in a housein Harley Street which contained some fine ornamentation by Angelica Kauffman, and, on moving to another quarter of the town, she loudly lamented the loss of her former drawing-room, "for it was so beautifully painted by Fra Angelico."

Mistakes of idiom are naturally the prolific parents of error, or, as Mrs. Lirriper said, with an admirable confusion of metaphors, breed fruitful hot water for all parties concerned. " The wines of this hotel leave one nothing to hope for," was the alluring advertisement of a Swiss innkeeper who thought that his vintage left nothing to be desired. Lady Dufferin, in her Reminiscences of Viceregal Life, has some excellent instances of the same sort. "Your Enormity" is a delightful variant on " Your Excellency," and there is something really pathetic in the Baboo's benediction, "You have been very good to us, and may Almighty God give you tit for tat." But to deride these errors of idiom scarcely lies in the mouth of an Englishman. A friend of mine, wishing to express his opinion that a Frenchman was an idiot, told

him that he was a " cretonne." Lord R , preaching

at the French Exhibition, implored his hearers to come and drink of the " eau de vie"; and a good-natured Cockney, complaining of the incivility of French drivers, said : " It is so uncalled for, because I always try to make things pleasant by beginning with 'Bonjour, Cochon.'" Even in our own tongue Englishmen sometimes come to grief over an idiomatic proverb. In a debate in Convocation at Oxford, Dr. Liddon, referring to a concession made by the opposite side, said, "It is proverbially ungracious to look a gift horse *in the face."* And though the undergraduates in the gallery roared " Mouth, sir ; mouth !" till they were hoarse, the Angelic Doctor never perceived the unmeaningness of his proverb.

Some years ago a complaint of inefficiency was pre- u 305 -

ferred against a workhouse - chaplain, and, when the Board of Guardians came to consider the case, one of the Guardians, defending the chaplain, observed that " Mr.

P was only fifty-two, and had a mother running

about." Commenting on this line of defence, a newspaper, which took the view hostile to the chaplain, caustically remarked : " On this principle, the more athletic or restless were a clergyman's relatives, the more valuable an acquisition would he himself be to the Church. Supposing that some Embertide a bishop were fortunate enough to secure among his candidates for ordination a a man who, in addition to ' a mother running about/ had a brother who gained prizes at Lillie Bridge, and a cousin who pulled in the 'Varsity Eight, and a nephew who was in the School Eleven, to say nothing of a grandmother who had St. Vitus's dance, and an aunt in the country whose mind wandered, then surely Dr. Liddon himself would have to look out for his laurels."

The " Things one would rather have expressed differently " for which reporters are responsible are of course legion. I forbear to quote such familiar instances *aa* "the shattered libertine of debate," applied to Mr. Ber- nal Osborne, and " the roaring loom of the *Times,"* when Mr. Lowell had spoken of the "roaring loom of time." I content myself with two which occurred in my own immediate circle. A clerical uncle of mine took the Blue Ribbon in his old age, and at a public meeting stated that his reason for so doing was that for thirty years he liad been trying to cure drunkards by making them drink in moderation, but had never once succeeded. He was thus reported : " The rev. gentleman stated that his reason for taking the Blue Ribbon was that for thirty years he had been trying to drink in moderation, but had never once succeeded." Another near relation of mine, protesting on a public platform against some misrepresentation by opponents, said : " The worst enemy that any cause can have to fight is a double lie in the shape of half a truth." The newspaper which reported the proceedings gave the sentiment thus : " The worst enemy that any cause can have to fight is a double eye in the shape of half a tooth." And, when an indignant remonstrance was addressed to the editor, he blandly said that he certainly had not understood the phrase, but imagined it must be a quotation from an old writer.

But, if journalistic reporting on which some care and thought are bestowed sometimes proves so misleading, common rumor is far more prolific of things which would have been better expressed differently. It is now (thank goodness!) a good many years since " spelling-bees" were a favorite amusement in London drawing-rooms. The late Lady Combermere, an octogenarian dame who retained a sempiternal taste for *les petits jeux innocents,* kindly invited a young curate whom she had been asked to befriend to take part in a "spelling-bee." He got on splendidly for a while and then broke down among the repeated "n's" in "drunkenness." Returuing crestfallen to his suburban parish, he was soon gratified by hearing the rumor that he had been turned out of a lady's house at the "VVest End for drunkenness.

Shy people are constantly getting into conversational scrapes, their tongues carrying them whither they know not; like the shy young man who was arguing with a charming and intellectual young lady.

Charming Young Lady: " The worst of me is that I am so apt to be run away with by an inference."

Shy Young Man: " Oh, how I wish I was an inference I"

When the late Dr. Woodford became Bishop of Ely, a rumor went before him in the diocese that he was a misogynist. He was staying, on his first round of Confirmations, at a country house, attended by an astonishingly mild yonng chaplain, very like the hero of *The Private Secretary.* In the evening the lady of the house said, archly, to this youthful Levite, " I hope you can contradict the story which we have heard about our new bishop, that he hates ladies." The chaplain, in much confusion, hastily replied, " Oh, that is quite an exaggeration ; but I do think his lordship feels safer with the married ladies."

Let me conclude with a personal reminiscence of a " Thing one would rather have left unsaid." A remarkably pompous clergyman who was a Diocesan Inspector of Schools showed me a theme on a Scriptural subject, written by a girl who was trying to pass from being a pupil-teacher to a school-mistress. The theme was full of absurd mistakes, over which the inspector snorted stertorously. "Well, what do you think of that?" he inquired, when I handed back the paper. " Oh," said I, in perfectly good faith, "the mistakes are bad enough, but the writing is far worse. It really is a disgrace." " Oh, *my* writing!" said the inspector: " I copied the theme out." Even after the lapse of twenty years I turn hot all over when I recall the sensations of that moment.

16

SECTION 16

XXXI

THE AET OF PUTTING THINGS

It was "A. K. H. B.," if I recollect aright, who wrote a popular essay on " The Art of Putting Things." As I know nothing of the essay beyond its title, and am not quite certain about that, I shall not be guilty of intentional plagiarism if I attempt to discuss the same subject. It is not identical with the theme which I have just handled, for " Things one would rather have expressed differently " are essentially things which one might have expressed better. If one is not conscious of this at the moment, Sheridan's "damned good-natured friend" is always at hand to point it out, and the poignancy of one's regret creates the zest of the situation. For example, when a German financier, contesting an English borough, drove over an old woman on the polling day, and affectionately pressed five shillings into her hand, saying, "Never mind, my tear, here's something to get drunk with," his agent instantly pointed out that she wore the Blue Bibbon, and that her husband was an influential class-leader among the Wesleyans.

But "The Art of Putting Things" includes also the things which one might have expressed worse, and covers the cases where a dexterous choice of words seems, at any rate to the speaker, to have extricated him from a conversational quandary. As an instance of this perilous art carried to high perfection, may be cited Abraham Lincoln's judgment on an nnreadably sentimental book:" People who like this sort of thing will find this the sort of thing they like" – humbly imitated by two eminent men on this side of the Atlantic, one of whom is in the habit of writing to struggling authors : " Thank you for sending me your book, which I shall lose no time in reading "; while the other prefers the less truthful but perhaps more flattering formula: " I hare read your blank verse, *and much like it."*

The late Mr. Walter Pater was once invited to admire a hideous wedding-present, compact of ormolu and malachite. Closing his eyes, the founder of modern aesthetics leaned back in his chair, and, waving away the offending object, murmured in his softest tone: " Oh, very rich, very handsome, very expensive, I am sure. *But they mustn't make any more of them."*

Dexterities of phrase sometimes recoil with dire effect npon their author. A very popular clergyman of my acquaintance prides himself on never forgetting an inhabitant of his parish. He was stopped one day in the street by an aggrieved parishioner whom, to use a homely phrase, he did not know from Adam. Ready in resource, he produced his pocket-book, and, hastily jotting down a memorandum of the parishioner's grievance, he said, with an insinuating smile, "It is so stupid of me, but I always forget how you spell your name." " J-0-N-E-S," was the gruff response; and the shepherd and the sheep went their several ways in mutual disgust. Perhaps the worst recorded attempt at an escape from a conversational difficulty was made by an East-end curate who specially cultivated the friendship of the artisans. One day a carpenter arrived in his room and, producing a photograph, said, "I've brought you my boy's likeness, as you said you'd like to have it."

Curate (rapturously): " How awfully good of you to remember! What a capital likeness! How is he ?"

Carpenter: "Why, sir, don't you remember? He's dead."

Curate: " Oh yes, of course, I know that. I mean, *how's the man who took the photograph ?"*

The art of disguising an unpleasant truth with a graceful phrase was well illustrated in the case of a friend of mine, not remarkable for physical courage, of whom a tactful phrenologist pronounced that he was "full of precaution against real or imaginary danger." It is not every one who dan tell a man he is an arrant coward without offending him. The same art, as applied by a man to his own shortcomings, is exemplified in the story of the ecclesiastical dignitary who gloried in his Presence of Mind. According to Dean Stanley, who knew him well, he used to narrate the incident in the following terms:

"A friend invited me to go out with him on the water. The sky was threatening, and I declined. At length he succeeded in persuading me, and we embarked. A squall came on, the boat lurched, and my friend fell overboard. Twice he sank, and twice he rose to the surface. He placed his hands on the prow and endeavored to climb in. There was great apprehension lest he should upset the boat. Providentially, I had brought my umbrella with me. I had the *presence of mind* to strike him two or three hard blows over the knuckles. He let go his hold, and sank. The boat righted itself, and we were saved."

The art of avoiding a conversational unpleasantness by a graceful way of putting things belongs, I suppose, in its highest perfection, to the East. When Lord Dufferin was Viceroy of India, he had a " shikarry," or sporting servant, whose special duty was to attend the visitors at the Viceregal Court on their shooting excursions. Returning one day from one of these expeditions theshikarry encountered the Viceroy, who, full of courteous solicitude for his guests' enjoyment, asked : " Well, what sort of sport has Lord had ?" " Oh," replied the scrupulously polite Indian, "the young Sahib shot divinely, but God was very merciful to the birds." Compare this honeyed speech with the terms in which an English gamekeeper would convey his opinion of a bad shot, and we are forced to admit the social superiority of Lord Salisbury's " black man."

But if we turn from the Orient to the Occident, and from our dependencies to the United Kingdom, the Art of Putting Things is found to flourish better on Irish than on Scotch or English soil. We all remember that Archbishop Whately is said to have thanked God on his death-bed that he had never given a penny in indiscriminate charity. Perhaps one might find more suitable subjects of moribund self - congratulation ; and I have always rejoiced in the mental picture of the Archbishop, in all the frigid pomp of Political Economy, waving off the Dublin beggar with " Go away ; go away. I never give to any one in the street," and receiving the instantaneous rejoinder: "Then where would your reverence have me wait on you ?" A lady of my acquaintance, who is a proprietress in county Galway, is in the habit of receiving her own rents. One day, when a tenant-farmer had pleaded long and unsuccessfully for an abatement, he exclaimed as he handed over his money: "Well, my lady, all I can say is that if I had my time over again it's not a tenant-farmer I'd be. I'd follow one of the learn'd professions." The proprietress gently replied that even in the learned professions there were losses as well as gains, and perhaps he would have found professional life as precarious as farming. " Ah, my lady, how can that be then ?" replied the son of St. Patrick. " If you're a lawyer – win or lose, you're paid. If yon're a doctor – kill or cure, you're paid. If you're a priest – heaven or hell, you're paid." Who can imagine an English farmer pleading the case for an abatement with this happy mixture of fun and satire ?

"Polite" and "urbane" are words which etymolog- ically bear witness that the ancient world, alike Greek and Roman, believed that the arts of courtesy were the products of the town rather than of the country. Something of the same distinction may occasionally be traced even in the civilization of modern England. The house-surgeon of a London hospital was attending to the injuries of a poor woman whose arm had been severely bitten. As he was dressing the wound he said : " I cannot make out what sort of creature bit you. This is too small for a horse's bite, and too large for a dog's." "Oh, sir," replied the patient, "it wasn't an animal; it was *another lydy."* Surely the force of Politeness or Urbanity could no further go. On the other hand, it was a country clergyman who, in view of the approaching Confirmation, announced that on the morning of the ceremony the young *ladies* would assemble at the Vicarage and the young *women* at the National School.

" Let us distinguish," said the philosopher, and certainly the arbitrary use of the term " lady " and " gentleman " suggests some curious studies in the Art of Putting Things. A good woman who let furnished apartments in a country town, describing a lodger who had apparently " known better days," said, " I am positive she was a real born lady, for she hadn't the least idea how to do hanything for herself; it took her hours to peel her potatoes." Carlyle has illustrated from the annals of our criminal jurisprudence the truly British conception of " a very respectable man " as one who keeps a gig ; and, similarly, I recollect that in the famous trial of Kerr and Benson, the turf - swindlers, twenty yearsago, a witness testified, with reference to one of the prisoners, that he had always considered him a "perfect gentleman " ; and, being pressed by counsel to give his reasons for this view, said, " He had rooms at the Langham Hotel, and dined with the Lord Mayor."

On the other hand, it would seem that in certain circles and contingencies the "grand old name of Gentleman" is regarded as a term of opprobrium. The late Lord Wriothesley Russell, who was for many years a Canon of Windsor, used to conduct a mission-service for the Household troops quartered there; and one of his converts, a stalwart trooper of the Blues, expressing his gratitude for these voluntary ministrations, and contrasting them with the officer-like and disciplinary methods of the army - chaplains, genially exclaimed, "But I always say there's not a bit of the gentleman about you, my lord." When Dr. Harold Browne became Bishop of Ely, he asked the head verger some questions as to where his predecessor had been accustomed to sit in the Cathedral, what part he had taken in the services, and so on. The verger proved quite unable to supply the required information, and said in self-excuse, "Well, you see, my lord, his late lordship wasn't at all a church-going gentleman "; which being interpreted meant that, on account of age and infirmities, Bishop Turton had long confined his ministrations to his private chapel.

Just after a change of Government not many years ago, an officer of the Royal Household was chatting with one of the Queen's old coachmen (whose name and location I, for obvious reasons, forbear to indicate). "Well, Whipcord, have you seen your new Master of the Horse yet ?" " Yes, sir, I have; and I should say that his lordship is more of *an in-doors man."* The phrase has a touch of genial contempt for a long-descended but effete aristocracy which tickles the democratic palate. It was notold "Whipcord, but a brother in the craft, who, when asked, during the Jubilee of 1887, if he was driving any of the Imperial and Royal guests then quartered at Buckingham Palace, replied, with calm self-respect: " No, sir; I am the Queen's coachman. I don't drive the *riff-raff."* I take this to be a sublime instance of the Art of Putting Things. Lingering for a moment on these back-stairs of history, let me tell the tragic tale of Mr. and Mrs. M-

Mr. M was one of the merchant-princes of London,

and Mrs. M had occasion to engage a new housekeeper for their palace in Park Lane. The outgoing official wrote to her incoming successor a detailed account of the house and its inmates. The butler was a very pleasant man. The *chef* was inclined to tipple. The lady's-maid gave herself airs; and the head housemaid was a very well principled young woman – and so on and so forth. After the signature, huddled away in a casual postscript, came the damning sentence, "As for Mr. and

Mrs. M , *they behave as well as they knoiv how."* Was

it by inadvertence, or from a desire to let people know their proper place, that the recipient of this letter allowed its contents to find their way to the children of the family ?

As incidentally indicated above, a free recourse to alcoholic stimulus used to be, in less temperate days, closely associated with thn culinary art; and one of the best cooks I ever knew was urged by her mistress to attend a great meeting for the propagation of the Blue Ribbon, to be held not a hundred miles from Southampton, and addressed by a famous preacher of total abstinence. The meeting was enthusiastic, and the Blue Ribbon was freely distributed. Next morning the lady anxiously asked her cook what effect the oratory had produced on her, and she replied, with the evident sense of narrow escape

from imminent danger, " Well, my lady, if Mr. hadgone on for five minutes more, I believe I should have taken the Ribbon too ; but, thank goodness ! he stopped in time."

So far, I find, I have chiefly dealt with the Art of Putting Things as practised by the " urbane " or town-bred classes. Let me give a few instances of "pagan" or countrified use. The blacksmith of my native village was describing to me with unaffected pathos the sudden death of his very aged father ; "and," he simply added, "the worst part of it was that I had to go and break it to my poor old mother." Genuinely entering into my friend's grief, I said: " Yes; that must have been terrible. How did you break it ?" " Well, I went into her cottage and I said, 'Dad's dead.' She said, 'What?' and I said, ' Dad's dead, and you may as well know it first as last.'" Breaking it! Truly a curious instance of the rural Art of Putting Things.

A laborer in Buckinghamshire, being asked how the rector of the village was, replied, "Well, he's getting wonderful old ; but they do tell me that his understanding's no worse than it always was" – a pagan synonym for the hackneyed phrase that one is in full possession of one's faculties. This entire avoidance of flattering circumlocutions, though it sometimes produces these rather startling effects, gives a peculiar raciness to rustic oratory. Not long ago a member for a rural constituency, who had always professed the most democratic sentiments, suddenly astonished his constituents by taking a peerage. During the election caused by his transmigration, one of his former supporters said at a public meeting : " Mr. says as how he's going to the House of

Lords to leaven it. I tell you he can't no more leaven the House of Lords than you can sweeten a cart-load of muck with a pot of marmalade." During the General Election of 1892 I heard an old laborer on a village green denouncing the evils of an Established Church. " I'll tell you how it is with one of these 'ere State parsons. If you take away his book, he can't preach ; and if you take away his gownd, he mus'n't preach ; and if you take away his screw, he'll be damned if he'll preach." The humor which underlies the roughness of countrified speech is often not only genuine but subtle. I have heard a story of a young laborer who, on his way to his day's work, called at the registrar's office to register his father's death. When the official asked the date of the event, the son replied, " He ain't dead yet, but he'll be dead before night, so I thought it would save me another journey if you would put it down now." "Oh, that won't do at all," said the registrar; " perhaps your father will live till to-morrow."

"Well, I don't know, sir; the doctor says as he won't; *and he knows what he has given him."*

The accomplished authoress of *Country Conversations* has put on record some delightful specimens of rural dialogue, culled chiefly from the laboring classes of Cheshire. And, rising in the social scale from the laborer to the farmer, what could be more life-like than this tale of an ill-starred wooing ? " My son Tom has met with a disappointment about getting married. You

know he's got that nice farm at H ; so he met a

young lady at a dance, and he was very much took up, and she seemed quite agreeable. So, as he heard she had Five Hundred, he wrote next day to purshue the acquaintance, and her father wrote and asked Tom to come

over to S . Eh, dear ! Poor fellow ! He went off

in such sperrits, and he looked so spruce in his best clothes, with a new tie and all. So next day, when I heard him come to the gate, I ran out as pleased as could be ; but I see in a moment he was sadly cast down. 'Why, Tom, my lad,' says I, 'what is it ?' 'Why, mother,' says he, ' she'd understood mine was a harable, *and she will not marry to a dairy.'"*

From Cheshire to East Anglia is a far cry, but let me give one more lesson in the Art of Putting Things, derived from that delightful writer, Dr. Jessopp. In one of his studies of rural life the Doctor tells in his own inimitable style a story of which the moral is the necessity of using plain words when you are preaching to the poor. The story runs that in the parish where he served his first curacy there was an old farmer on whom had fallen all the troubles of Job – loss of stock, loss of capital, eviction from his holding, the death of his wife, and the failure of his own health. The well-meaning young curate, though full of compassion, could find no more novel topic of consolation than to say that all these trials were the dispensations of Providence. On this the poor old victim brightened up and said with a cheerful smile, " Ah yes, sir; I know that right enough. That old Providence has been against me all along; but I reckon *there's One above* that will put a stopper on him if he goes too far." Evidently, as Dr. Jessopp observes, "Providence" was to the good old man a learned synonym for the devil.

17

SECTION 17

XXXII

CHILDREN

The humors of childhood include in rich abundance both Things which would have been better left unsaid and Things which might have been expressed differently. But just now they lack their sacred bard. There is no one to observe and chronicle them. It is a pity, for the "heart that watches and receives" will often find in the pleasantries of childhood a good deal that deserves perpetuation.

The children of fiction are a mixed company, some life-like and some eminently the reverse. In *Joan* Miss Rhoda Broughton drew with unequalled skill a family of odious children. Henry Kingsley took a more genial view of his subject, and sketched some pleasant children in *Austin Elliot,* and some delightful ones in the last chapter of *Ravenshoe.* The " Last of the Neros" in *Barchestcr Towers* is admirably drawn, and all elderly bachelors must have sympathized with good Mr. Thome when, by way of making himself agreeable to the mother, Signora Vesey-Neroni, he took the child upon his knee, jumping her up and down, saying, " Diddle, diddle, diddle," and was rewarded with, " I don't want to be did- dle-diddle-diddled. Let me go, yon naughty old man." Dickens's children are by common consent intolerable, but a quarter of a century ago we were all thrilled by Miss Montgomery's *Misunderstood.* It is credibly reported that an earlier and more susceptible generationwas moved to tears by the sinfulness of Topsy and the saintliness of Eva; and the adventures of the *Fairclrild Family* enjoy a deserved popularity among all lovers of unintentional humor. But the "sacred bard" of child- life was John Leech, whose twofold skill immortalized it with pen and with pencil. The childish incidents and sayings which Leech illustrated were, I believe, always taken from real life. His sisters "kept an establishment," as Mr. Dombey said – the very duplicate of that to which little Paul was sent. "' It is not a Preparatory School by any means. Should I express my meaning,' said Miss Tox with peculiar sweetness, ' if I designated it an infantine boarding - house of a very select description ?'

"' On an exceedingly limited and particular scale/ suggested Mrs. Chick, with a glance at her brother. " ' Oh ! exclusion itself/ said Miss Tox." The analogy may be even more closely pressed, for, as at Mrs. Pipchin's, so at Miss Leech's, "'juvenile nobility itself was no stranger to the establishment." Miss Tox told Mr. Dombey that " the humble individual who now addressed him was once under Mrs. Pipchin's charge "; and, similarly, the obscure writer of these papers was once under Miss Leech's. Her school supplied the originals of all the little boys, whether greedy or gracious, grave or gay, on foot or on pony-back, in knickerbockers or in nightshirts, who figure so frequently in *Punch* between 1850 and 1864; and one of the pleasant- est recollections of those distant days is the kindness with which the great artist used to receive us when, as the supreme reward of exceptionally good conduct, we were taken to see him in his studio at Kensington. It is my rule not to quote at length from what is readily accessible, and therefore I cull only one delightful episode from Leech's *Sketches of Life and Character.* Twolittle chaps are discussing the age of a third, and the one reflectively remarks: " Well, I don't 'zactly know how old Charlie is; but he must be very old, for he blows his own nose." Happy and far-distant days, when such an accomplishment seemed to be characteristic of a remotely future age ! " Mamma," inquired an infant aristocrat of a superlatively refined mother, " when shall I be old enough to eat bread and cheese with a knife, and put the knife in my month ?" But the answer is not recorded.

The vagueness of the young with respect to the age of their elders is pleasingly illustrated by the early history of a nobleman who recently represented a division of Manchester in Parliament. His mother had a maid, who seemed to childish eyes extremely old. The children of the family longed to know her age, but were much too well - bred to ask a question which they felt would be painful; so they sought to attain the desired end by a system of ingenious traps. The future Member for Manchester chanced in a lucky hour to find in his *Book of Useful Knoialedge* the tradition that the aloe flowers only once in a hundred years. He instantly saw his opportunity, and, accosting the maid with winning air and wheedling accent, asked insinuatingly, "Dunn, have you often seen the aloe flower ?"

The *Enfant Terrible,* though his name is imported from France, is an indigenous growth of English soil. A young husband and wife of my acquaintance were conversing in the comfortable belief that "Tommy didn't understand," when Tommy looked up from his toys and said, reprovingly, "Mamma, oughtn't you to have said that in French ?"

The late Lord , who had a deformed foot, was going to visit the Queen at Osborne, and before his arrival the Queen and Prince Albert debated whether it would be better to warn the Prince of Wales and the Princess Royal of his physical peculiarity, so as to avoid embarrassing remarks, or to leave it to their own good feeling. The latter course was adopted. Lord duly arrived. The foot elicited no remarks from the Royal children, and the visit passed off anxiously but with success. Next day the Princess Royal asked the Queen, "Where is Lord ?" " He has gone back to London, dear." "Oh ! what a pity ! He had promised to show Bertie and me his foot!" They had caught him in the corridor, and made their own terms with their captive.

In more recent years the little daughter of one of the Queen's most confidential advisers had the unexampled honor of being invited to luncheon with Her Majesty. During the meal, an Illustrious Lady, negotiating a pigeon after the German fashion, took up one of its bones with her finger and thumb. The little visitor, whose sense of British propriety was stronger than her awe of Courts, regarded the proceeding with wonder- dilated eyes, and then burst out: " Oh, Piggy-wiggy, Piggy-wiggy! You *are* Piggy-wiggy." Probably she is now languishing in the dungeon-keep of Windsor Castle.

If the essence of the *Enfant Terrible* is that he or she causes profound embarrassment to the surrounding adults, the palm of pre-eminence must be assigned to the children of a famous diplomatist, who, some twenty years ago, organized a charade and performed it without assistance from their elders. The scene displayed a Crusader knight returning from the wars to his ancestral castle. At the castle gate he was welcomed by his beautiful and rejoicing wife, to whom, after tender salutations, he recounted his triumphs on the tented field and the number of paynim whom he had slain. "And I, too, my lord," replied his wife, pointing with conscious prideto a long row of dolls of various sizes – " and I, too, my lord, have not been idle." *Tableau* indeed !

The argumentative child is scarcely less trying than the *Enfant Terrible.* Miss Sellon, the foundress of English sisterhoods, adopted and brought up in her convent at Devonport a little Irish waif who had been made an orphan by the outbreak of cholera in 1849. The infant's customs and manners, especially at table, were a perpetual trial to a community of refined old maids. " Chew your food, Aileen," said Miss Sellon. " If you please, mother, the whale didn't chew Jonah," was the prompt reply of the little Romanist, who had been taught that the examples of Holy Writ were for our imitation. Answers made in examinations I forbear, as a rule, to quote, but one I must give, because it so beautifully illustrates the value of ecclesiastical observances in our elementary schools:

Vicar: "Now, my dear, do yon know what happened on Ascension Day ? "

Child: " Yes, sir, please. We had buns and a swing."

Natural childhood should know nothing of social forms, and the coachman's son who described his father's master as " the man that rides in dad's carriage," showed a finely democratic instinct. But the boastful child is a very unpleasant product of nature or of art. " We've got a private master comes to teach us at home, but we ain't proud, because Ma says it's sinful," quoth Morleena Kenwigs, under her mother's instructions, when Nicholas Nickleby gave her French lessons. The infant daughter of a country clergyman, drinking tea in the nursery of the episcopal palace, boasted that at the vicarage they had a hen which laid an egg every day. " Oh, that's nothing," retorted the bishop's daughter ; " Papa lays a foundation-stone every week."

The precocious child, even when thoroughly wellmeaning, is a source of terror by virtue of its intense earnestness. In the days when Maurice first discredited the doctrine of Eternal Punishment, some learned and theological people were discussing, in a country-house near Oxford, the abstract credibility of endless pain. Suddenly the child of the house (now its owner), who was playing on the hearth-rug, looked up and said, " But how am I to know that it isn't hell already, and that I am not in it ?" – a question which threw a lurid light on his educational and disciplinary experiences. Some of my readers will probably recollect the "Japanese Village " at Knightsbridge – a pretty show of Oriental wares which was burned down, just at the height of its popularity, a few years ago. On the day of its destruction I was at the house of a famous financier, whose children had been to see the show only two days before. One of them, an urchin of eight, immensely interested by the news of the fire, asked, not if the pretty things were burned or the people hurt, but this one question: "Mamma, was it insured ?" Verily, *bon chat chasse de race.* An excellent story of commercial precocity reaches me from one of the many correspondents who have been good enough to write to me in connection with this series of papers. It may be specially commended to the promoters of that class of company which is specially affected by the widow, the orphan, and the curate. Two small boys, walking down Tottenham Court Road, passed a tobacconist's shop. The bigger remarked, " I say, Bill, I've got a ha'penny, and if you've got one too, we'll have a penny smoke between us." Bill produced his copper, and Tommy, diving into the shop, promptly reappeared with a penny cigar in his mouth. The boys walked side by side for a few minutes, when the smaller mildly said, " I say, Tom, when am I to have a puff ? The weed's half mine." " Oh, you shut up," was the business-like reply." I'm the chairman of this company, and yon are only a shareholder. *You can spit."*

The joys of childhood are a theme on which a good deal of verse has been expended. I am far from denying that they are real, but I contend that they take commonly a form which is quite inconsistent with poetry, and that the poet (like heaven) "lies about us in our infancy." " I wish every day in the year was a pot of jam/' was the obviously sincere exclamation of a fat little boy whom I knew, and whom Leech would have delighted to draw. Two little London girls who had been sent by the kindness of the vicar's wife to have "a happy day in the country," narrating their experiences on their return, said, " Oh yes ! mum, we *did* 'ave a 'appy day. We saw two pigs killed and a gentleman buried." And the little boy who was asked if he thought he should like a hymn- book for his birthday present replied that "he *thought* he should like a hymn-book, but he *Tcnew* he should like a squirt." A small cousin of mine, hearing his big brothers describe their experiences at a Public School, observed with unction, " If ever I have a fag of my own, I will stick pins into him." But now we are leaving childhood behind, and attaining to the riper joys of full- blooded boyhood.

" O running stream of sparkling joy

To be a soaring human boy 1"

exclaimed Mr. Chadband in a moment of inspiration. " In the strictest sense a boy," was Mr. Gladstone's expressive phrase in his controversy with Colonel Dopping. For my own part, I confess to a frank dislike of boys. I dislike them equally whether they are priggish boys, like Kenelm Chillingly, who asked his mother if she was never overpowered by a sense of her own identity; or sentimental boys, like Dibbins in *Basil the Schoolboy,*

who, discussing with a friend how to spend a whole
holiday, said, " Let us go to Dingley Dell and talk about
Byron"; or manly boys like Tom Tulliver, of whom it
is excellently said that he was the kind of boy who is
commonly spoken of as being very fond of animals –
that is, very fond of throwing stones at them.
Whatever their type,

" I've seemed of late
To shrink from happy boyhood – boys
Have grown so noisy, and I hate
A noise.
They fright me when the beech is green,
By swarming up its stem for eggs;
They drive their horrid hoops between
My legs.
It's idle to repine, I know ;
I'll tell you what I'll do instead :
I'll drink my arrow-root, and go
To bed."

But before I do so let me tell one boy-story, connected with the Eton and Harrow match, which has always struck me as rather pleasing. In the year 1866, when F. C. Cobden, who was afterwards so famous for his bowling in the Cambridge Eleven, was playing for Harrow, an affable father, by way of making conversation for a little Harrow boy at Lord's, asked, " Is your Cob- den any relation to the great Cobden ?" " Why, he *is* the great Cobden," was the simple and swift reply. There spoke the true spirit of hero-worship.

SECTION 18

I1

XXXIII

LETTER-WRITING

" Odd men write odd letters." This rather platitudinous sentence, from an otherwise excellent essay of the late Bishop Thorold's, is abundantly illustrated alike by my Collections and by my Recollections. I plunge at random into my subject, and immediately encounter the following letter from a Protestant clergyman in the north of Ireland, written in response to a suggestion that he might with advantage study Mr. Gladstone's magnificent Speech on the Second Reading of the Affirmation Bill in 1883 :

"MY Dear Sir, – I have received your recommendation to read carefully the speech of Mr. Gladstone in favor of admitting the infidel Bradlaugh into Parliament. I did so when it was delivered, and I must say that the strength of argument rests with the opposition. I fully expect, in the event of a dissolution, the Government will lose between fifty and sixty seats. Any conclusion can be arrived at, according to the premises laid down. Mr. G. avoided the Scriptural lines and followed his own. All parties knew the feeling of the country on the subject, and, notwithstanding the bullying and majority of Gladstone, he was defeated. Before the Irish Church was robbed, I was nominated to the Deanery of Tuam, but, Mr. Disraeli resigning, I was defrauded of my just right by Mr. Gladstone, and my wife, Lady, the only surviving child of an Earl, was sadly disappointed ; but there is a just Judge above. The letter of nomination is still in my possession.

" I am, dear sir, yours faithfully,

It is highly characteristic of Mr. Gladstone that, when this letter was shown to him by its recipient as a specimen of epistolary oddity, he read it, not with a smile, but with a portentous frown, and, handing it back, sternly asked, " What does the fellow mean by quoting an engagement entered into by my predecessor as bind- iug on me ?"

It is not only clergy " defrauded " of expected dignities that write odd letters. Young curates in search of benefices often seek to gratify their innocent ambitions by the most ingenious appeals. Here is a letter received not many years ago by the Prime Minister of the day :

" I have no donbt but that your time is fully occupied. I will therefore compress as much as possible what I wish to say, and frame my request in a few words. Some time ago my mother wrote to her brother,

Lord , asking him to try and do something for me in

the way of obtaining a living. The reply from Lady

was that my uncle could do nothing to help me.

I naturally thought that a Premier possessed of such a plenitude of power as yourself could find it a matter of less difficulty to transform a curate into a rector or vicar than to create a peer. My name is in the Chancellor's List – a proceeding, as far as results, somewhat suggestive, I fear, of the Greek Kalends. . . . My future father- in-law is a member of the City Liberal Club, in which a *large bust* of yourself was unveiled last year. I am thirtyone years of age ; a High Churchman ; musical, etc. ;

graduate of . If I had a living I conld marry. . . .

I am very anxious to marry, but I am very poor, and a living would help me very much. Being a Southerner, fond of music and of books, I naturally would like to be somewhere near town. I hope you will be able to help me in this respect, and thus afford much happiness to more than one."

There is great force in that appeal to the " large bust."

Here is are quest which Bishop Thorold received from an

admirer, who unfortunately omitted to give his address:

" Rev. And Learned Sir, – Coming into your presence through the medium of a letter, I do so in the spirit of respect dne to you as a gentleman and a scholar. I unfortunately am a scholar, but a blackguard. I heard you preach a few times, and thought you might pity the position I have brought myself to. I should be grateful to you for an old coat or an old pair of boots."

And, while the seekers after emolument write odd letters, odd letters are also written by their admirers on their behalf. A few years ago one of the principal benefices in West London was vacated, and, the presentation lapsing to the Crown, the Prime Minister was favored with the following appeal:

" Sir, – Doubtless you do not often get a letter from a working man on the subject of clerical appointments, but as I here you have got to find a minister for to fill Mr.

Boyd Carpenter's place, allow me to ask you to just go some Sunday afternoon and here our little curate, Mr.

, at St. Matthew's Church – he is a good, Earnest

little man, and a genuine little Fellow ; got no humbugabout him, but a sound Churchman, is an Extempor Preacher, and deserves promotion. Nobody knows I am writing to you, and it is not a matter of kiss and go by favor, but simply asking you to take a run over and here him, and then put him a stept higher – he deserves it. I know Mr. Sulivau will give him a good character, and so will Mr. Alcroft, the Patron. Now do go over and here him before you make a choice. We working men will be sorry to lose him, but we think he ought not to be missed promotion, as he is a good fellow. " Your obediently servant."

Ladies, as might naturally be expected, are even more enthusiastic in advocating the claims of their favorite divines. Writing lately on the Agreeableness of Clergymen, I described some of the Canons of St. Paul's and Westminster, and casually referred to the handsome presence of Dr. Duckworth. I immediately received the following effusion, which, wishing to oblige the writer, and having no access to the *Church Family Newspaper,* I now make public :

" A member of the Rev. Canon Duckworth's congregation for *more than* twenty-five *years* has been much pained by the scant and curious manner in which he is mentioned by you, and begs to say that his Gospel teaching, his scholarly and yet simple and charitable discourses (and teaching), his courteous and sympathetic and prompt answers to his people's requests and inquiries, his energetic and constant work in his parish, are beyond praise. Added to all is his clear and sonorous voice in his rendering of the prayer and praise amongst us. A grateful parishioner hopes and *asks* for some further recognition of his position in the Church of Christ, in the *Church Family Newspaper,* June 12."

So far the Church. I now turn to the world.

In the second volume of Lord Beaconsfield's *Endymion* will be found a description, by a hand which was never excelled in that sort of business, of that grotesque revival of mediasval mummery, the Tournament at Eglin- tonn Castle in 1839. But the writer, conceding something to the requirements of art, ignores the fact that the splendid pageant was spoiled by rain. Two years' preparation and enormous expense were thrown away. A grand cavalcade, in which Prince Louis Napoleon rode as one of the knights, lefb Eglintoun Castle on August 28 at two in the afternoon, with heralds, banners, pursuivants, the knight-marshal, the jester, the King of the Tournament, the Queen of Beauty, and a glowing assemblage of knights and ladies, seneschals, chamberlains, esquires, pages, and men-at-arms, and took their way in procession to the lists, which were overlooked by galleries in which nearly two thousand spectators were accommodated ; but all the while the rain came down in bucketsful, never ceased while the tourney proceeded, and brought the proceedings to a premature and ignominious close. I only mention the occurrence here because the Queen of Beauty, elected to that high honor by unanimous acclamation, was Jane Sheridan, Lady Seymour; and there is all the charm of vivid contrast in turning from the reckless expenditure and fantastic brilliancy of 1839 to the following correspondence, which was published in the newspapers in the early part of 1840.

Anne, Lady Shuckburgh, was the wife of Sir Francis Shuckburgh, a Northamptonshire baronet, and to her the Queen of Beauty, forsaking the triumphs of chivalry for the duties of domestic economy, addressed the following letter:

"Lady Seymour presents her compliments to Lady Shuckburgh, and would be obliged to her for the character of Mary Stedman, who states that she lived twelve months, and still is, in Lady Shuckburgh's establishment. Can Mary Stedman cook plain dishes well ? make bread ? and is she honest, good-tempered, sober, willing, and cleanly ? Lady Seymour would also like to know the reason why she leaves Lady Shnckburgh's service ? Direct, under cover to Lord Seymour, Maiden Bradley."

To this polite and business-like inquiry Lady Shuck- burgh replied as follows:

" Lady Shuckburgh presents her compliments to Lady Seymour. Her ladyship's note, dated October 28, only reached her yesterday, November 3. Lady Shuckburgh was unacquainted with the name of the kitchan-maid until mentioned by Lady Seymour, as it is her custom neither to apply for or give characters to any of the under servants, this being always done by the housekeeper, Mrs. Conch – and this was well known to the young woman ; therefore Lady Shuckburgh is surprised at her referring any lady to her for a character. Lady Shuckburgh having a professed cook, as well as a housekeeper, in her establishment, it is not very likely she herself should know anything of the abilities or merits of the under servants; therefore she is unable to answer Lady Seymour's note. Lady Shuckburgh cannot imagine Mary Stedman to be capable of cooking for any except the servants'-hall table.

" *November* 4, Pavilion, Hans Place."

But Sheridan's granddaughter was quite the wrong subject for these experiments in fine-ladyism, and she lost no time in replying as follows :

"Lady Seymour presents her compliments to Lady Shuckburgh, and begs she will order her housekeeper, Mrs. Pouch, to send the girl's character without delay; otherwise another young woman will be sought for elsewhere, as Lady Seymour's children cannot remain without their dinners because Lady Shuckburgh, keeping a 'professed cook and a housekeeper,'thinks a knowledge of the details of her establishment beneath her notice. Lady Seymour understands from Stedman that, in addition to her other talents, she was actually capable of dressing food fit for the little Shuckburghs to partake of when hungry."

To this note was appended a pen-and-ink vignette by Lady Seymour representing the three " little Shuck- burghs," with large heads and cauliflower wigs, sitting at a round table and voraciously scrambling for mutton chops dressed by Mary Stedman, who was seen looking on with supreme satisfaction, while Lady Shuckburgh appeared in the distance in evident dismay. A crushing rejoinder closed this correspondence:

" Madam, – Lady Shuckburgh has directed me to acquaint you that she declines answering your note, the vulgarity of which is beneath contempt; and although it may be the characteristic of the Sheridans to be vulgar, coarse, and witty, it is not that of a ' lady,' unless she happens to have been born in a garret and bred in a kitchen. Mary Stedman informs me that your ladyship does not keep either a cook or a housekeeper, and that you only require a girl who can cook a mutton chop. If so, I apprehend that Mary Stedman, or any other scullion, will be found fully equal to cook for or manage the establishment of the Queen of Beauty. I am, your Ladyship, &c.,

"elizabeth Couch (not Pouch)."

"Odd men," quoth Bishop Thorold, "write odd letters," and so do odd women. The original of the following epistle to Mr. Gladstone lies before me. It is dated Cannes, March 15, 1893 :

" Far away from my native Land, my bitter indignation as a *Welshwoman* prompts me to reproach you, you *bad, wicked, false,* treacherous Old Man ! for your iniquitous scheme to *rob* and overthrow the dearly beloved Old Church of my Country. You have no conscience, but I pray that God may even yet give you one that will sorely *smart* and trouble you before you die. You pretend to be religious, you old hypocrite ! that you may more successfully pander to the evil passions of the lowest and most ignorant of the Welsh people. But you neither care for nor respect the principles of Religion, or you would not distress the minds of all true Christian people by instigating a mob to commit the awful sin of Sacrilege. You think you will shine in History, but it will be a notoriety similar to that of *Nero.* I see some one pays you the unintentional compliment of comparing you to Pontius Pilate, and I am sorry, for Pilate, though a political time-server, was, with all his faults, a very respectable man in comparison with you. And he did not, like you, profess the Christian Religion. You are certainly *clever.* So also is your lord and master the Devil. And I cannot regard it as sinful to hate and despise you, any more than it is sinful to abhor Him. So with full measure of contempt and detestation, accept these compliments from

" A Daughter Of Old Wales."

It is a triumph of female perseverance and ingenuity that the whole of the foregoing is compressed into a single post-card.

Some letters, like the foregoing, are odd from their extraordinary rudeness. Others – not usually, it must beadmitted, Englishmen's letters – are odd from their excessive civility. An Italian priest working in London wrote to a Roman Catholic M. P., asking for an order of admission to the House of Commons, and, on receiving it, acknowledged it as follows :

" *To the Hon. Mr. , M. P.*

" Hon. Sir, Son in Jesu Christ, I beg most respectfully you, Hon. Sir, to accept the very deep gratitude for the ticket which you, Hon. Sir, with noble kindness favored me by post to-day. May the Blessing of God Almighty come upon you, Hon. Sir, and may he preserve you, Hon. Sir, for ever and ever, Amen. With all due respect, I have the honor to be, Hon. Sir, your most " humble and obedient servant,

Surely the British Constituent might take a lesson from this extremely polite letter-writer when his long- suffering member has squeezed him into the Strangers' Gallery.

Some letters, again, are odd from their excess of candor. A gentleman, unknown to me, soliciting pecuniary assistance, informed me that, having " sought relief from trouble in dissipation," he " committed an act which sent him into Penal Servitude," and shortly after his release " wrote a book containing many suggestions for the reform of prison discipline." A lady, widely known for the benevolent use she makes of great wealth, received a letter from an absolute stranger, setting forth that he had been so unfortunate as to overdraw his account at his banker's, and adding, "As I know that it will only cost you a scratch of the pen to set this right, I make no apology for asking you to do so."

Among " odd men " might certainly be reckoned the late Archdeacon Denison, and he displayed his oddnessvery characteristically when, having quarrelled with the Committee of Council on Education, he refused to have his parish schools inspected, and thus intimated his resolve to the inspector :

" My Dear Bellairs, – I love you very much ; but, if yon ever come here again to inspect, I lock the door of the school, and tell the boys to put yon in the pond."

I am not sure whether the great Duke of Wellington can probably be described as an " odd man," but beyond question he wrote odd letters. I have already quoted from his reply to Mrs. Norton, when she asked leave to dedicate a song to him – " I have made it a rule to have nothing dedicated to me, and have kept it in every instance, though I have been Chancellor of the University of Oxford, and in other situations *much exposed to authors."* The Duke replied to every letter that he received, but his replies were not always acceptable to their recipients. When a philanthropist begged him to present some petitions to the House of Lords on behalf of the wretched chimney-sweeps, the Duke wrote back : "Mr. Stevens had *thought fit* to leave some petitions at Apsley House. They will be found with the porter." The Duke's correspondence with "Miss J.," which was published by Mr. Fisher Unwin some ten years ago, and is much less known than it deserves to be, contains some gems of composition. Miss J. consulted the Duke about her duty when a fellow-passenger in the stage-coach swore, and he wrote: "I don't consider with yon that it is necessary to enter into a disputation with every wandering Blasphemer. Much must depend upon the circumstances." And when the good lady mixed flirtation with piety, and irritability with both, he wrote : "The Duke of Wellington presents His Compliments to Miss J. She is quite mistaken. He has no Lock of Hair of Hers. He never had one."

Curtness in letter-writing does not necessarily indicate oddity. It often is the most judicious method of avoiding interminable correspondence. When one of Bishop Thorold's clergy wrote to beg leave of absence from his duties in order that he might make a long tour in the

East, he received for all reply: " Dear , Go to

Jericho. – Yours, A. W. R." At a moment when scarlet- fever was ravaging Haileybury, and suggestions for treatment were pouring in by every post, the Head Master had a lithographed answer prepared, which ran: " Dear Sir, – I am obliged by your opinions, and retain my own." An admirable answer was made by another Head Master to a pompous matron, who wrote that, before she sent her boy to his school, she must ask if he was very particular about the social antecedents of his pupils: "Dear madam, as long as your son behaves himself and his fees are paid, no questions will be asked about his social antecedents."

Sydney Smith's reply, when Lord Houghton, then young "Dicky Milnes," wrote him an angry letter about some supposed unfriendliness, was a model of mature and genial wisdom: "Dear Milnes, – Never lose your good temper, which is one of your best qualities." When the then Dean of Hereford wrote a solemn and elaborate letter to Lord John Russell, announcing that he and his colleagues would refuse to elect Dr. Hampden to the See, Lord John replied: "Sir, – I have had the honor to receive your letter of the 22d inst., in which you intimate to me your intention of violating the law." Some

years ago Lady , who is well known as an ardent
worker in the interests of the Roman Church, wrote
to the Duke of , who was equally known as a sturdy
Protestant, that she was greatly interested in a Roman Catholic charity, and, knowing the Dnke's wide benevolence, had ventured to put down his name for $100. The Duke wrote back : " Dear Lady , – It is a curious coincidence that, just before I got your letter, I had put down your name for a like sum to the English Mission for Converting Irish Catholics; so no money need pass between us." But perhaps the supreme honors of curt correspondence belong to Mr. Bright. Let one instance suffice. Having been calumniated by a Tory orator at Barrow, Mr. Bright wrote as follows about his traducer : " He may not know that he is ignorant, but he cannot be ignorant that he lies. And after such a speech the meeting thanked him – I presume because they enjoyed what ho had given them. I think the speaker was named Smith. He is a discredit to the *numerous family of that name."* XXXIV

OFFICIALDOM

The announcements relating to the first Cabinet of the winter set me thinking whether my readers might be interested in seeing what I have "collected" as to the daily life and labors of Her Majesty's Ministers. I decided that I would try the experiment, and, acting on the principle which I have professed before – that when once one has deliberately chosen certain words to express one's meaning one cannot, as a rule, alter them with advantage – I have obtained the kind permission of the editor of the *Windsor Magazine* to borrow from some former writings of my own.

The Cabinet is the Board of Directors of the British Empire. All its members are theoretically equal; but, as at other Boards, the effective power really resides in three or four. At the present moment Manchester is represented by one of these potent few. Saturday is the usual day for the meeting of the Cabinet, though it may be convened at any moment as special occasion arises. Describing the potato-disease which settled the repeal of the Corn Laws, Lord Beaconsfield wrote: " This mysterious but universal sickness of a single root changed the history of the world. 'There is no gambling like politics,5 said Lord Roehampton, as he glanced at the *Times:* ' four Cabinets in one week ! The Government must be more sick than the potatoes !'"

Twelve is the usual hour for the meeting of the Cabinet, and the business is generally over by two. At the Cabinets held during November the legislative programme for next session is settled, and the preparation of each measure is assigned to a sub-committee of Ministers specially conversant with the subject-matter. Lord Salisbury holds his Cabinets at the Foreign Office; but the old place of meeting was the official residence of the First Lord of the Treasury at 10 Downing Street, in a pillared room looking over the Horse Guards Parade, and hung with portraits of departed First Lords.

In theory, of course, the proceedings of the Cabinet are absolutely secret. The Privy Councillor's oath prohibits all disclosures. No record is kept of the business done. The door is guarded by vigilant attendants against possible eavesdroppers. The despatch-boxes which constantly circulate between Cabinet Ministers, carrying confidential matters, are locked with special keys, said to date from the administration of Mr. Pitt; and the possession of these keys constitutes admission into what Lord Beaconsfield called "the circles of high initiation." Yet in reality more leaks out than is supposed.

In the Cabinet of 1880-5 the leakage to the press was systematic and continuous. Even Mr. Gladstone, the stiffest of sticklers for official reticence, held that a Cabinet Minister might impart his secrets to his wife and his Private Secretary. The wives of official men are not always as trustworthy as Mrs. Bucket in *Blealc House,* and some of the Private Secretaries in the Government of 1880 were little more than boys. Two members of the Cabinet were notorious for their free communications to the press, and it was often remarked that the *Birmingham Daily Post* was peculiarly well informed. A noble lord who held a high office, and who, though the most pompous, was not the wisest of mankind, was habitually a victim to a certainjournalist of known enterprise, who used to waylay him outside Downing Street and accost him with jaunty

confidence : " Well, Lord , so you have settled on

so-and-so, after all ?" The. noble lord, astonished that the Cabinet's decision was already public property, would reply: " As you know so much, there can be 110 harm in telling the rest"; and the journalist, grinning like a dog, ran off to print the precious morsel in a special edition of the *Millbank Gazette.* Mr. Justin M'Carthy could, I believe, tell a curious story of a highly important piece of foreign intelligence communicated by a Minister to the *Daily News,* of a resulting question in the House of Commons, and of the same Minister's emphatic declaration that no effort should be wanting to trace this violator of official confidence and bring him to condign punishment.

While it is true that outsiders sometimes become possessed by these dodges of official secrets, it is not less true that Cabinet Ministers are often curiously in the dark about great and even startling events. A political lady once said to me: " Do you in your party think

much of my neighbor, Mr. ?" As in duty bound,

I replied, "Oh yes, a great deal." She rejoined: "I shouldn't have thought it, for when the boys are shouting any startling news in the special editions I see him run out without his hat to buy an evening paper. *That doesn't look well for a Cabinet Minister."* On the evening of May 6,1882,1 dined in company with Mr. Bright. He stayed late, but never heard a word of the Phcenix Park murders, went off quietly to bed, and read of them as news in the next morning's *Observer.*

But, after all, attendance at the Cabinet, though a most important, is only an occasional, event in the life of one of Her Majesty's Ministers. Let us consider the ordinary routine of his day's work during the sessionof Parliament. The truly virtuous Minister, we may presume, struggles down to the dining-room to read prayers and to breakfast in the bosom of his family between 9 and 10 A. m. But the self-indulgent bachelor declines to be called, and sleeps his sleep out. Mr. Arthur Balfour invariably breakfasts at 12 ; and more politicians than would admit it consume their tea and toast in bed. Mercifully, the dreadful habit of giving breakfast-parties, though sanctioned by the memories of Holland and Macaulay and Rogers and Houghton, virtually died out with the disappearance of Mr. Gladstone.

" Men who breakfast out are generally Liberals," says Lady St. Julians in *SyMl. "* Have not you observed that *?"*

" I wonder why ?"

" It shows a restless, revolutionary mind," said Lady Firebrace, " that can settle to nothing, but must be running after gossip the moment they are awake."

" Yes," said Lady St. Julians, " I think those men who breakfast out, or who give breakfasts, are generally dangerous characters; at least I would not trust them."

And Lady St. Julians' doctrine, though half a century old, applies with perfect exactness to those enemies of the human race who endeavor to keep alive or to resuscitate this desperate tradition. Juvenal described the untimely fate of the man who went into his bath with an undigested peacock in his system. Scarcely pleasanter are the sensations of the Minister or the M. P. who goes from a breakfast-party, full of buttered muffins and broiled salmon to the sedentary desk-work of his office or the fusty wrangles of a Grand Committee.

Breakfast over, the Minister's fancy lightly turns to thoughts of exercise. If he is a man of active habits and strenuous tastes, he may take a gentle breather np Highgate Hill, like Mr. Gladstone, or play tennis, likeSir Edward Grey. Lord Spencer when in office might be seen any morning cantering up St. James's Street on a hack, or pounding round Hyde Park in high naval debate with Sir Ughtred Kay-Shuttleworth. Lord Rose- bery drives himself in a cab; Mr. Asquith is driven; both occasionally survey the riding world over the railings of Rotten Row; and even Lord Salisbury may be found prowling about the Green Park, to which his house in Arlington Street has a private access. Mr. Balfour, as we all know, is a devotee of the cycle, and his example is catching; but Mr. Chamberlain holds fast to the soothing belief that when a man has walked upstairs to bed he has made as much demand on his physical energies as is good for him, and that exercise was invented by the doctors in order to bring grist to their mill.

Whichever of these examples our Minister prefers to follow, his exercise or his lounge must be over by 12 o'clock. The Grand Committees meet at that hour; on "Wednesday the House meets then ; and, if he is not required by departmental business to attend either the Committee or the House, he will probably be at his office by mid-day. The exterior aspect of the Government offices in Whitehall is sufficiently well known, and any peculiarities which it may present are referable to the fact that the execution of an Italian design was intrusted by the wisdom of Parliament to a Gothic architect. Inside, their leading characteristics are the abundance and steepness of the stairs, the total absence of light, and an atmosphere densely charged with Irish stew. Why the servants of the British Government should live exclusively on this delicacy, and why its odors should prevail with equal pungency "from morn to noon, from noon to dewy eve," are matters of speculation too recondite for a popular sketch like this.

The Minister's own room is probably on the first floor; perhaps looking into Whitehall, perhaps into the Foreign Office Square, perhaps on to the Horse Guards Parade. It is a large room, with immense windows, and a fireplace ingeniously contrived to send all its heat up the chimney. If the office is one of the older ones, the room probably contains some good pieces of furniture derived from a less penurious age than ours – a bureau or bookcase of mahogany dark with years, showing in its staid ornamentation traces of Chippendale or Sheraton ; a big clock in a handsome case; and an interesting portrait of some historic statesmen who presided over the department two centuries ago. But in the more modern offices all is barren. Since the late Mr. Ayrton was First Commissioner of Works a squalid cheapness has reigned supreme. Deal and paint are everywhere; doors that won't shut, bells that won't ring, and curtains that won't meet. In two articles alone there is prodigality – books and stationery. *Hansard's Debates,* the *Statutes at Large,* treatises illustrating the work of the office, and books of reference innumerable are there ; and the stationery shows a delightful variety of shape, size, and texture, adapted to every conceivable exigency of official correspondence.

It is, indeed, in the item of stationery, and in that alone, that the grand old constitutional system of perquisites survives. Morbidly conscientious Ministers sometimes keep a supply of their private letter-paper on their office-table and use it for their private correspondence. But the more frankly human sort write all their letters on official paper. On whatever paper written, Ministers' letters go free from the office and the House of Commons ; and certain artful correspondents outside, knowing that a letter to a public office need not be stamped, write to the Minister at his official address andsave their penny. In days gone by each Secretary of State received on his appointment a silver inkstand, which he could hand down as a keepsake to his children. Mr. Gladstone, when he was Chancellor of the Exchequer, abolished this little perquisite, and the only token of office which an outgoing Minister can now take with him is his despatch-box. The wife of a Minister who had long occupied an official residence said with a pensive sigh on being evicted from office, " I hope I am not avaricious, but I must say, when one was hanging up pictures, it was very pleasant to have the Board of Works' carpenter and a bag of the largest nails for nothing."

The late Sir William Gregory used to narrate how, when a child, he was taken by his grandfather, who was Under-Secretary for Ireland, to see the Chief Secretary, Lord Melbourne, in his official room. The good-natured old Whig asked the boy if there was anything in the room that he would like; and he chose a large stick of sealing-wax. " That's right," said Lord Melbourne, pressing a bundle of pens into his hand, " begin life early; all these things belong to the public, and your business must always be to get out of the public as much as you can." There spoke the true spirit of our great governing families.

And now our Minister, seated at his official table, touches his pneumatic bell. His Private Secretary appears with a pile of papers, and the day's work begins. That work, of course, differs enormously in amount, nature, importance, and interest with different offices. To the outside world probably one office is much the same as another, but the difference in the esoteric view is wide indeed. When the Revised Version of the New Testament came out, an accomplished gentleman who had once been Mr. Gladstone's Private Secretary, andhad been appointed by him to an important post in the permanent Civil Service, said : " Mr. Gladstone I have been looking at the Revised Version, and I think it distinctly inferior to the old one."

" Indeed," said Mr. Gladstone, with all his theological ardor roused at once; " I am very much interested to hear you say so. Pray give me an instance."

"Well," replied the Permanent Official, " look at the first verse of the second chapter of St. Luke. That verse used to run, ' There went out a decree from Caesar Augustus that all the world should be taxed.' Well, I always thought that a splendid idea – a tax levied on the whole world by a single Act – a grand stroke, worthy of a great empire and an imperial treasury. But in the Revised Version I find, ' There went out a decree that all the world should be enrolled' – a mere counting ! a census ! the sort of thing the Local Government Board could do ! Will any one tell me that the new version is as good as the old one in this passage ?"

This story aptly illustrates the sentiments with which the more powerful and more ancient departments regard those later births of time, the Board of Trade, the Local Government Board, the Board of Agriculture, and even the Scotch Office – though this last is redeemed from utter contempt by the irritable patriotism of our Scottish fellow-citizens, and by the beautiful house in which it is lodged. For a Minister who loves an arbitrary and single-handed authority the India Office is the most attractive of all. The Secretary of State for India is (except in financial matters, where he is controlled by his Council) a pure despot. He has the Viceroy at the end of a telegraph-wire, and the Queen's three hundred millions of Indian subjects under his thumb. His salary is not voted by the House of Commons ; very few M. P.'s care a rap about India ; and he is practically free from Parliamentary control. The Foreign Office, of course, is full of interest, and its social traditions have always been of the most dignified sort – from the days when Mr. Ran- ville-Ranville used to frequent Mrs. Perkins's Balls to the existing reign of Sir Thomas Sanderson and Mr. Eric Barrington.

The Treasury has its finger in every departmental pie except the Indian one, for no Minister and no department can carry out reforms or even discharge its ordinary routine without public money, and of public money the Treasury is the vigilant and inflexible guardian. " I am directed to acquaint you that My Lords do not see their way to comply with your suggestion, inasmuch as to do so would be to *open a serious door."* This delightful formula, with its dread suggestion of a flippant door and all the mischief to which it might lead, is daily employed to check the ardor of Ministers who are seeking to advance the benefit of the race (including their own popularity among their constituents) by a judicious expenditure of public money. Bnt whatever be the scope and function of the office, and whatever the nature of the work done there, the mode of doing it is pretty much the same. Whether the matter in question originates inside the office by some direction or inquiry of the chief, or comes by letter from outside, it is referred to the particular department of the office which is concerned with it. A clerk makes a careful minute, giving the facts of the case and the practice of the office as bearing on it. The paper is then sent to any other department or person in the office that can possibly have any concern with it. It is minuted by each, and it gradually passes up by more or fewer official gradations to the Under-Secretary of State, who reads, or is supposed to read, all that has been written on the paper in its earlier stages, balances the perhaps conflicting views of different annotators, and, if the matter is too important for his own decision, sums up in a minute of recommendation to the chief. The ultimate decision, however, is probably less affected by the Under-Secretary's minute than by the oral advice of a much more important personage, the Permanent Head of the office.

It would be beyond my present scope to discuss the composition and powers of the permanent Civil Service, whose chiefs have been, at least since the days of Bage- hot, recognized as the real rulers of this country. In absolute knowledge of their business, in self-denying devotion to duty, in ability, patience, courtesy, and readiness to help the fleeting Political Official, the permanent chiefs of the Civil Service are worthy of the highest honor. That they are conservative to the core is only to say that they are human. On being appointed to permanent office the extremest theorists, like the bees in the famous epigram, " cease to hum" their revolutionary airs, and settle down into the profound conviction that things are well as they are. All the more remarkable is the entire equanimity with which the Permanent Official accepts the unpalatable decision of a chief who is strong enough to override him, and the absolute loyalty with which he will carry out a policy which he cordially disapproves.

Much of a Minister's comfort and success depends upon his Private Secretary. Some Ministers import for this function a young gentleman of fashion whom they know at home – a picturesque butterfly who flits gayly through the dusty air of the office, making, by the splendor of his raiment, sunshine in its shady places, and daintily passing on the work to unrecognized and unrewarded clerks. But the better practice is to appoint as Private Secretary one of the permanent staff of the office. He supplies his chief with official information, hunts upnecessary references, writes his letters, and interviews his bores.

When the late Lord Ampthill was a junior clerk in the Foreign Office, Lord Palmerston, then Foreign Secretary, introduced an innovation whereby, instead of being solemnly summoned by a verbal message, the clerks were expected to answer his bell. Some haughty spirits rebelled against being treated like footmen, and tried to organize resistance ; but Odo Russell, as he then was, refused to join the rebellious movement, saying that whatever method apprised him most quickly of Lord Pal- merston's wishes was the method which he preferred. The aggrieved clerks regarded him as a traitor to his order – but he died an ambassador. Trollope described the wounded feelings of a young clerk whose chief sent him to fetch his slippers ; and in our own day a Private Secretary, who had patiently taken tickets for the play for his chief's daughters, drew the line when he was told to take the chief's razors to be ground. But such assertions of independence are extremely rare, and as a rule the Private Secretary is the most cheerful and the most alert of ministering spirits.

But it is time to return from this personal digression to the routine of the day's work. Among the most important of the morning's duties is the preparation of answers to be given in the House of Commons, and it is often necessary to have answers ready by three o'clock to questions which have only appeared that morning on the notice-paper. The range of questions is infinite, and all the resources of the office are taxed in order to prepare answers at once accurate in fact and wise in policy, to pass them under the Minister's review, and to get them fairly copied out before the House meets. As a rule the Minister, knowing something of the temper of Parliament, wishes to give a full, explicit, and intelligibleanswer, or even to go a little beyond the strict terms of the question if he sees what his interrogator is driving at. But this policy is abhorrent to the Permanent Official. The traditions of the Circumlocution Office are by no means dead, and the crime of "wanting to know, you know," is one of the most heinous that the M. P. can commit. The answers, therefore, as prepared for the Minister are generally jejune, often barely civil, sometimes actually misleading. But the Minister, if he be a wise man, edits them into a more informing shape, and, after long and careful deliberation as to the probable effect of his words and the reception which they will have from his questioner, he sends the bundle of written answers away to be fair-copied and turns to his correspondence.

And here the practice of Ministers varies exceedingly. Lord Salisbury writes almost everything with his own hand. Mr. Balfour dictates to a short-hand clerk. Most Ministers write a great deal by their Private Secretaries. Letters of any importance are usually transcribed into a copying-book. A Minister whom I knew used to burn the fragment of blotting-paper with which he had blotted his letter, and laid it down as an axiom that, if a constituent wrote and asked a member to vote for a particular measure, the member should on no account give a more precise reply than, " I shall have great pleasure in voting in the sense you desire." For, as this expert observed with great truth, "unless the constituent has kept a copy of his letter – and the chances are twenty to one against that – there will be nothing to prove what the sense he desired was, and you will be perfectly safe in voting as you like."

The letters received by a Minister are many, various, and surprising. Of course a great proportion of them relate to public business, and a considerable number tothe affairs of his constituency. But, in addition to all this, lunatics, cranks, and impostors mark a Minister for their own, and their applications for loans, gifts, and offices of profit would exhaust the total patronage of the Crown and break the Bank of England. When the day's official papers have been dealt with, answers to questions settled, correspondence read, and the replies written or dictated, it is very likely time to go to a conference on some Bill with which the office is concerned. This conference will consist of the Minister in charge of the Bill, two or three of his colleagues who have special knowledge of the subject, the Permanent Officials, the Parliamentary draftsman, and perhaps one of the Law Officers. At the conference the amendments on the paper are carefully discussed, together with the objects for which they were presumably put down, their probable effect, their merits or demerits, and the best mode of meeting them. An hour soon passes in this kind of anticipatory debate, and the Minister is called away to receive a deputation.

The scene is exactly like that which Matthew Arnold described at the Social Science Congress – the large bare room, dusty air, and jaded light, serried ranks of men with bald heads and women in spectacles; the local M. P., like Mr. Gregsbury in *Nicholas Nickleby,* full of affability and importance, introducing the selected spokesmen – "Our worthy mayor"; "Our leading employer of labor"; "Miss Twoshoes, a philanthropic worker in all good causes " – the Minister, profoundly ignorant of the whole subject, smiling blandly, or gazing earnestly from his padded chair ; the Permanent Official at his elbow murmuring what the "practice of the department" has been, what his predecessor said on a similar occasion ten years ago, and why the object of the deputation is equally mischievous and impossible; and the Minister finally expressing sympathy and promising earnest consideration. Mr. Bright, though the laziest of mankind at official work, was the ideal hand at receiving deputations. Some Ministers scold or snub or harangue, but he let them talk their full, listened patiently, smiled pleasantly, said very little, treated the subject with gravity or banter as its nature required, paid the introducing member a compliment on his assiduity and public spirit, and sent them all away on excellent terms with themselves and highly gratified by their intelligent and courteous reception.

So far we have described our Minister's purely departmental duties. But perhaps the Cabinet meets at twelve, and at the Cabinet he must, to use Mr. Gladstone's phrase, " throw his mind into the common stock " with his fellow-Ministers, and take part in the discussions and decisions which govern the Empire. By two o'clock or thereabouts the Cabinet is over. The labors of the morning are now beginning to tell, and exhausted nature rings her luncheon-bell. Here again men's habits widely differ. If our Minister has breakfasted late, he will go on till four or five, and then have tea and toast, and perhaps a poached egg; but if he is an early man ho craves for nutriment more substantial. He must not go out to luncheon at a friend's house, for he will be tempted to eat and drink too much, and absence from official territory in the middle of the day has a bad look of idleness and self-indulgence. The *dura ilia* of the present Duke of Devonshire could always cope with a slice of the office- joint, a hunch of the office-bread, a glass of the office- sherry. But, as a rule, if a man cannot manage to get back to the family meal in South Kensington or Cavendish Square, he turns into a club, has a cutlet and a glass of claret, and goes back to his office for another hour's work before going to the House.

At 3.30 questions begin, and every Minister is in his place, unless, indeed, there is a Levee or a Drawing-room, when a certain number of Ministers, besides the great Officers of State, are expected to be present. The Minister lets himself into the House by a private door – of which Ministers alone have the key – at the back of the Chair. For an hour and a half, or perhaps longer, the storm of questions rages, and then the Minister, if he is in charge of the Bill under discussion, settles himself on the Treasury Bench to spend the remainder of the day in a hand-to-hand encounter with the banded forces of the Opposition, which will tax to their utmost his brain, nerve, and physical endurance. If, however, he is not directly concerned with the business, he goes out perhaps for a breath of air and a cup of tea on the Terrace, and then buries himself in his private room – generally a miserable little dog-hole in the basement of the House of Commons – where he finds a pile of office-boxes, containing papers which must be read, minuted, and returned to the office with all convenient despatch. From these labors he is suddenly summoned by the shrill ting-ting of the division-bell and the raucous bellow of the policeman to take part in a division. He rushes upstairs two steps at a time, and squeezes himself into the House through the almost closed doors. " What are we ?" he shouts to the Whip. "Ayes" or "Noes" is the hurried answer; and he stalks through the lobby to discharge this intelligent function, dives down to his room again, only, if the House is in Committee, to be dragged up again ten minutes afterwards for another repetition of the same farce, and so on indefinitely.

It may be asked why a Minister should undergo all this worry of running up and down and in and out, laying down his work and taking it up again, dropping threads, and losing touch, and wasting time, all to give a purely party vote, settled for him by his colleague in charge of the Bill, on a subject with which he is personally unfamiliar. If the Government is in peril, of course every vote is wanted; but, with a normal majority, Ministers' votes might surely be "taken as read," and assumed to be given to the side to which they belong. But the traditions of Government require Ministers to vote. It is a point of honor for each man to be in as many divisions as possible.

A record is kept of all the divisions of the session and of the week, and a list is sent round every Monday morning showing in how many each Minister has voted.

The Whips, who must live and move and have their being in the House, naturally head the list, and their colleagues follow in a rather uncertain order. A Minister's place in this list is mainly governed by the question whether he dines at the House or not. If he dines away and " pairs," of course he does not in the least jeopardize his party or embarrass his colleagues, but " pairs " are not indicated in the list of divisions, and as divisions have an awkward knack of happening between nine and ten, the habitual diner - out naturally sinks in the list. If he is a married man, the claims of the home are to a certain extent recognized by his Whips; but woe to the bachelor who, with no domestic excuse, steals away for two hours' relaxation. The good Minister therefore stays at the House and dines there. Perhaps he is entertaining ladies in the crypt-like dining-rooms which look on the Terrace, and in that case the charms of society may neutralize the discomforts of the room and the unattractive character of the food. But if he dine upstairs at the Ministerial table, few indeed are the alleviations of his lot. In the first place, he must dine with the colleagues with whom his whole waking life is passed – excellent fellows and capital company – but nature demands an occasional enlargement of the mental horizon. Then, if by chance he has onespecial bugbear – a bore or an egotist, a man with dirty hands or a churlish temper – that man will inevitably come and sit down beside him and insist on being affectionate and fraternal.

The room is very hot; dinners have been going on in it for the last two hours ; the *Kvlm)* – the odor of roast meat, which the gods loved, but which most men dislike – pervades the atmosphere ; your next-door neighbor is eating a rather high grouse while you. are at your apple- tart, or the perfumes of a deliquescent Camembert mingle with your coffee. As to beverages, you may, if you choose, follow the example of Lord Cross, who, when he was Sir Richard, drank beer in its native pewter; or of Mr. Radcliffe Cooke, who tries to popularize cider; or you may venture on that thickest, blackest, and most potent of vintages which a few years back still went by the name of " Mr. Disraeli's port." But as a rule these heroic draughts are eschewed by the modern Minister. Perhaps, if he is in good spirits after making a successful speech or fighting his Estimates through Committee, he will indulge himself with an imperial pint of champagne; but more often a whiskey-and-soda or a half- bottle of Zeltinger quenches his modest thirst.

On Wednesday and Saturday our Minister, if he is not out of London, probably dines at a large dinner-party. Once a session he must dine in full dress with the Speaker; once he must dine at or give a full-dress dinner " to celebrate Her Majesty's birthday." On the eve of the meeting of Parliament he must dine again in full dress with the Leader of the House, to hear the rehearsal of the "gracious Speech from the Throne." But, as a rule, his fate on Wednesday and Saturday is a ceremonious banquet at a colleague's house, and a party strictly political – perhaps the Prime Minister as the main attraction, reinforced by Lord and Lady Decimns Tite - Barnacle, Mr. and Mrs. Stiltstalking, Sir John Taper, and yonng Mr. Tadpole. A political dinner of thirty colleagues, male and female, in the dog- days is only a shade less intolerable than the greasy rations and mephitic vapors of the Honse of Commons dining-room.

At the political dinner, " shop" is the order of the day. Conversation turns on Brown's successfnl speech, Jones's palpable falling-off, Robinson's chance of office, the explanation of a recent by-election, or the prospects of an impending division. And, to fill the cnp of boredom to the brim, the political dinner is usually followed by a political evening-party. On Saturday the Minister probably does two hours' work at his office and has some boxes sent to his house, but the afternoon he spends in cycling, or golfing, or riding, or boating, or he leaves London till Monday morning. On Wednesday he is at the House till six, and then escapes for a breath of air before dinner. But on Monday, Tuesday, Thursday, and Friday, as a rule, he is at the Honse from its meeting at three till it adjourns at any hour after midnight. After dinner he smokes and reads and tries to work in his room, and goes to sleep and wakes again, and towards midnight is unnaturally lively. Outsiders believe in the " twelve o'clock rule," but insiders know that, as & matter of fact, it is suspended as often as an Irish member in the '80 Parliament. Whoever else slopes homewards, the Government must stay. Before now a Minister has been fetched out of his bed, to which he had surreptitiously retired, by a messenger in a hansom, and taken back to the House to defend his estimates at three in the morning.

"There they sit with ranks unbroken, cheering on the fierce debate,

Till the sunrise lights them homeward as they tramp through Storey's Gate,

Racked with headache, pale and haggard, worn by nights of endless talk, While the early sparrows twitter all along the Birdcage Walk."

Some ardent souls there are who, if report speaks true, are not content with even this amount of exertion and excitement, but finish the night, or begin the day, with a rubber at the club or even a turn at baccarat. However, we are describing not choice spirits or chartered *viveurs,* but the blameless Minister, whose whole life during the Parliamentary session is the undeviating and conscientious discharge of unexciting duty; and he, when he lays his head upon his respectable pillow any time after 1 A. m., may surely go to sleep in the comfortable consciousness that he has done a fair day's work for a not exorbitant remuneration.

19

SECTION 19

XXXV

AN OLD PHOTOGRAPH-BOOK

The diary from which these Recollections have been gathered dates from my thirteenth year, and it has lately received some unexpected illustration. In turning out the contents of a neglected cupboard, I stumbled on an old photograph-book, which I filled when I was a boy at a Public School. That school has lately been described under the name of Lyonness, and the name will serve as well as another. The book had been mislaid years ago, and when it accidentally came to light a strange aroma of old times seemed still to hang about it. Liside and out it was reminiscent of a life which may still be going on – I never go to Lyonness now, and therefore I cannot tell – but which certainly existed once, and in which I bore my part. Externally the book bore manifest traces of a schoolboy's ownership, in broken corners, plentiful ink-stains; from exercises and punishments; droppings of illicit candle-grease, consumed long after curfew-time; round marks like fairy-rings on a greensward, which indicated the stand-point of extinct jam-pots – where are those jam-pots now ? But while the outside of the book spoke thus, as it were, by innuendo and suggestion, the inside seemed to shout with joyous laughter or chuckle with irreverent mirth ; or murmured, in tones lower perhaps, but certainly not less distinct, of things which were neither joyous nor amusing.

The book had been carefully arranged. As I turned over the leaves there came back the memory of holidayevenings and the interested questionings of sisters over each new face or scene ; and the kind fingers which did the pastings-in; and the care with which we made portrait and landscape fit into and illustrate one another. And what memories, what impressions, strong and clear as yesterday's, clung to each succeeding view ! The spire – that "pinnacle perched on a precipice" – with its embosoming trees, as one had so often seen it from the North-Western Railway, while the finger of fate, protruding from the carriage window, pointed it out with – "There's where you will go to school." And, years later, came the day when one travelled for the first time by a train which did not rush through Lyonness Station (then how small), but stopped there, and disgorged its crowd of boys and their confusion of luggage, and one's self among the rest, and one's father just as excited and anxious and eager as his son.

A scurry for a seat on the omnibus or a tramp uphill, and we find ourselves abruptly in the village street. Then did each page as I turned it over bring some fresh recollections of one's unspeakable sense of newness and desolation ; the haunting fear of doing something ludicrous ; the morbid dread of chaff and of being "greened," which even in my time had, happily, supplanted the old terrors of being tossed in a blanket or roasted at a fire. Even less, I venture to think, was one thrilled by the heroic ambitions, the magnificent visions of struggle and success, which stir the heroes of schoolboy-novels on the day of their arrival.

Here was a view of the School Library, with its patch of greensward separating it from the dust and traffic of the road. There was the Old School with its Fourth Form Room, of which one had heard so much that the actual sight of it made one half inclined to laugh and half to cry with surprise and disappointment. Therewas the twisting High Street, with its precipitous cause- way; there was the faithful presentment of the fashionable "tuck-shop," with two boys standing in the road, and the leg of a third caught by the camera as he hurried past; and, wandering through all these scenes in the album, as one had wandered through them in real life, I reached at last my boarding-house, then a place of mystery and wonderful expectations and untried experiences ; now full of memories, some bright, some sad, but all gathering enchantment from their retrospective distance; and in every brick and beam and cupboard and corner as familiar as home itself.

The next picture, a view of the School Bathing-place, carried me a stage onward in memory, to my first summer-quarter. Two terms of school-life had inured one to a new existence, and one began to know the pleasures, as well as the pains, of a Public School. It was a time of cloudless skies, and abundant "strawberry mashes," and *dolce far niente* in that sweetly shaded pool, when the sky was at its bluest, and the air at its hottest, and the water at its most inviting temperature.

And then the Old Speech-Room, so ugly, so incommodious, where we stood penned together like sheep for the slaughter, under the gallery, to hear our fate on the first morning of our school-life, and where, when he had made his way up the school, the budding scholar received his prize or declaimed his verses on Speech-day. That was the crowning day of the young orator's ambition, where there was an arch of evergreens reared over the school gate, and Lyonness was all alive with carriages, and relations, and grandees,

"And, as Lear, ho pour'd forth the deep imprecation,
By his daughters of kingdom and reason deprived,
Till, fired by loud plaudits and self-adulation,
He regarded himself as a Garrick revived."

Opposite the old Speech-Room was the interior of the Chapel, with its roof still echoing the thunder of the Parting Hymn; and the pulpit, with its unforgotten pleadings for truthfulness and purity; and the organ, still vocal with those glorious psalms. And, high over all, the churchyard hill, with its heaven-pointing spire, and the Poet's Tomb; and, below, the incomparable expanse of pasture and woodland stretching right away to the "proud keep with its double belt of kindred and coeval towers."

" Still does yon bank its living Lues unfold,
With bloomy wealth of amethyst and gold ;
How oft at eve we watched, while there we lay,
The flaming sun lead down the dying day,
Soothed by the breeze that wandered to and fro
Through the glad foliage musically low.
Still stands that tree, and rears its stately form
In rugged strength, and mocks the winter storm;
There, while of slender shade and sapling growth,
We carved our schoolboy names, a mutual troth.
All, all, revives a bliss too bright to last,
And every leaflet whispers of the past."

And while the views of places were thus eloquent of the old days, assuredly not less so were the portraits. There was the revered presence of the Head Master in his silken robes, looking exactly as he did when

" In studious ranks around, the listening throng
Drank the deep wisdom of his learned tongue ;
Nor guessed his love, but only feared his power:
A friend for life – the terror of an hour."

And there was the Mathematical Master – the Rev. Rhadamanthus Rhomboid – compared with whom his classical namesake was a lenient judge. An admirable example was old Mr. Rhomboid of a pedagogic type which, I am told, is passing away – precise, accurate, stern, solid ; knowing very little, but that little thoroughly ; never overlooking a slip, but seldom guilty of an injustice ; sternest and most unbending of prehistoric Tories, both in matters political and educational; yet carrying concealed somewhere under the square-cut waistcoat a heart which knew how to sympathize with boy-flesh and the many ills which it is heir to. Good old Mr. Rhom- boid ! I wonder if he is still alive.

Facing him in the album, and most appropriately contrasted, was the portrait of a young master – the embodiment of all that Mr. Rhomboid most heartily loathed. We will call him Vivian Grey. Vivian Grey was an Oxford Double First of unusual brilliancy, and therefore found a special charm and a satisfying sense of being suitably employed in his duty at Lyonness, which was to instil T-ujitw and *Phcedrus* into the five-and- thirty little wiseacres who constituted the lowest form. Over the heads of these sages his political and metaphysical utterances rolled like harmless thunder, for he was at once a transcendentalist in philosophy and a utilitarian Radical of the purest dye. All of which mattered singularly little to his five - and - thirty disciples, but caused infinite commotion and annoyance to the Rhomboids and Rhadamanthuses. Vivian Grey at Oxford had belonged to that school which has been described as professing " one Kant with a K, and many a cant with a c." At Lyonness he was currently supposed to have helped to break the railings of Hyde Park and to be a Head Centre of the Fenian Brotherhood. In personal appearance Mr. Grey was bearded like the pard – and in those days the scholastic order shaved – while his taste in dress made it likely that he was the " Man in the Red Tie" whom we remember at the Oxford Commemoration some five-and-twenty years ago. In short, he was the very embodiment of all that was most abhorrent to the oldtraditions of the school - master's profession ; and proportionately great was the appositeness of a practical joke which was played me on my second or third morning at Lyonness. I was told to go for my mathematical lesson to Mr. Bhoniboid, who tenanted a room in the Old School. Next door to his room was Mr. Grey's, and I need not say that the first boy whom I asked for guidance playfully directed me to the wrong door. I enter, and the Third Form suspend their *Phcedrus.* " Please, sir, are you Mr. Rhomboid ?" I ask, amid unsmother- able laughter. Never shall I forget the indignant ferocity with which the professor of the new lights drove me from the room, nor the tranquil austerity with which Mr. Khomboid, when I reached him, set me "fifty lines" before he asked me my name.

On the same page I find the portrait of two men who have before now figured in the world of school - fiction under the names of Rose and Gordon. Of Mr. Rose I will say no more than that he was an excellent schoolmaster and a most true saint, and that to his influence and warnings many a man can, in the long retrospect, trace his escape from moral ruin. He died the death of the Just – ten years ago. Mr. Gordon is now a decorous Dean, but at Lyonness he was the most brilliant, the most irregular, and the most fascinating of teachers. He spoiled me for a whole quarter. I loved him for it then, and I thank him even now.

These more distinguished portraits, of cabinet dimensions, were scattered up and down among the miscellaneous herd of *cartes de visile.* The art of Messrs. Hills and Saunders was denoted by the pretentious character of the chairs introduced – the ecclesiastical Glastonbury for masters, and velvet-backs studded with gilt nails for boys. The productions of the rival photographer were distinguished by a pillar of variegated marble, or possibly scagliola, on which the person portrayed leaned, bent, and propped himself in every phase of graceful discomfort. The athletes and members of the School Eleven, dressed in appropriate flannel, were depicted as a rule with their arms crossed over the backs of chairs, and brought very much into focus, so as to display the muscular development in high relief. The more studious portion of the community, " with leaden eye that loved the ground," scanned small photograph-books with absorbing interest; while a group of editors, of whom I was one, were gathered round a small table, with pens, ink, and paper, the finger pressed on the forehead, and on the floor proofs of the journal which we edited – was it the *Tyro* or the *Triumvirate?*

Among the athletes I instantly recognize Biceps Max., captain of the Cricket Eleven, and practically autocrat of my house – " Charity's" the house was called, in allusion to a prominent feature of my tutor's character. Well, at Charity's we did not think much of intellectual distinction in those days, and little recked that Biceps was " unworthy to be classed " in the terminal examination. We were much more concerned with the fact that he made the highest score at Lord's; that we at Charity's were absolutely under his thumb, in the most literal acceptation of that phrase; that he beat us into mummies if we evaded cricket-fagging; and that if we burned his toast he chastised us with a tea-tray. Where is Biceps now, and what ? If he took Orders, I am sure he must be a Muscular Christian of the most aggressive type. If he is an Old Bailey barrister, I pity the timid witness whom he cross-examines. Why do I never meet him at the club or in society ? It would be a refreshing novelty to sit at dinner opposite a man who corrected your juvenile shortcomings with a tea-tray! Would he attempt it again if I contradicted him in conversation, or confuted him in argument, or capped his best story with a better ?

Next comes Longbow – Old Longbow, as we called him, I suppose as a term of endearment, for there was no young Longbow. He was an Irishman, and the established wit, buffoon, or jester of the school. Innumerable stories are still told of his youthful escapades, of his audacity and skill in cribbing, of his dexterity in getting out of scrapes, of his repartees to masters and persons in authority. He it was who took up the same exercise in algebra to Mr. Rhomboid all the time he was in the Sixth Form, and obtained marks, ostensibly for a French exercise, with a composition called *De camelo qualis sit.* He alone of created boys could joke in the rarefied air of the Head Master's schoolroom, and had power to "chase away the passing frown" with some audacious witticism, for which an English boy would have been punished. Longbow was ploughed three times at Oxford, and once rusticated. But he is now the very orthodox vicar of a West-end parish, a centre of moral good, and a pattern of ecclesiastical propriety. Then, leaving these heroic figures and coming to my own contemporaries, I discern little Paley, esteemed a prodigy of parts – Paley, who won an Entrance Scholarship while still in knickerbockers ; Paley, who ran up the school faster than any boy on record; Paley, who was popularly supposed never to have been turned in a " rep" or to have made a false quantity ; Paley, for whom his tutor and the whole magisterial body were never tired of predicting a miraculous success in after life. Poor Paley ! He is at this moment languishing in the Temple, consoling himself for professional failure by contemplating the largest extant collection of Lyonness prize-books. I knew Paley, as boys say, " at home," and when he had been a few years at the Bar, I asked his mother if he had got any briefs yet." Yes," she answered, with maternal pride; " he has been very lucky in that way." "And has he got a verdict ?" I asked. " Oh no," replied the simple soul; "we don't aspire to anything so grand as that."

Next to Paley in my book is Roderick Random, the cricketer. Dear Random, my contemporary, my form- fellow and house-fellow; partaker with me in the ignominy of Biceps's tea-tray and the tedium of Mr. Rhomboid's problems; my sympathetic companion in every amusement, and the pleasant drag on every intellectual effort – Random, who never knew a lesson, nor could answer a question ; who never could get up in time for the First School nor lay his hand on his own Virgil – Random, who spent more of his half-holidays in Extra School than any boy of his day, and had acquired by long practice the power of writing the "record" number of lines in an hour; who never told a lie, nor bullied a weaker boy, nor dropped an unkind jest, nor uttered a shameful word – Random, for whom every one in authority predicted ruin, speedy and inevitable; who is, therefore, the best of landlords and the most popular of country gentlemen ; who was the most promising officer in the Guards till duty called him elsewhere, and at the last election came in at the top of the poll for his native county.

Then what shall we say for Lncian Gay, whose bright eyes and curly hair greet me on the same page, with the attractive charm which won me when we stood together under the Speech-room gallery on the first morning of our school-life ? Gay was often at the top of his form, yet sometimes near the bottom; wrote, apparently by inspiration, the most brilliant verses; and never could put two and two together in Mr. Rhomboid's schoolroom. He had the most astonishing memory on record, and an inventive faculty which often did him even better service. He was the soul of every intellectual enterprise in the school, the best speaker at the Debating Society; the best performer on Speech-day; who knew nothing about ye and less about *fiiv* and *& ;* who composed satirical choruses when he should have been taking notes on Tacitus; edited a School Journal with surprising brilliancy ; failed to conjugate the verbs in p during his last fortnight in the school; and won the Balliol Scholarship when he was seventeen. I trust, if this meets his eye, he will accept it as a tribute of affectionate recollection from one who worked with him, idled with him, and joked with him for five happy years.

Under another face, marked by a more spiritual grace, I find written *Requiescat.* None who ever knew them will forget that bright and pure beauty, those eyes of strange, supernatural light, that voice which thrilled and vibrated with an unearthly charm. All who were his contemporaries remember that dauntless courage, that heroic virtue, that stainless purity of thought and speech, before which all evil things seemed to shrink away abashed. We remember how the outward beauty of body seemed only the visible symbol of a goodness which dwelt within, and how moral and intellectual excellence grew up together, blending into a perfect whole. We remember the School Concert, and the enchanting voice, and the words of the song which afterwards sounded like a warning prophecy, and the last walk together in the gloaming of a June holiday, and the loving, thrilling companionship, and the tender talk of home. And then for a day or two we missed the accustomed presence, and dimly caught a word of dangerous illness; and then came the agony of the parting scene, and the clear, hard, pitiless school-bell, cutting on our hearts the sense of an irreparable loss, as it thrilled through the sultry darkness of the summer night.

Here I shut the book. And with the memories which that picture called up I may well bring these Recollections to a close. It is something to remember, amid the bustle and bitterness of active life, that one once had youth, and hope, and eagerness, and large opportunities, and generous friends. A tender and regretful sentiment seems to cling to the very walls and trees among which one cherished such bright ambitions and felt the passionate sympathy of such loving hearts. The innocence and the confidence of boyhood pass away soon enough, and thrice happy is he who has contrived to keep " the young lamb's heart among the full-grown flocks."

" O'er twenty leagues of morning dew,
Across the cheery breezes,
Can fairies fail to whisper true
What youth and fancy pleases ?
As strength decays with after days,
And eyes have ceased to glisten,
Those souls alone, not older grown,
Will have the ears to listen.
Keep youth a guest of heart and breast,
Aud though the hair be whiter –
Ho ho ! ha ha ! Tra la la la!
You hear them all the brighter 1"

Lightning Source UK Ltd.
Milton Keynes UK
UKOW050205260612

195052UK00002B/265/P